To

Pat & Dave,

This was indeed a season beyond our wildest dreams.

Here's to 2006/07.

Best wishes.

Doreen & Brian

SEASON OF DREAMS

Wigan Athletic's historic campaign in the **Premiership 2005/06**

WIGAN Observer The voice of Wigan for 153 years

SEASON OF DREAMS

Wigan Athletic's historic campaign in the **Premiership 2005/06**

Edited by Phil Wilkinson

First published in Great Britain in 2006 by
The Breedon Books Publishing Company Limited
Breedon House, 3 The Parker Centre,
Derby, DE21 4SZ.

ISBN 1 85983 514 7

Printed and bound by Cromwell Press, Trowbridge, Wiltshire.

Contents

‘They are the story of the season.
They are Wigan Athletic.’

– Sky Sports commentator Martin Tyler

Preface

Dave Whelan, Chairman Wigan Athletic AFC

The 2005–06 Premiership campaign, Wigan Athletic's first ever in the top flight of English football, lived up to all the dreams and expectations that we could ever have hoped for.

From the pulsating opening day encounter with the champions Chelsea, to the curtain coming down in historic fashion with the final game at Highbury against Arsenal, the season had everything.

This season really saw Wigan Athletic come of age. The JJB Stadium was full to bursting for the vast majority of the campaign, with record crowds seeing the club do battle with the biggest names in the world. The Carling Cup adventure put Latics on the global stage like never before and helped the town of Wigan gain recognition in every corner of the planet.

Everyone who played their part in this fairytale story, from the boardroom to the manager, players, staff and of course our brilliant fans, can be very proud of themselves – and look back on the season with pride and joy.

I'm sure the experience will live long in the memory and you will never tire of seeing the images of this historic season over and over again.

Dave Whelan
May 2006

Acknowledgements

Thanks to all the people who have helped with the production of *Season Of Dreams.*

Photographers Gary Brunskill, Nick Fairhurst, Paul Greenwood, Gary Kelman, John Leatherbarrow and Frank Orrell for their pictures… and patience.

Janet Wilson and Gillian Gray for their guidance, Jean Fisher for her endless supply of caffeine, and Emma Shawcross, Emma Turner, Alison Hughes and Traci Robbins for promoting *Season of Dreams* and co-ordinating subscriptions.

Susan Last and everyone at Breedon Publishing, as well as Today's Community Church for their kind sponsorship.

Stuart Maconie for so readily agreeing to write the foreword, and to the several hundred people who subscribed to *Season Of Dreams* before it was published.

Finally, to the players, manager, officials (particularly Matt McCann and Geoff Lea), chairman and fans of Wigan Athletic – for a story which you'd be hard pressed to make up.

Foreword

Stuart Maconie, BBC broadcaster and lifelong Wigan supporter

I think it might have been against Goole Town, and I'm pretty sure it was Jimmy Savage. But it was definitely a frosty Tuesday night under the slightly-less-than state-of-the-art floodlights at Springfield Park, and as it was about 1973, I should certainly have been at home doing my homework. But I remember the goal as if it were yesterday; a brilliant snap shot from the halfway line that had the crowd dancing for joy. All two hundred of us, I imagine.

I remembered Jimmy Savage's goal – one of the abiding glorious memories of my early Latics supporting days – as I sat in my seat at the very state-of-the-art JJB and watched Shaun Wright-Phillips, Joe Cole and Hernan Crespo warming up in front of me. It was the opening game of the 2005–06 season and Wigan Athletic were playing Premiership champions Chelsea in their opening game in the top flight of the world's most glamorous Football League. With all due respect to Goole Town, this was truly the stuff of dreams.

We were told that the dream couldn't last. Rodney Marsh said we wouldn't get 40 corners, let alone 40 points. I think he collects glasses in Goose Green Labour Club on Tuesday nights now. Others sneered at the fact that a working-class town from the Industrial North had the temerity to stray into the spotlight usually reserved for football's elite. Well, no one's sneering now.

Is it a fairytale? No. It's a story of how commitment, belief and hard work can bring you success. There are no genies or magic wands here. Just the vision of Dave Whelan and the passion of Paul Jewell and his players. Our players. Because in a way this is our story too, the town and the people, and the first of many seasons of dreams.

Stuart Maconie
May 2006

1: Introduction

'NO MONEY, no fans,' declared the *Sunday Times*, in their pre-season forecast of how Wigan would cope with the rigours of the Premiership. 'Will need a miracle if they are to survive. Prediction: 20th.'

Wigan did so much more than survive in their elevated status among the world's leading clubs. Their knack of continuing to build history, week in, week out, put the town on the map and established the club as a real force in English football. Let nobody tell you Paul Jewell did not perform a modern miracle. Let no one forget just what a fabulously improbable season they enjoyed.

Arjan De Zeeuw brought authority to a hard-working team.

The significance of Wigan's historic campaign was not lost on this fan.

Assistant manager Chris Hutchings was an unsung hero of Wigan's blistering campaign.

Matt Jackson says farewell to Arsenal legend Dennis Bergkamp.

They brought the romance back to the Carling Cup and then became the first club to record a top-10 finish in their first-ever Premiership campaign. Whichever way you look at it, Wigan Athletic's debut in the top flight was one of the most extraordinary stories in football.

'When you sit back in years to come you'll think "what a season that was",' reflected Jewell, casually dressed in blue jeans and black T-shirt. Chatting outside the Christopher Park training camp on a beautifully warm day, in the days immediately after the final game at Highbury, Jewell was kicking back, learning what it was like to relax again after a frantic past few months.

'Funnily enough, my son said to me he's looking forward to watching the *Premiership Years* which they show on Sky Sports. When you look back there were some great games, some great moments and some wonderful scenes. It's been a wonderful season for us. I knew I was good, but I didn't know I was this good! But all jokes aside, aiming to finish 17th was all we could ever hope for. To finish in the top 10 though, was a fantastic achievement. It's been a great story – it would be one you couldn't make up.'

The journey of Wigan Athletic has been told many, many times before. And like all good fishing tales, it becomes more remarkable each time.

Just 27 years before they rubbed shoulders with champions Chelsea in front of the world, Wigan were non-League. Less than two decades before they were preparing for Roman Abramovich's helicopter landing in town, fans were being serenaded to the rattle of bucket collections after matches, asking for donations for the club's survival. Gasping for life in the bottom division, with little more than 1,500 hardy fans cheering on at their spartan Springfield Park, local entrepreneur Dave Whelan bought the club in 1995 and immediately declared,

Arsene Wenger and Paul Jewell exchanged views on four occasions.

tongue in cheek, that he was going to take Wigan into the Premiership. Everybody laughed.

Whelan continued to pour money into the club and, though never paying over-the-top salaries, it smoothed the way for Jewell to transform Wigan. Two promotions later, and with attendances rocketing, the phenomenon of Wigan Athletic warmed even the cold-hearted. 'The club has grown so much over the last three or four years, more than any other I would think,' Jewell continued. 'In the second division we were getting gates of five and six thousand. We got out of that division when we won the Championship and I said we could establish ourselves as a mid-table team at the next level. But we did more than that. We've kept on surprising ourselves. It's difficult to keep on pulling rabbits out of the hat. Now we've proved we're good enough to compete on an equal footing in the Premiership and we are now getting gates of more than 20,000 – it's fantastic.'

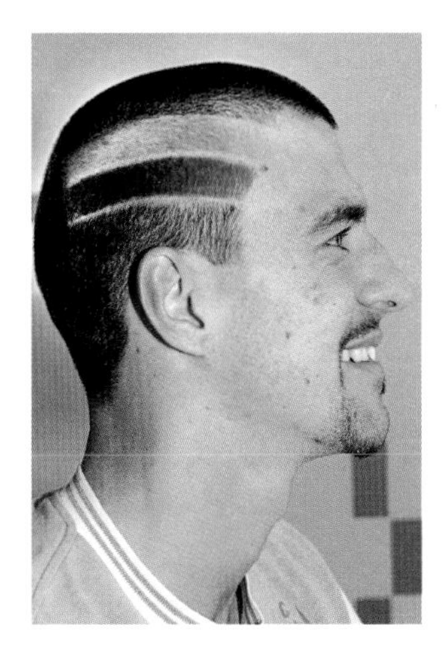

Paul Scharner proved he was a true blue.

Less than a year earlier, Jewell spoke with the same tinge of excitement but not the same optimism. He was frustrated. Having guided his side to the Promised Land, he discovered the lure of Premiership football alone was not enough to attract the quality players he wanted. 'A lot of players didn't want to come here last year for reasons that I totally understood,' he says. 'It's no point in me telling lies about it. If I was a top player I'd ask myself if I'd go to Wigan, thinking they'd probably have one year in the Premiership and then "Little Old Wigan" would disappear without a trace.'

Highbury hero Mike Pollitt and Gary Teale celebrate reaching the Carling Cup Final.

His struggle only gave his critics more ammunition to shoot down Wigan Athletic's prospects. The prophecies of doom and gloom that welcomed the club into the spotlight were disconcerting, and challenged the faith of every fan. Predictions that Wigan would never climb off the bottom spot were widespread. The press truly believed Wigan would be relegated. 'It must be the worst feeling in the world,' reported the *News of The World*, Britain's best-selling newspaper. 'Knowing relegation waits just eight months away. Nobody expects Wigan to beat the drop after a long, hard season.'

Indeed, the few brave souls who voiced opinions that Latics could, actually, thrive in the competition were dismissed as naive, optimistic souls. Or just plain crazy. 'No one gave us a chance at the start of the season. No one,' recalled captain Arjan De Zeeuw. 'We were seen as "Little Old Wigan" who didn't deserve to be in the Premiership and that really hurt us.'

But after just one game, Wigan were already Premiership legends. The televised thrashing that millions had believed would befall the Premiership newcomers never materialised. Wigan were supposed to be humiliated, but they forced reigning champions Chelsea into a humbling retreat until they escaped with the luckiest of wins. No one could remember the last time a team had made Jose Mourinho's men appear mortal. Ordinary, even. Here was a club that thought nothing of spending £21 million of their billionaire owner's money on a winger, Shaun Wright-Phillips, a few weeks earlier. Paul Jewell's entire line-up had been assembled for a snip above £7 million. Yet their performance oozed passion and persistence, and earned Jewell gushing praise for not only forging a team with such internal discipline... but also for concocting the side from virtually nothing.

The following May, the season closed with another defeat and a walk-on part in an equally historic occasion (for once, their opponents took centre stage). And during that time, in nine magical months, Wigan's fearless, scintillating brand of

ROBERTS

(Previous page) Jason Roberts proved he had the credentials to mix it with the best.

The JJB Stadium welcomed Wayne Rooney and Manchester United. The Reds won 2-1 despite having just one shot on target!

football had captured the hearts of the footballing world. 'There have been so many highlights,' Jewell smiled. 'The semi-final in the Carling Cup at Highbury, when Jason scored in the last minute, really stands out. That was a tremendous journey home. But the season as a whole has been fantastic. There were lots of highlights when you look back.'

Latics were still in the top six in February and looked on course to try to claim a UEFA Cup spot. But the fatigue of an unforgiving schedule punished Jewell's side, and three wins out of the last 11 saw their hopes slip away. 'People think our season tailed off and looking at results that was the case,' added Jewell. 'We just didn't score enough goals. The three relegated teams the year before nearly scored more goals than we did. Our goal return wasn't good enough. We finished with a goal difference of minus seven and we were in the top 10. But no one can criticise the

These Wigan fans recorded their own memories of their historic Premiership season on camera.

Wigan fans at Highbury on the last day of the season.

When Dave Whelan took over Wigan a decade earlier he said he would take the club to the Premiership. Everyone laughed at him.

effort the players and my staff put in throughout the season – they were a credit to everyone.'

For Whelan, the season really was the culmination of a decade's loyal, generous support. And faith. 'It's been unbelievable,' he enthused, his eyes lighting up. 'We've had an unbelievable season. It has seen an eruption in support for Wigan Athletic and we are enjoying the backing of the town which we could have only ever dreamed of. It's truly phenomenal.'

Like the club's legion of dedicated fans, *Season of Dreams* has trekked from one side of the country to the other and made fortnightly trips up and down the nation's motorways following, and documenting, Wigan Athletic's campaign. There have been hours spent kicking heels in the Christopher Park entrance, Sunday mornings agonising over analysis of the previous day's events, countless phone calls and endless rewrites.

This book does not detail every tackle and does not include every shot. Those blow-by-blow, detailed accounts serve a purpose – usually in the immediate hours and days after a game. Instead, we hope to bring out the human stories, the occasional disappointments and the frequent triumphs, as well as provide a rare insight into the inner workings of a club and reveal the diverse, often colourful characters. A chance to see at close-quarters the players after every game, coping with the breakneck speed that is the Premiership.

Paul Jewell takes a lap of honour to celebrate Latics' achievements this season.

This young fan gets in the party mood.

Nothing will ever, ever come close to matching the excitement of Wigan Athletic's first season in the Premiership, no matter what the future has in store. Hopefully, this book will help preserve the euphoria and prevent the passing months and years eroding a season's memories which deserve to be treasured.

It has been written so that, in years to come, fans can dip into the book at random (for those doing that, Wigan's imperious run through September and October or Phil O'Brien's humourous *On The Road* chapter would be good starting points).

As for the title, *Season Of Dreams* was selected last July as it would stand the test of time. Even if the team were relegated, the cynic inside us argued, it would still have been a dream season as no one ever, really, expected Wigan to be competing on the same level as Chelsea, Arsenal, Liverpool and Manchester United. Besides, Wigan weren't going to be relegated, we assured ourselves.

But even such bullish confidence ahead of the opening game against Chelsea could never have prepared us for what was to come. The rest, as they say, is history.

Our history.

We hope you enjoy reliving it as much as we enjoyed documenting the most fascinating season of our lives...

Wigan's season in numbers

227,000,000	the amount in pounds Dave Whelan is worth, according to the *Sunday Times*.
93,300,000	the difference in pounds between the cost of Wigan's team and Manchester United's in the Carling Cup Final.
70,000,000	the amount in pounds Dave Whelan had ploughed into Latics before the start of the season.
11,000,000	the amount in pounds the local economy benefited from Latics' Premiership campaign.
6,000,000	the price tag in pounds slapped on Pascal Chimbonda after the final game of the season.
3,000,001	the amount in pounds paid by West Brom for Nathan Ellington in August.
3,000,000	the amount in pounds paid for Wolves striker Henri Camara last August, making him a club record buy.
2,500,000	the amount in pounds spent by Jewell in the January transfer window on Paul Scharner (David Thompson was a free, Neil Mellor and Reto Ziegler were on loan).
1,037,109	the total number of fans who watched Wigan in all their Premiership matches in 2005–06.
350,000	the amount in pounds that JJB's shirt sponsorship deal is worth with Wigan, putting the club joint 15th on the value with Portsmouth and West Brom. West Ham and Blackburn are lowest, with deals worth £300,000 each.
270,000	the amount in pounds that Wigan owed the police before the Premiership season started.
100,000	pounds spent by Dave Whelan relaying the JJB Stadium turf in December.
25,017	the new stadium record of the JJB Stadium after the South Stand's capacity was slightly increased.
20,610	the average League home gate at the JJB Stadium in their debut Premiership season.
12,000	season tickets sold before the first match.
2,374	number of miles travelled by Latics fans if they attended every away game.
545	the number of minutes before Wigan conceded their first goal in this season's Carling Cup.
470	miles clocked up by the Wigan family from Kent for each home match. They attend every Latics home game.
390	the total number of minutes played by Matt Jackson in the season's Carling Cup.
254	pence it cost in electricity closing the Millennium Stadium roof for the Carling Cup Final.
123	consecutive League starts by Jimmy Bullard before his club record run was ended at Chelsea in December.
120	the number of journalists at the

opening day match against Chelsea – 84 more than for their opening-day fixture the previous season.

88 seconds that Andreas Johansson was on the pitch at Highbury before being sent off.

74 seconds, the length of Sir Alex Ferguson's press conference previewing Manchester United's game with Wigan.

57 references to Wigan Pier in the national newspapers in the week leading up to the Wigan game.

54 seconds before Jason Roberts netted a spot-kick to register the club's first goal in the Premier League.

40 minutes gone when David Connolly netted Wigan's first away goal, and first goal in open play, in the Premier League.

34 seconds remaining of injury time when Chelsea's Herman Crespo struck to deny Latics a 0–0 draw in their opening game.

25 points from the available 33 in the opening 11 games, giving Wigan the best run in Europe and the best start from a promoted side since Nottingham Forest in 1994.

23 the amount in pounds Dave Whelan received for playing in the 1960 FA Cup Final. It would have been £34 if Blackburn had won.

14 goals scored by Jason Roberts in all competitions during Wigan's debut season.

12 seconds played before referee Steve Bennett awarded Latics the quickest-ever penalty against Sunderland in their third game of the season.

11 games remaining when Wigan reached the fabled 40-point safety mark.

10 Wigan's final League position. After September they were never out of the top half.

9 games missed by Henri Camara due to his Senegal commitments in the African Nations Cup.

7 goals on Boxing Day, with Wigan edging out Manchester City 4–3.

6 the number of goals Wigan scored in the last 10 minutes or in extra-time in this season's Carling Cup ties.

5 goals conceded in the opening 11 games, giving Wigan the best defence in the Premier League.

4 the number of Premiership clubs Latics had never faced in a competitive match before this season. They were Charlton, Manchester United, Tottenham Hotspur and Arsenal.

2 the number of goals conceded by Wigan in the six games that took them to the Carling Cup Final.

1 shot on target by Manchester United at the JJB in March, despite winning 2–1. The winning goal was from a Pascal Chimbonda own goal.

1 person allowed into the chairman's suite while wearing jeans... Roman Abramovich.

2: Preparing for the Premiership

PAUL JEWELL'S feverish efforts to bolster his squad during the summer of 2005 fed the hungry tabloids a string of stories. But behind the headlines and photocalls, staff worked tirelessly to prepare Wigan – and the JJB Stadium – for the glamour and glitz of the biggest domestic football competition in the world...

Trainer Joey Gallanagh puts Emerson Thome through his paces at Christopher Park.

'DANCE Ali, get off the ropes. Move your feet, man, MOVE YOUR FEET!'

Joey Gallanagh barked instructions, as Emerson Thome landed blow after blow on the pad pressed tightly against the trainer's body. Thome was wearing his typical training gear but had also donned a new addition to his kit: boxing gloves. It was a hot Tuesday morning in July, and the duo were in the new but still barren gym at the Christopher Park training ground. Gallanagh, a chirpy Australian, was putting Thome through an extra session of boxing training at the defender's request.

'The players love boxing,' Gallanagh said. 'It's a great blow out, it teaches the mind to react quicker… and it separates the men from the boys.'

Dave Whelan casts his eyes over the Premiership fixtures during the summer months at the JJB Stadium.

Five weeks before the start of the new season, Gallanagh was pleased with the progress the players were making. The squad had reported back for training two weeks earlier although, in truth, pre-season began a month before that.

'Some people have this idea that when the season finishes, players can spend the summer on the drink,' smiled Steve McMillan. 'But it's not like that any more. Apart from a couple of weeks off relaxing, all the boys have to do their own training and look after themselves.'

Gallanagh, born in Ireland but raised in Perth on the west Australian coast, was appointed to his role at Wigan during their first season in the Championship, having cut his teeth at Salford Reds, Wigan Warriors and Newcastle Knights in Australia. This bloke strips fat off players, loves it too, and considered himself fortunate to not only have a role with one of the 20 Premiership clubs, but also to have a manager who was proud to have such fit players.

The step up to the Premiership meant stepping up the fitness. Shortly after Latics had secured promotion, Gallanagh began looking for records of fitness levels at other top-flight clubs to see how fit their players were. After a frustrating search and more than 100 phone calls – such fitness records were hard to come by – he obtained a copy of AC Milan's figures from the previous year. The document highlighted how fit their players were, their recovery rates and their body fat indexes.

He read it, digested it... and then he worked out a way to beat it.

'The way we see it,' he explained, 'is that other clubs can beat us for personnel, they can beat us for revenue and they can beat us for facilities. But when it comes to fitness, no one should be able to beat us. That's one thing we control.'

Wigan Athletic's new PR representative, Matt McCann, at the JJB Stadium.

Although Sunday 8 May was the day etched in scores of fans' memories as the day Wigan sealed promotion to the Premiership, for some of the staff and coaches at the club, adapting to life in the top flight started much earlier.

Chief executive Brenda Spencer began holding talks with Premier League officials several weeks into 2005, while work to upgrade the training ground at a cost of £500,000 – as well as the appointment of Gallanagh – took place the previous year.

The bulk of the work, though, took place in the summer months of 2005. The changes were sweeping, and ranged from the massive (renovating large parts of the JJB Stadium) to the miniscule (installing a short metal chain to separate the substitutes from the backroom staff) to the secretive (taking delivery of the secure Noc list which contains each Premier League manager's phone number).

'People said when we got promoted we'd notice a big difference in the workload,' admitted Spencer, who joined Wigan as a secretary in 1986. 'I thought, "How could it be different to the Championship?" But believe me it was. There was so much organising to do – it was nearly twice what we'd been used to.'

As well as meeting with the Premier League to find out the requirements of the competition, Spencer's duties included dealing with Sky Sports, drawing up season ticket plans, increasing advertising and ensuring the building developments were completed in time.

The smell of sawdust perfumed the stadium's corridors two weeks before the start of the season, as workmen toiled to finish the refurbishments. 'Being in the Premiership demands certain things of us,' said Matt McCann, the club spokesman. 'The calibre of celebrity will be much greater.'

Some of the improvements were due to Premiership regulations – or the more

Wigan Athletic's new football co-ordinator Bill Green with manager Paul Jewell and chief executive Brenda Spencer.

friendly sounding 'recommendations', as they prefer to call them. But many more were cosmetic, and completed to satisfy Wigan Athletic's own self-pride.

'A lot was just for vanity's sake,' said McCann. 'There was an onus on us to make sure we impressed this season – we were keen not to be left behind and thought of as "little Wigan". It also helps attract players to the club when we can show them around a stadium that is geared to the Premiership. I think it has been a success. The opening gambit on Radio 5 Live on the opening day of the season was, "What a lovely stadium it is". We took that as a triumph for all the work we'd done.'

Reception at the JJB Stadium.

The new players' lounge.

McCann was assisted in the PR offices by Geoff Lea, the matchday press officer, programme editor Ed Jones – a former sports writer for the *Wigan Reporter*, and better known in Wigan circles for playing bass guitar for The Tansads – and webmaster Andy Hudson.

All, with the exception of McCann, worked part-time for Wigan. And though effective, the size of the crew was over-shadowed by bigger Premiership outfits: Chelsea brought nine members of their media team to the JJB Stadium on the opening day of the season.

McCann and Jones also proved their durability ahead of the new season. While many big clubs employ player liaison officers, Wigan turned to their two communications workers to show new players around apartments and houses, and generally help them adjust to English customs and local cultures.

Jones speaks fluent French, which allowed him to serve as a translator and tutor for Pascal Chimbonda and Henri Camara, and the favours did not end there.

When the club was negotiating with Turkish striker Fatih Tekke at the start of their Championship season, they again avoided having to employ a costly translation agency by asking a Turkish waiter from the JJB Stadium's Rigaletto's restaurant to translate the conversation. 'I think it's an attribute of the club,' McCann offered. 'It helps create warmth.'

Inside the players' lounge.

Not all Wigan's summer arrivals arrived from overseas. Stephane Henchoz, though Swiss, had been playing at Celtic but had been released at the end of the season and Jewell invited him to train with Wigan and travel with them on their pre-season tour. Ryan Taylor was lured from Tranmere for £750,000, a signing that was trumpeted as a coup as he was also being targeted by Everton.

'Keeper Mike Pollitt was recruited from Rotherham for £200,000 and midfielder Damien Francis, relegated at the end of summer with Norwich, was bought for £1.5 million. Inevitably a few had to leave, with Jason Jarrett, Ian Breckin and Nicky Eaden among those who made way.

Paul Jewell also brought in Bill Green to help scout for players, negotiate with agents and organise contracts. This gave Jewell more time to do what he loved – he always regarded himself as a training pitch manager, rather than an office manager.

The media interview room.

Some of the biggest changes during the summer of 2005 were made to accommodate the media. The press box, the prime area directly in front of the directors where journalists watch the game, was expanded to accommodate 86 reporters – the average the previous season was 30. At the end of each row plasma screen TVs to show a live feed of the game – as well as replays of key incidents – were installed, a key requirement of the Premier League.

To make room for the two extra rows of press benches, 46 season-ticket holders, of Wigan Athletic and Wigan Warriors, had to be relocated to other seats (incidentally, a solitary Warriors fan protested by continuing to sit among the working journalists until the season was over).

A foreign broadcast area, independent of the English press so as not to distract them, was also erected on the gantry. The media suite, which accommodates the press and broadcasters before and after each game, was relocated deep in the belly of the West Stand. Three times the size of the previous facility, it included a small stage at the front to separate the manager from the media and workstations with power, internet and ISDN access points.

The new manager's office.

The site of the new media facility had been two dressing rooms, one for the cheerleaders and one for the referees. But the need to have the officials' room within sight of the players' dressing room – and the realisation that a large dressing room for the cheerleaders wasn't really needed – prompted the change. This allowed the old, cramped media room to be split in two to create an interview room, for TV and radio, and a new office for Paul Jewell – his previous one was not much bigger than a single bedroom – to host the opposition manager after the game.

His new room comprised a plasma screen TV, leather suites and food and drink, with the decor tastefully finished in varnished oak. As part of the new set-up, a

Ryan Taylor arrived in the summer of 2005.

The changing rooms corridor.

separate photographers' room was built and numbered bibs were ordered (the Premier League fiercely police the use of photographs to ensure they do not breach the image rights of the competition) and down the corridors of the JJB Stadium, new A2-sized boxed pictures decorated the walls, half depicting Warriors, half Latics.

'They can be picked up and moved, to help them feel like it's their stadium,' McCann explained. 'Our players didn't want to run out with pictures of Warriors players staring at them, and it's the same the other way around.'

In the dugout, the Premier League insisted on 11 seats for each team (five for the substitutes and six for the management and staff). Wigan had three rows of five, and consequently had to install a new bench of six seats for Jewell, Chris Hutchings, a physio, a kitman (in case of a bloodied or torn shirt), conditioner Joey Gallanagh and either goalkeeping coach Gary Walsh (if he was not a substitute) or another physio.

A new players' bar was also built. In previous seasons, the players' bar was located on the second floor, where Blue Chip members also enjoyed a post-match drink. But in the celebrity-mad era, a new, luxury lounge finished in stylish leather and wood was built on the ground floor nearer to the dressing rooms, to save players the challenge of navigating hordes of autograph-hungry fans or – even worse – angry supporters keen to vent their frustrations. 'A lot of the players are global stars,' McCann pointed out. 'They would be mobbed if they went up there.'

The view players have as they walk out onto the pitch.

Fans queue to snap up their season tickets.

Promotion to the Premiership also forced Wigan to change their stand allocation for visiting supporters, who were moved from the larger East Stand to the smaller North Stand behind the goal. That meant moving fans who had season tickets in the North Stand to the South, and the South to the East. Confused? So were the fans, which prompted Wigan to have an open day to explain what seating was available.

But in the months that followed no one suggested a more sensible choice, even though Wigan lost the chance to capitalise on the income-generating potential of using the Marquee as a corporate facility due to policing restrictions (all the other corporate facilities were sold out weeks before the start of the Premier League season).

Jewell's influence was felt most strongly at the Christopher Park training ground. When he first arrived at Wigan, only the assortment of luxury BMWs and Mercedes cars distinguished the facility as that of a rich, professional club. The nicest way to describe it was as spartan. Or homely.

'Let's be honest, it was a dump,' McCann said frankly. 'It was archaic – there used to be a toaster, a microwave and a kettle in an old kitchen. Now, there is a full canteen and professional advice on diet. Few of the stadium changes were driven by Paul, but he took personal pride in the training facilities. Paul used to say the only thing that gave it away as a Premiership club was the carpark! He often talks of leaving a legacy at the club.'

The Christopher Park training ground does not compete with Chelsea's or Manchester United's, but it is largely unrecognisable from the shambles it once was. And according to Gallanagh, it has everything they would like except for a swimming pool on site.

'But we have access to the pool at the JJB gym, so it's not a problem,' he added. 'Paul's been very hands-on with what he has done here, and we're happy with what we've got. If we are showing prospective players around they want to see a club with good facilities.'

Latics fan Dale Holford, from Orrell, plants a smacker on his season tickets.

What they said before a ball was even kicked...

JAMES FLETCHER, ***News of the World***: 'It must be the worst feeling in the world... knowing relegation waits just eight months away. Nobody expects Wigan to beat the drop after a long, hard season.'

Sunday Times: 'No money, no fans. Will need a miracle if they are to survive. Prediction: 20th.'

MARTIN SAMUEL, ***News of the World***: 'The colours of Wigan Athletic came first at a Football Furlong horse race last week. No offence, lads. But make the most of it.'

BRIAN READE, ***Daily Mirror***: 'In response to the defiant post 7/7 website wearenotafraid.com, a follow-up has appeared called iamf*****gafraid.com, whose home page asks us to 'join in showing the world how s*** scared we are.' This puzzles me. I've checked it several times, and amazingly I can't find one message from a Wigan fan.'

HARRY REDKNAPP: 'I am sure Wigan will have a real go, especially with a chairman who has backed the manager and given him cash to spend.'

Independent: 'Wigan Athletic v Chelsea; Arsenal v Wigan Athletic: Hans Christian Andersen must have been operating the fixtures computer.'

Guardian: 'Paul Jewell has a cannonball head and cherubic grin of an improbably jovial and popular prison officer. Wigan's turnover in managers rivalled JJB's turnover in shirts before Jewell earned the board's respect.'

PAUL JEWELL: 'I was in a Premier League managers' meeting last week and David O'Leary of Aston Villa said to me, "Good luck, I hope you stay up" and I turned round to him and said "I hope you do too".'

Pundit RODNEY MARSH: 'The Wigan people have been pathetic in their non-support of the football team. I don't think they'll fill the stadium more than four or five times this year and I don't think they'll win more than eight games.'

Independent: 'This Lancashire town is the sort of can-do place where people take a joke and turn it into an astonishing success. And the latest, most dramatic example of that, is the football team. Dreams, and jokes, do come true in Wigan.'

PAUL WILSON, ***The Observer***: 'The fixture computer was having a laugh when it came up with the idea of sending newly-crowned champions Chelsea to newly-promoted Wigan's humble abode on the opening weekend of the Premiership season.'

MARTIN TARBUCK, author of ***Pies and Prejudice***: 'Premier League – we're not having a laugh, we're living the dream. Bring it on.'

JOHN HEELEY, editor of cockneylatic website: 'What Paul's achieved is nothing short of incredible. Where will we finish? Somewhere between halfway and the relegation zone.'

MARTIN SAMUEL, ***News of the World*** (again): 'So many clubs have no money and lowly Wigan have a budget of £25 million but have struggled to get players to join them. I feel sorry for Paul Jewell and fear they will go straight down. Prediction: 20th.'

The Sun: 'Wigan's boss Paul Jewell said this week, "Right now I don't know my best team". Didn't know you had one to be honest, mate.'

JEWELL again: 'I'll tell you now we will not go down.'

DANNY FULLBROOK, ***Daily Star***: 'Of the three promoted sides Wigan will do the best.'

Gary Lineker, Alan Hansen and Kenny Dalglish with Dave Whelan at Wigan Golf Club. Lineker gave them 'a shot' at survival.

MATT DENVER, ***Independent on Sunday***: 'With funds to strengthen in January if need be they might just do it.'

SIR BOBBY ROBSON: 'It's certainly going to be hard for Wigan with the smaller crowds they get. If they're to stay up they'll need to win their home games.'

The Times: 'Paul Jewell will find out whether he has a realistic chance of staging a successful campaign to stay up over the next 30 days.'

FourFourTwo magazine: 'Wigan will take heart from the Robbo-inspired exploits of West Brom. Predict: 17th.'

BRUCE RIOCH: 'Last year's experience will stand them in good stead and can spur them on. I hope Wigan do well and I think they will.'

DAVE WHELAN: 'We aren't in the Premiership to collect autographs. I'm letting Roman Abramovich land his helicopter on my pad near the stadium but I've told him, "Don't assume you'll be taking three points home".'

Then-Warriors coach IAN MILLWARD: 'I think they're going to struggle. Football is the only major sport that operates without a salary cap and it's wrong.'

England legend GARY LINEKER: 'Wigan, naturally, will be long odds-on to go down but I know their chairman Dave Whelan really well and he is an experienced football man who knows what is needed. He also has a good young manager in Paul Jewell, who has been through this before. So I give (them) a shot.'

SIMON MULLOCK, ***Sunday Mirror***: 'I just hope Wigan can beat the odds, the prejudice and the drop.'

3: August: The fairytale business

A WEEK before the big one, and Paul Jewell was in a defiant, defensive mood. Wigan's prospects of producing a competitive performance against Chelsea were being written off by the national media, who ridiculed and provoked Wigan Athletic mercilessly.

The critics did little to dampen the spirits around Wigan, however. More than 12,000 season tickets had been sold (the same figure as the club's average attendance during their promotion season in the Championship), replica shirts were flying off the shelves at the local JJB stores and newspaper supplements and posters fuelled the Chelsea fever that dominated conversations in pubs, clubs, at home and by the office water coolers.

The euphoria must have provided some comfort for the Wigan staff, but even so, Jewell was becoming increasingly frustrated with their portrayal in the national media. He had guided a team from the old second division to the Premiership, and though he was lauded locally, there was a distinct lack of respect nationally. No one dared ask him quite how many times he had been asked about relegation, being written off and fairytales. 'I am not in the business of fairytales,' he pointed out.

In his previous four years in charge, Jewell often stated that he never read the papers, though only fools took his claim as an invitation to insult or question him

Head of Communications and Media Matt McCann explains the procedure for the photocall to Paul Jewell and Dave Whelan.

and his team, at least without justification. His theory, and one he voiced on numerous occasions, was that he should be the only one allowed to criticise his team, in the same way only a husband should be able to say what he feels about his wife.

'I know that no-one outside the club gives us a prayer,' said Jewell, fighting to restore some credibility for his side's remarkable achievement. 'But we have not written to *Jim'll Fix It* to play Chelsea. It all comes down to getting the players organised.'

His thoughtful remarks did little to deflect the mocking, though, with *The Sun* newspaper reacting to his remark that he didn't know his strongest team just a few days before the game by cheekily stating: 'Didn't know you had one to be honest, mate.'

With his squad not complete, the last thing Jewell needed was a distraction. But that is what he got, as rumours began to creep out that star striker Nathan Ellington was attracting interest from West Brom. Ellington's contract had been the subject of various stories over the summer, with his pay demands seemingly the stumbling block for a new, extended deal, although his advisor Tony Finnigan repeatedly stressed during the close season that it was ambition – not money – that drove the striker.

Jewell was not the only one who could have done without a sub-plot to the historic opening weekend. Matt McCann worked with Wish FM before joining Wigan Athletic in April 2005 to oversee the club's publicity. Although Leicester born-and-bred, he is an honorary Wiganer, and over the summer worked so tirelessly to improve the club's image that he was often seen juggling two mobile phones. Always moving, always on the go. Think the Duracell bunny… but not as cuddly.

Matt was tiring of reading the regurgitated same old clichés that tied Wigan to a stereotyped image of being a northern mill town full of men wearing flat caps and owning ferrets. He was, understandably, left speechless for perhaps the first time when the Premier League sent him a welcome pack that included a pie. 'I don't know whether everyone got one or whether they're taking the mick,' he said, after recovering from the shock.

PRODIGAL son Arjan De Zeeuw was given more than a hero's welcome after returning to the Latics – Paul Jewell also handed the 35-year-old the captaincy. In his own words, De Zeeuw recalls the epic opening day encounter against Chelsea after three years away from Wigan...

I thought it might be a bit awkward coming back after so long away. But it was like 'welcome home from everyone here' and I was delighted.

When I was handed the armband, I felt really bad for Jacko (Matt Jackson) because he's been the captain here while I've been away and has been very inspirational.

It was hard for him to take, but he's a good pro. I approached him before the game and said I was sorry, but he said he was just delighted to still be here and be in the Premiership.

If he was not playing, someone had got to take the armband and I was more than willing to take it.

As for the game, it was a cruel blow. Everyone was gobsmacked. We had two great breaks at the end and we could have won it.

Latics new signing Arjan De Zeeuw.

It just shows you what happens at this level if you don't take your chances.

I was gutted that Crespo scored from there with his left foot. We worked so hard and defended magnificently in the second half.

It showed our early promise. When I was at Portsmouth we played fantastic against Arsenal and then a week later we got hammered 3–0 at Aston Villa, so we had to continue and keep it going. We just needed that extra bit of quality.

The young lads showed a few nerves. But after the performance against Chelsea, it showed they had no reason to be worried about anyone.

Though Ellington's talks with West Brom dampened the anticipation ahead of the Chelsea match a little, another transfer development was more warmly received in the parish. Arjan De Zeeuw, who served Wigan so stoically as captain in the old Division Two, had successfully requested that he be transfer-listed after falling down the pecking order under Alain Perrin at Portsmouth.

Jewell needed little persuasion to lure him back to the JJB Stadium. Was De Zeeuw happy to return? That was evident from the phone conversation he had with the *Wigan Observer*'s Matt Swindells:

'Hello.'

'Arry, it's Matt Swindells at the *Wigan Observer*. Just ringing to see what stage the talks are at...'

'I'm sorry Matt, you'll have to ring me back. I'm not having talks with the gaffer until this afternoon.'

'Erm... the only problem is our deadline is 11.30am. Is there anything I can put?'

'Just put in that I'm back in Wigan, and that I'm ready to re-sign for the club that I love.' Top man, that Arjan De Zeeuw.

He duly did re-sign for the club, though his move took place amid claims and counter-claims between the two clubs that the Dutch defender had been tapped up, an accusation Jewell furiously denied. 'We went through the correct channels,' he insisted, before firing, 'I think they have a communication problem at that club [Portsmouth].'

Media interest in the week leading up to the Chelsea game gathered momentum, to the point that when Wigan staged a press conference – their first in their new, swish media suite inside the West Stand – Al-Jazeera TV, which rocketed into the global eye for broadcasting Al-Qaeda's statements, was in attendance covering the event. The Premiership's newest club was seemingly popular in the Middle East.

When Jewell entered, he acknowledged a couple of local reporters, and a couple of older, respected writers he first met while in charge at Bradford.

'Would you settle for a 1–0 defeat to Chelsea?' someone asked. 'No I bloody wouldn't,' he replied. 'I'd be happy with a 1–0 win.'

And he was serious. Deadly serious.

Jewell answered all the journalists' questions, but not all sections of the media were behaving themselves. A reporter claiming to be from the *Daily Mail* had been phoning around offering to pay money for players' phone numbers for a feature about their wives. No one quite knew what kind of piece, exactly, they wanted to run, although the sprinkling of articles and news features comparing Wigan's northern image with that of Chelsea's bourgeois, elitist squad – the minnows and the millionaires – led to suspicions. The news infuriated McCann, whose temper was fraying with each passing minute.

The following day, Bryan Robson revealed that a £3 million bid for Nathan Ellington had been accepted by Wigan Athletic. Robson claimed he had been made aware by a newspaper story of a clause in Ellington's contract that he could talk to other clubs if they offered more than £3 million.

The Midlands club's offer was for £1 more than that amount, leaving Wigan with little choice but to allow Ellington to hold negotiations with the Baggies. Wigan did, however, have a choice about David Graham, a striker who had a

A new signing at the Hawthorns as Nathan Ellington, seen with manager Bryan Robson, joins West Bromwich Albion.

difficult first season with limited chances after signing from Torquay the previous summer. But Jewell accepted that Graham would again be restricted to a bit-part role in the Premier League, and sold him to Sheffield Wednesday – the club where he himself endured his darkest days of management – for a £250,000 fee.

Two days before the Chelsea match, Ellington completed his switch to West Brom to leave Wigan with a desperate shortage of fire-power. Only Henri Camara and Jason Roberts were available, and though a £5 million strike-force could not be described as weak, the strength in depth – or more precisely, the distinct lack of it – had Latics fans worried.

Their concerns were channelled into anger towards Ellington over his move, with message boards and local newspaper letters pages bombarded with insults and remarks. But even the Duke, who became Wigan's club record buy and had left the JJB Stadium with a legacy of wonderful goals, was playing second fiddle to the Chelsea game.

The night before their opening, historic match, Wigan were featured on BBC One's flagship *Six'O'Clock News*. Inevitably, there were the northern mill town clichés – workers from Uncle Joe's were even asked their thoughts – but there were no cobbled streets, and with the England cricket team's Ashes heroics the only other sports story, no one was complaining.

Sunday 14 August was the day that Premiership football arrived in Wigan. All the preparations had been completed, from the new facilities down to the dress code of the chairman's lounge (the ban on jeans was lifted for Chelsea's millionaire owner Roman Abramovich). The crowds flooded into the JJB Stadium on a glorious summer day. As the BBC put it, it was the day that 'Latics won the hearts of the nation', the day Chelsea went so, so agonisingly close to receiving an opening day bloody nose. Hernan Crespo's sweetly struck 93rd-minute goal defied sporting justice, and Jose Mourinho graciously admitted afterwards, 'It was unfair, they played better than us.' Paul Jewell's response at the time? 'That's life. That's football.'

But it was so much more than that. It was an exhilarating, brilliant exhibition from Wigan that was just 36 seconds short of rekindling the romance of the beautiful game.

At the after-match press conference, Jewell took his seat and was immediately asked by one journalist bluntly, 'How did you feel after Crespo scored, Paul?'

Dave Whelan looks gutted and Roman Abramovich looks bemused by the result at the final whistle.

Sunday 14 August 2005

Wigan 0 Chelsea 1

WIGAN: Pollitt 8, Chimbonda 9, Henchoz 8, De Zeeuw 9, Baines 7, Teale 7, Francis 8, Bullard 8, Mahon 6, Roberts 7, Camara 7. Sub: Johansson 6 (for Mahon 86). Wigan star man: De Zeeuw.

CHELSEA: Cech 7, Ferreira 7, Gallas 7, Terry 7, Del Horno 7, Duff 6, Lampard 6, Makelele 6, Robben 7, Drogba 6, Gudjohnsen 6. Subs: Cole 7 (for Robben 45), Wright-Phillips 7 (for Gudjohnsen 45), Crespo 8 (for Duff 60).

Goal: Crespo (90)
Half-time: 0–0
Referee: Mark Clattenburg
Attendance: 23,575

What the opposition said...

'They have a good manager who prepares his team well. Wigan have a great spirit and determination. I wasn't surprised by Wigan's performance. I watched a lot of videos on Wigan before the game and I knew they were a good side. My scouts followed them during the pre-season. I thought Wigan played better than us and didn't deserve to lose.' – Chelsea manager Jose Mourinho.

What the Wigan fan said...

'I've literally been to hundreds of Wigan games but this was the biggest of them all and the pre-game hype was akin to England playing in a World Cup Final – it wasn't a let down! The result apart, it will be one day that will remain etched in my memory as long as I breathe.' – *Cockney Latics* fanzine editor John Heeley.

	P	W	D	L	F	A	Pts
Charlton	1	1	0	0	3	1	3
West Ham	1	1	0	0	3	1	3
Arsenal	1	1	0	0	2	0	3
Man Utd	1	1	0	0	2	0	3
Tottenham	1	1	0	0	2	0	3
Chelsea	1	1	0	0	1	0	3
Aston Villa	1	0	1	0	2	2	1
Bolton	1	0	1	0	2	2	1
Birm'ham	1	0	1	0	0	0	1
Fulham	1	0	1	0	0	0	1
Liverpool	1	0	1	0	0	0	1
Man City	1	0	1	0	0	0	1
Middlesb'h	1	0	1	0	0	0	1
West Brom	1	0	1	0	0	0	1
Wigan	1	0	0	1	0	1	0
Blackburn	1	0	0	1	1	3	0
Sunderl'd	1	0	0	1	1	3	0
Everton	1	0	0	1	0	2	0
Newcastle	1	0	0	1	0	2	0
Portsm'th	1	0	0	1	0	2	0

'Great, lovely, delighted – it was a smashing feeling,' came the reply from the clearly deflated scouser. 'How do you think I felt? I was gutted, pig sick. I was sick for the players more than anything because they gave everything. They can't walk away from the stadium with anything other than their chests stuck out after that.'

Jewell spoke for everyone in Wigan colours. No, correct that – for everyone in the country not wearing Chelsea's colours. Any doubts over whether Wigan had what it took to survive against the best clubs in the land were answered in 90 breathtaking minutes. They battled, scrapped and mixed it with the best team this country has to offer – all £160 million of them.

'This is a moral victory,' Jewell said. 'It should get easier after this, shouldn't it? This has to be a benchmark. If we can do it against Chelsea we can do it against every other team.'

Latics went toe to toe, traded blows and slugged it out with Roman's superstars all the way to the death. And with an ounce more luck 'Little Old Wigan' could have walked off with a win or, at the least, one of the most famous 0–0 draws ever. Chances came and went as Chelsea were quite clearly rattled by the intensity, drive and determination of Jewell's outfit.

It was intimidating stuff, right from the first whistle as Jason Roberts kicked off Wigan's Premiership campaign with the clock showing 4.02pm. But the JJB Stadium turned to ice as the opening day dreams of holding the champions to a 0–0 draw were shattered in an instant. You don't always get what you deserve in this game and Latics certainly didn't deserve to walk off the pitch with nothing to show for their efforts.

Leighton Baines tangles with Shaun Wright-Phillips.

Admittedly, Hernan Crespo's winner with just 36 seconds of action remaining was worthy of winning any game. But this was Brian Deane revisited from a little over a year previously, when West Ham's late goal denied Wigan a place in the play-offs.

'We're all absolutely gutted,' Jimmy Bullard said, as he held back the tears afterwards. 'We gave it our all and we could have won the game. To lose it in that way it is just so hard to take. We had Chelsea frightened and we could sense that out there. Every one of our players rose to the challenge and proved they've got what it takes.'

For Bullard, in particular, it was proof that although his career path never took the direct route of Chelsea's Joe Cole and Frank Lampard, both former teammates at West Ham, he had the ability to justify his place in the top flight. Mourinho saluted the efforts of referee Mark Clattenburg at the final whistle. But there was one question on everyone's lips as he blew for full-time: Where on earth did he get three added minutes from? There were two substitutions in the second half for one extra minute, but adding on two more for free-kicks boggled minds.

Matt Jackson applauds the players off at the end of the game.

Abramovich wasn't complaining though, sitting in the director's box. A smug grin, a quick handshake with Dave Whelan and the Russian was off with his bodyguards to the heli-pad located a mile away in the JJB Sports headquarters to catch his luxury lift home.

'We were lucky, just one of those days,' chief executive Peter Kenyon admitted, as he applauded the Wigan troops as they left the field.

There were heroic performances throughout the Wigan side, as well as highly encouraging displays from the five debutants. The action itself was edge of the seat stuff, and after a frantic opening and just three minutes gone, Latics should have been ahead. Imagine that – Wigan one up against Chelsea inside five minutes. And at the end, substitute Andreas Johansson had two glorious chances on the counter-attack as the clock dwindled down.

'I was disappointed we didn't make more of them,' admitted Jewell, though not oblivious to how surreal his statement seemed in the context of the occasion. 'We had three against two and we could have won the game.'

From the resulting goal-kick the ball was quickly back in the Wigan half and in the blink of an eye in the back of Mike Pollitt's net. Cruel? It didn't come close.

But Wigan's bold and brilliant pursuit of a result against Chelsea assured the club the unofficial title as many people's second favourite team. And their wounds were nursed by lavish praise from the previously sceptical national media. Days earlier the media had been suspicious about Wigan's place among the country's elite. After their opening match, they eulogised about the drama without restraint.

'Chelsea made some interesting signings but no one realised they had signed Lady Luck as well,' wrote Henry Winter in the *Daily Telegraph*. 'Wigan's ascent to the Premiership may be mind boggling,' volunteered Kevin McCarra in *The Guardian*, 'but it was Chelsea who hardly knew where they were.' Richard Tanner wrote in the *Daily Express*: 'If ever a team deserved a point it was Wigan, after matching Chelsea stride for stride, pass for pass and chance for chance.'

The opening game, between the Premiership champions and the Premiership new boys, attracted the chief football writers of all the national newspapers and even triggered a debate over whether Crespo's late cannonball would be the goal of the season that was about to unfold.

'Already beyond doubt though,' offered Matt Dickinson in *The Times,* 'is that no team will lose more cruelly all year than Wigan Athletic did.' Even respected *Daily Mirror* writer Oliver Holt, who once compared Dave Whelan to a dinosaur, wrote, 'Wigan have got a smart manager, a great stadium, brilliant fans and an army of courteous, helpful stewards and officials. Their players aren't bad, either. They are a class act on and off the pitch and a great addition to the Premiership. I think boss Paul Jewell might be right: They're going to surprise a few people this season.'

Jewell handled the defeat with grace and professionalism, yet despite the media's response, he was hurt. Proud, but hurt. It didn't help that, the following day, Ellington rubbed salt into the proverbial wound when he was unveiled at West Brom.

'No disrespect to Wigan,' he commented, 'but West Brom are a bigger club who want to go to the next step.'

Not surprisingly, Ellington's remarks were as welcome as Rodney Marsh's presence at a Wigan Athletic Supporters' Club meeting would be. Chairman Dave Whelan responded by criticising the striker's adviser for engineering the move against his wishes, while Jewell said the Championship's top scorer had been in 'floods of tears' when he left.

Within a day or two, though, the Wigan players had recovered. Midfielder Graham Kavanagh summed up the buoyant, vibrant mood after being made aware of a *Wigan Observer* article in which Latics' Australian fitness coach, Joey Gallanagh, referred to Kavanagh as 'Wigan's second best boxer behind John Filan.'

'That's a laugh,' Kavanagh grinned, his eyes lighting up. 'I could take Filo with my eyes closed!'

The confidence that had followed their spirited performance against Chelsea was dented a little when Henri Camara was ruled out of Wigan's next game, against Charlton, with an injury. Jewell described the fixture as 'tougher than Chelsea', a statement in itself that was tempting to ridicule, but one that he justified by pointing out just how crucial the enthusiasm and energy had been against the Blues. 'The whole world was watching that game, so it's easier to raise yourself,' he said.

Certainly, with no Camara, Jewell's task was made all the more difficult. He stepped up his attempts to sign a striker and was widely linked with Dean Ashton, but the Norwich forward clarified his position with the Canaries by signing an extension to his contract, leaving Jewell no choice but to use Jason Roberts as the sole forward against Charlton at the Valley.

Latics lost 1–0 for the second time in six days, though any similarities between their loss to Charlton and the previous week's game against Chelsea ended with the scoreline. The verve and vigour that had served Wigan so well against the champions abandoned them in the capital. Even Jewell admitted that the final scoreline flattered Wigan, with goalkeeper Mike Pollitt and Arjan De Zeeuw the only players to emerge with enhanced reputations.

Saturday 20 August 2005

Charlton 1 Wigan 0

CHARLTON: Anderson 6, Young 7, Hreidarsson 7, Perry 7, Powell 8, Smertin 8, Murphy 9, Kishishev 7, Thomas 8, Rommedahl 8, Bent 7. Subs: Johansson (for Rommedahl 77), Bartlett (for Thomas 83), Hughes (for Murphy 85).

WIGAN: Pollit 8, Chimbonda 7, Henchoz 6, De Zeeuw 7, Baines 6, Teale 6, Francis 6, Bullard 6, Mahon 5, Johansson 6, Roberts 6. Subs: McMillan (for Mahon 45) 6, Taylor (for Teale 63) 6. Wigan star man: Pollitt.

Goal: Bent (42)
Half-time: 1–0
Referee: Rob Styles
Attendance: 23,453

What the opposition said...
'You know what you're going to get with Wigan. They've got some good players with lots of work rate and lots of enthusiasm. They made it difficult for us and they will against a lot of teams in this division. Paul Jewell is no stranger to the Premiership – many people will recall the great job he did at Bradford City. He got them up to the top flight and kept them there.' – Charlton manager Alan Curbishley.

Jewell had just 16 fit players (Latics' bench at the Valley comprised a goalkeeper and four defenders) and if any more members of the squad had cried off injured, Jewell would have been forced to select untried youngsters Luke Joyce or Kevin Lee for their second Premier League contest.

The lack of firepower told as Wigan didn't record a single shot on target, though

Wigan's Andreas Johansson leaves Charlton's Radostin Kishishev.

What the Wigan fan said...
'It was a disappointing performance following last week's mighty display at home. Danny Murphy caused real problems for Baines. Latics forged some half chances but in the end it was a fair result. With Camara sidelined our lack of firepower was a telling factor.' – Caroline Molyneux, chairperson of Wigan Athletic's Supporters Club.

Jewell was concerned that signs of complacency had begun to creep in. He combatted those fears head on, keeping his players in the dressing room for 20 minutes after the final whistle as he handed out the hairdryer treatment.

'It was a big difference from the Chelsea game,' admitted De Zeeuw. 'We didn't keep the ball well at all and we were too hesitant. Charlton had long spells when they were on top of us. The gaffer warned us before the game not to be complacent. We never really went for it and didn't create enough opportunities to score. The squad isn't big enough and the gaffer knows it.'

The skipper believed the defeat doubled the importance of the following weekend's game at home to Sunderland. 'This puts a much greater emphasis on it now,' he offered. 'There's a lot of pressure on this game, but it's not all doom and gloom. We've had a hard start. Chelsea at home, we had nothing to lose and I've never got anything better than a draw at Charlton.'

Charlton dominated possession with Latics penned inside their own half for the majority of the contest. Jason Roberts worked tirelessly on his own up front, but to no avail. Wigan didn't have an answer to the impressive Danny Murphy, who pulled strings like a puppetmaster. Pollitt had to produce two smart saves to keep Jerome Thomas and then Darren Bent out, though he stood no chance of keeping Bent's

	P	W	D	L	F	A	Pts
Tottenham	2	2	0	0	4	0	6
Charlton	2	2	0	0	4	1	6
Man Utd	2	2	0	0	3	0	6
Chelsea	2	2	0	0	2	0	6
West Ham	2	1	1	0	3	1	4
Man City	2	1	1	0	2	1	4
West Brom	2	1	1	0	2	1	4
Liverpool	2	1	1	0	1	0	4
Arsenal	2	1	0	1	2	1	3
Blackburn	2	1	0	1	3	4	3
Everton	2	1	0	1	1	2	3
Aston Villa	2	0	1	1	2	3	1
Bolton	2	0	1	1	2	3	1
Birm'ham	2	0	1	1	1	2	1
Fulham	2	0	1	1	1	2	1
Middlesb'h	2	0	1	1	0	2	1
Newcastle	2	0	1	1	0	2	1
Wigan	2	0	0	2	0	2	0
Portsm'th	2	0	0	2	1	4	0
Sunderl'd	2	0	0	2	1	4	0

Wigan's Ryan Taylor faces Charlton's Chris Powell.

second effort from crossing the line three minutes from the break from Murphy's deadly accurate cross.

Bullard had one sight of goal a minute after the restart, but fired into the crowd. Charlton remained in the ascendancy and had two claims for penalties as Stephane Henchoz pulled Rommedahl back and Steve McMillan handled the Dane's cross. Roberts's diving header with nine minutes left, which rolled three yards wide, was as good as it got.

Their performance was featured on Saturday's *Match of the Day* for the first time, though Gary Lineker and Alan Hansen spent barely a minute discussing the game. Hansen, who was at Liverpool when Jewell was a young apprentice, said Wigan would be able to strengthen in the January transfer window if they were struggling by Christmas.

Jewell continued the post-mortem on television when he made his first appearance on *Goals on Sunday*. He joined Sky Sports studio hosts Rob McCaffrey and Chris Kamara, along with former Bradford midfielder Stuart McCall, to discuss the weekend's action. He was typically frank in his assessment of Wigan's performance against Charlton.

'That sort of performance won't keep us in this division,' he admitted. 'We lacked a lot of firepower and we were nowhere near our best. The players looked like they didn't believe they could win the game or score a goal. We've got to be stronger than that all over the park.'

The following day, Wigan made the back page of the *Daily Mirror* after Whelan's daring move to bring Real Madrid striker Michael Owen to England leaked out. At first, the story was dismissed as being either a publicity stunt or so far off the mark it would need a NASA radar to pick it up. But no. Senior sources at Wigan confirmed it was true.

A conversation with Paul Jewell later that day all but confirmed it when he point-blank refused to discuss Owen, other than to admit he was 'a decent player'. Jewell has always appreciated the chance to set the record straight on the endless number of rumours and tabloid stories linking various players with the club.

Sometimes, though, talks are at a delicate stage and he is unable to divulge too much information. In these instances, other managers and clubs often blatantly lie, but Jewell is a man who is stoically honest, and as such there is an occasional conflict between not jeopardising a move and not lying, in which case he usually tries to deflect the question with a joke, or instead offer a simple 'no comment'.

Not long after he arrived at Wigan the local media managed to devise a three-pronged key to digest his responses: if he isn't interested in a player, he says so; if he is interested in a player but it is at an early stage, he says 'no comment'; if he is interested in a player and he is confident of completing the signing, he will talk about it. Over the years that tool has proved a simple but effective means of assessing the credibility of rumours and tabloid transfer gossip. Using that key, even a fool could translate the following question and answer session from his regular Monday lunchtime press conference with the local hacks:

'There has been a report that you are trying to sign Michael Owen. Is it true?'

'No comment. I don't comment on newspaper speculation.'

'There have also been stories linking Wigan with Fatih Tekke…'

'Yes, we would like to sign Tekke and it's one we are pursuing.'

As precise as science.

Though resigned to Owen going elsewhere, Wigan defender Ryan Taylor said the attempt to sign him underlined the determination to establish Wigan as a serious force in the Premiership.

'Michael Owen is a fantastic player – just look at his record,' said the former Tranmere player, a die-hard Kop fan. 'For Wigan to try to sign a player of his calibre just shows what the manager is trying to do here. That bid showed pretty quickly that the manager and chairman are so ambitious.'

Owen, unsurprisingly, joined Newcastle, despite his admission that he wanted to return to Anfield, which prompted 'Swindonlatic' to write on the Cockneylatic message board, surely with tongue firmly in cheek, that: 'Owen has an overinflated ego and is simply not worth that kind of money. Thank God there was no way he was going to join us!'

Australian midfielder Josip Skoko arrived in Wigan after his long-standing problem with the Home Office was resolved. Skoko's visa had to work its way through the usual, drawn-out process despite his 40 caps for the Socceroos, but he trained with the squad for the first time and, after recovering from his jetlag, found an ally in John Filan, his fellow countryman, ahead of the start of the fourth Ashes Test the following day. 'We'll be watching the cricket this week and hope England get thrashed,' grinned the Melbourne-raised midfielder.

Skoko's arrival handed McCann another task – finding him a house. The Wigan PR had to balance his media commitments with helping new players settle in. Just days before he had viewed an apartment in Manchester with Pascal Chimbonda, and McCann reported back that the previous tenant was actor Patrick Stewart, better known for playing Jean-Luc Picard in *Star Trek*. Inevitably, the news was greeted with cheeky satisfaction by some of his teammates, who spent the next week ribbing the Frenchman with chants of: 'Beam me up Chimmy.'

Charlton's manager Alan Curbishley licks his lips at the match against Wigan.

Wigan's manager Paul Jewell after another defeat, this time at the Valley.

Wigan Athletic's new boy Josip Skoko, bottom right, in training with Arjan De Zeeuw and the rest of the Latics squad.

Saturday 27 August 2005

Wigan 1
Sunderland 0

WIGAN: Pollitt 9, Chimbonda 7, Henchoz 8, De Zeeuw 7, Baines 7, Taylor 7, Francis 6, Kavanagh 6, McCulloch 6, Bullard 6, Roberts 6. Subs: Mahon (for Kavanagh 70), Jackson (for Henchoz 86). Wigan star man: Pollitt.

SUNDERLAND: Davis 7, Nosworthy 7, Breen 6, Stubbs 6, Arca 7, Elliott 7, Le Tallec 7, Whitehead 8, Miller 7, Welsh 8, Stead 7. Subs: Woods 6 (for Welsh 63), Gray 6 (for Stead 63).

Goal: Roberts (1)
Half-time: 1–0
Referee: Steve Bennett
Attendance: 17,223

On the transfer front, Jewell's attempt to sign Turkish striker Fatih Tekke was faltering and he turned his attention to Bradford's veteran striker Dean Windass. Jewell said Windass, who opted to stay at Bradford, still had 'Premiership quality', but that did not stop criticism from some fickle fans, who were impatiently waiting for new signings.

'I've been getting fed up of supporters saying we're not doing this or we're not doing that,' Jewell snapped. 'We've been trying to spend money. I want our supporters to trust me rather than complaining all the time. We've been trying to get players in.'

He sought refuge in his impeccable record of unearthing quality, often from the obscurity of the lower leagues, as well as his two promotions in three years.

'If my best isn't good enough then maybe someone else should have a go,' he continued. 'I won't be swayed by the opinions of these so-called experts. I'm good at my job and I can pick a player. If we get into Europe I might just quieten one or two of them down. Sometimes you wonder if you're appreciated for the job you do here.'

On Saturday 27 August – nearly two weeks after opening their season – Latics won their first Premiership game with a 1–0 home win against Sunderland. Referee Steve Bennett awarded the home side a penalty after just 12 seconds, the quickest ever recorded in the history of the Premier League, and the visitors never recovered.

Fittingly, it was Jason Roberts who stroked home the spot-kick. Here was a player who, having turned up from West Brom, fired in the third quickest debut goal in English football in just 34 seconds at Preston. But he was not content to just live off that glorious statistic. His goal secured him a place in Wigan folklore as the player to net the club's opening goal in the top flight, when it rolled over the line after 54 seconds.

'It's nice to get the first goal in the Premiership with Wigan,' he said. 'Hopefully this will be the first of many for me.'

Roberts's last goal at Premiership level had been on 13 December 2003 for Portsmouth in a 2–1 defeat against Everton. His first for Wigan was a gift. Jimmy Bullard sent the ball forward from the kick-off, Gary Breen made a hash of a simple header and Lee McCulloch knocked the ball through for Roberts to chase. Mick McCarthy, unsurprisingly, reckoned Breen's clumsy challenge on Roberts wasn't a penalty, but the defender's lack of complaint to Steve Bennett said it all. There were no shortage of takers for the resulting spot-kick, but Roberts made sure he grabbed the ball.

'When the referee pointed to the spot I was trying to get the ball to take it,' admitted former Tranmere penalty taker Ryan Taylor. 'But there's a big queue here. Jason's got a good record with penalties and I knew he'd score.'

A little shimmy and a firm stroke of the right boot saw Kelvin Davis fall to his left and Roberts plant the ball in the opposite corner.

'Breen leant right into me and brought me down – there was no doubt it was a penalty,' Roberts insisted. 'If you start thinking about penalties too much you will miss them. I knew how important it was to score. It would have been a long two weeks without any points on the board. To get the victory was so important for us.'

Wigan's first win in the Premiership had arrived, and it brought with it more than three points. It brought confidence. Bags of it.

'It's great to have got the monkey off our back – we're up and running now,' smiled Graham Kavanagh. 'This will give us the confidence. We need to knuckle down and try to grind out results.'

Dave Whelan admitted there was an element of luck to their first win in the Premiership. 'We deserved three points against Chelsea and we were lucky against Sunderland which shows this game levels itself out,' he said.

Ryan Taylor and Martin Woods tangle.

What the opposition said...

'It couldn't have been a worse start for us. We gave Wigan an easy start to score and that was the only difference between the two sides. I think the penalty was harsh and Jason Roberts made a meal of it. My players didn't get the reward for their efforts. The two teams are going to find it hard to score goals this season – the last thing we needed to do was give them one on a plate.' – Sunderland manager Mick McCarthy.

What the Wigan fan said...

'We got off to a great start scoring in the first minute, but then it got a bit scrappy in stages and there wasn't much quality from either side. We looked nervous in possession and kept giving the ball away which was giving Sunderland the advantage. Chimbonda stood out for me.' – season-ticket holder Mark Fulton.

	P	W	D	L	F	A	Pts
Chelsea	4	4	0	0	8	0	12
Man City	4	3	1	0	6	3	10
Charlton	3	3	0	0	7	1	9
Man Utd	3	3	0	0	5	0	9
Bolton	4	2	1	1	6	4	7
Tottenham	4	2	1	1	4	2	7
Arsenal	3	2	0	1	6	2	6
Aston Villa	4	1	2	1	4	4	5
West Ham	3	1	1	1	4	3	4
Liverpool	2	1	1	0	1	0	4
Blackburn	4	1	1	2	3	5	4
Middlesb'h	4	1	1	2	3	5	4
Birm'ham	4	1	1	2	4	7	4
Fulham	4	1	1	2	3	6	4
West Brom	4	1	1	2	4	8	4
Wigan	3	1	0	2	1	2	3
Everton	3	1	0	2	1	3	3
Portsm'th	4	0	1	3	3	7	1
Newcastle	4	0	1	3	0	6	1
Sunderl'd	4	0	0	4	2	7	0

Arjan De Zeeuw congratulates a beaming Roberts after scoring Wigan's first Premiership goal.

Sunderland were comfortable in possession, but simply didn't have the class going forward to cause any lasting damage. And when they did get sight of goal, Pollitt again proved it would have to be a decent effort to get anything past him.

After Latics' glorious opening they could have gone behind and would have done but for Stephane Henchoz. The Swiss defender blocked Anthony Le Tallec's shot superbly and then cleared Alan Stubbs's header off the line, all within the opening five minutes. But then the game fizzled out slightly. Lee McCulloch, brought back in to replace Alan Mahon, put himself about but it was Pollitt who shone brightest, producing another fine save to keep Jon Stead out from close range.

As the game moved into stoppage time, the whistles from the crowd were amplified around the electric JJB Stadium. There was a quick punch of the air from Jewell when Sunderland's last attack rolled out for a goal-kick. Pollitt's resulting punt upfield was the last play of a ground-breaking game. For Pollitt, it was a moment to savour. He was rescued from Rotherham just weeks before the season kicked off and the 1–0 win over Sunderland was his first clean sheet at the highest level.

'I think I've done well over the first three games,' he said. 'I've not been feeling any nerves and I've made some important saves. It's strange now that I'm sitting at home on a Saturday night watching myself playing in the Premiership on *Match of the Day*. But I do feel a lot sharper than I ever have done.'

Days after the game, Whelan spoke publicly about how Wigan would have signed Owen had he not gone to Newcastle or Liverpool and also revealed a bonus scheme to reward his players if they retained their Premiership status. 'I'll be paying the players £2 million if we stay up this season,' he declared.

As the clock ticked down to the 31 August transfer window deadline, Jewell dispatched his scouts across Europe and even flew to France himself to watch Monaco take on Lens.

'To be honest I'm not a big fan of the transfer window,' he admitted. 'In fact I'd quite like to throw a brick through it at the moment. Chasing players abroad adds its difficulties and I can tell you I've covered some miles in the past few weeks. We've been to Norway, Denmark, Bulgaria, Poland, Germany and other far-flung places. We should get Alan Whicker on board.'

Despite his airmiles, Jewell found his man not in Lyon or Lisbon, but in Leicester. David Connolly beat the transfer deadline by nine hours to sign at the JJB Stadium in a £2 million deal from the Foxes. It came after unsuccessful attempts to

Jason Roberts is congratulated by more of his teammates on scoring his penalty.

Paul Jewell and Mick McCarthy.

sign Fatih Tekke, Dean Ashton, Dean Windass, Robert Earnshaw and Michael Owen, but Jewell stressed he was not a panic buy.

'We had to wait until deadline day itself but I feel we've landed a top-quality forward who will give us something different from what we already have,' Jewell said.

Jewell also wanted to bring back Brett Ormerod after a successful one-month loan spell the previous season, but a deal for the Southampton hit man couldn't be completed in time. 'In the end the clock beat us,' Jewell said. 'But we still had enough quality to compete and survive at this level.'

Pascal Chimbonda is fouled.

Wigan defender Steve McMillan kept a diary leading up to the glamorous opening day game against Chelsea...

Monday 8 August

It's the photoshoot at the stadium at 9.30am. I look around at the players I'm with and it gives me confidence – I know they can do a job. After the picture, we go training but it's a light session. We played a friendly on the weekend so it was just a chance to get the legs working again. We played a game of eight v eight, just to get the ball rolling for the week. It seems everywhere I go everyone asks me the same question: 'Are you ready for Chelsea?' Some people don't quite word it like that – they say things like 'You must be quaking in your boots.' I'm not, and I don't think any of the other Wigan players are. We're looking forward to the game. This is what we've dreamed of.

Tuesday 9 August

I turn up for training and someone tells me that Arry (Arjan De Zeeuw) is having a medical, but I haven't seen him. My seven-year-old son, Lewis, is down from Scotland and he comes along. He loves it! The training picks up intensity. Joey (Gallanagh) has come in and he's been really good for us – we've never been fitter. We broke into three teams of six and played games, with the Gaffer (Paul Jewell) controlling it. He's the referee – but no one dare talk back to him! He takes great delight in punishing the losing team with forfeits. Usually it's shuttle runs to the halfway line, then the 18-yard line and on and on... unfortunately I was on the losing side. We train a lot like we play – we don't go for a long leisurely run, instead we're at it for two hours at full pace.

This year it's been a little different with the foreign lads joining us but there isn't really a language barrier. We've had foreign players before but the difference is Arry and Per Frandsen speak English better than most of the British players! This year we have Henri Camara and Pascal (Chimbonda) who are still learning the language. But Pascal knows more English than he lets on... he certainly knew what the words 'day off' meant!

Wednesday 10 August

We trained today, and trained well. Arry joins the squad and it's like he's never been away. It's good to see him again. Arry was the captain when I signed for Wigan and I don't hesitate to say he's one of the most professional players I've ever been involved with. He's 35 but he's as fit as anyone. He's a good bloke Arry... but I won't be sitting next to him on the team bus. He is a qualified doctor and some of the medical journals he reads are baffling! They're certainly not John Grisham. We play 11 on 11 with the gaffer again the ref, and after training, we all go for lunch together and then we go our separate ways. I've had quite a few text messages from mates and some members of my family... and quite a few are asking for tickets to the game!

Thursday 11 August

It's our day off today. With such a big game coming up, the gaffer has told us to go easy and relax. Often on days off, some of the boys go playing golf but I'm not a golfer and in any case, ahead of a big game the boys know they're better off doing nothing. All the players are very close. I wouldn't say any one of them was my best friend, but the spirit is incredible. Today my kids – Lewis and Emma, who is two – are at Alton Towers with their mum, so I travel down there to have a day with them. They're down from Scotland before the summer holidays end and they've had a great time. Lewis is beginning to realise what a big deal it is that we're playing Chelsea and Man U, and teams like that. He asks all the questions. He's a great kid and he's loved being at training with me – Jimmy Bullard keeps making him laugh. Lewis calls him 'daft Jimmy'. He's a smart boy, my son.

Friday 12 August

The gaffer named his side for the Chelsea game... and I'm not in it. He opted for Leighton Baines at left-back, with me on the bench. I'm disappointed. In a way, I saw it coming. Paul took me to one side and explained why he was doing it. He said Bainesy played a big part in last season and he deserved his chance, and I respect that. Though we are fighting for the same position, Bainesy and I get on great and no one spits the dummy out when they don't get named – you can't afford to. We're all in this together, and I know I'll get my chance at some point. All the team trained together and today we looked at Chelsea's shape and their plan, and we adapted our game to cope with that. We set ourselves up 11 v 11 and go through each scenario. The club scouted Chelsea just like any other side, and we worked on ways to frustrate them and match them head to head. Afterwards, we relaxed. You've got to take it easy before a big game – that even means laying off the shopping!

Saturday 13 August

We trained this morning, but it was a light session. We went over our set pieces, our corners and throw-ins, and played a wee game of eight against eight for fun, and we did some shadow play as well. Even though I've been named on the bench I have to prepare as if I was playing, because you never know what can happen. Overnight, someone could be taken ill or they could injure themselves during the opening minute of the game.

The afternoon before the game I force myself to laze

at home. Today, I watched the football on TV in the afternoon – like many footballers, I'm a huge fan of the game, although I'm not really a fan of any one club. I always look out for my former club Motherwell because I still have some mates there. That's the great thing about football – you have friends all over the place, so it's interesting to see how they're getting on. I'm always getting texts off mates wishing me well. Flynny [former teammate Mike Flynn] is a good lad – a bit mad, mind – but I've kept in touch with him since he left Wigan. He played for Gillingham and they drew 1–1. The Chelsea game is all over the TV and the papers and it's impossible to ignore it, though you have to try. We know how good we are, and we're still confident in ourselves.

Sunday 14 August

On a game day I always get up at around 10.30am, have a couple of weetabix and some toast, and that's it. It's a bit of a boring routine, but it works for me so I still do it. I drove to the ground and I couldn't believe it when I got there – literally thousands of fans. There was a real buzz about the place. I checked in and got changed, and there were no withdrawals. I was on the bench. I've never been a player to get really nervous before a game – except for the hour leading up to the kick-off. Everyone is different. Jason Roberts always says a little prayer, but for me, I just can't wait for it to start. Once the whistle goes, though, I'm fine. The game itself was great – and we got their tactics spot on. We knew no one would beat us in a battle, it would need something really special from them – and they got it in the 93rd minute.

Everyone was gutted. But the important thing is it was a wonder-goal – it didn't come from one of our errors – and it is goals like that which is why Crespo is paid £100,000 a week! Football is all about highs and lows but despite the positives, the dressing room had a sombre mood afterwards. We were all gutted. The gaffer got us together and told us he was proud to be our manager and that we can leave with our heads held high, and that helped. Arry got named the man of the match and before he went out to do the Sky TV interview he took a bottle of Lucozade with him. It's a little-known secret that players get £500 from Lucozade every time their drink is on screen – even if it's on the training pitch. It can add up over a season: at the end of last season Portsmouth got £50,000! Arry didn't do it for the money, of course, but to raise the team spirits – he put the money straight into the kitty!

I turned on my mobile and there were dozens of new messages, all from mates and members of my family who had seen the game. They were all saying the same thing – that we were desperately unlucky. After the game we went into the new players' bar – and very nice it is, too. But the Chelsea players didn't come in, they were straight on the team bus and back to London after the game.

There was little interaction between both camps. Jimmy [Bullard] knows Frank Lampard and Joe Cole from their days at West Ham and they had a chat afterwards, but that was it. Although they are famous players it's important not to be over-awed by them – ultimately, they are just footballers like us. Having said that, I came out of the dressing room and who did I see? Graham Kavanagh posing for a picture with them!

The Premiership Trophy was in town and Latics' players were keen to get close up to it. Pictured with the famous trophy are Ryan Taylor and Steve McMillan.

4: September: 'Who Needs Mourinho, we've got Paul Jewellio'

TWO DAYS after the transfer deadline closed, new signing David Connolly was paraded at Christopher Park. The assembled media, including local TV, Sky Sports and numerous print and radio journalists, waited patiently as he practiced his ball

Paul Jewell keeps an eye on David Connolly in training.

skills for 20 minutes, before being told the press conference would be a rapid affair as Connolly had a flight to London to catch to tie up loose ends.

Under such tight constraints, interviews commonly follow a structured routine, particularly when the national press are involved. The local press will ask the nice questions about their thoughts of signing for their new club... and then the tabloids will try and lure the player into firing a parting shot at their former club.

Many of the Premiership's biggest stars have become increasingly wary of such a practice, aware that one slip can lead to a screaming back-page headline. To counter this, they often fall back on any one of an assortment of stock cliché answers. Connolly, a victim in the past of unfair stories regarding his international career with Ireland, was understandably on his guard against the direct line of questioning.

'Do you think you are worth £2 million?'

'Do you think you can fill the boots of Nathan Ellington?'

To his merit, he answered the questions thoughtfully, modestly and tactfully. 'The transfer fee is of no concern to me,' he said. 'Wigan think I'm worth the money and now it's down to me to repay that faith and score goals for the club. Nathan Ellington did really well for Wigan when he was here and I was very impressed with the partnership he had with Jason Roberts. But I'm here now and I'm aiming to push my way into the team against West Brom on Saturday and score goals.'

Connolly's arrival followed failed attempts to land Michael Owen, Fatih Tekke, Dean Ashton, Dean Windass, Brett Ormerod and Robert Earnshaw. But Jewell, who had always taken great pride in the quality of his signings, furiously denied suggestions he had broken his own strict rule of not making panic buys.

'I will never buy players for the sake of it,' he insisted. 'There weren't too many out there who I wanted, although we did miss out on a couple. Connolly is a proven striker and I've seen enough of him to know he will score goals at this level. He's a natural finisher and he's always caused us problems when he's played against us.'

As the days rumbled on, fans used website message boards, talkback radio and newspaper letters pages to vent their frustrations at the lack of strength in the squad. Jewell even received letters from fans who questioned his ability in the transfer market. Not surprisingly, given Jewell's near impeccable track record, they provoked an angry response.

'Some people need to grow up and have a reality check,' he stormed, in his second broadside at some sections of fans in the opening month of the Premier League. 'I'm disappointed in some people's reactions and some arrogant comments from fans about it being another typical week at Wigan Athletic.

'We were closer than people think to getting Michael Owen in. A £5 million bid went in for Fatih Tekke and Dean Ashton. We made a seven million euro bid for Johan Elmander at Brondby, but they are in the UEFA Cup and they didn't want to sell him. We made one bid for Dean Windass of £350,000 – we didn't go back with another offer. He didn't think he could play in the Premiership every week and I disagreed with him. It must be a terrible week for us here.

'We're in the Premiership, we've got four players away on international duty and we've got record crowds. It must have been great here 10 years ago.

'We haven't brought in too many full English internationals for some people's liking. Wigan Athletic is a big catch isn't it? We're only competing against the likes of United, Arsenal, Chelsea and Liverpool.'

Despite failed attempts to land Michael Owen, Fatih Tekke, Dean Ashton, Dean Windass, Brett Ormerod and Robert Earnshaw, manager Paul Jewell managed one signing in September. He received a special shirt to mark his birthday.

With a vacant weekend for the World Cup qualifiers – England scraped to a 1–0 win over Wales with a highly-contested 4–5–1 formation – Wigan used their time wisely. The squad was given some time off to relax, though Jewell did not enjoy such a luxury. The closure of the transfer window stopped him signing players from other clubs, though the rule did not affect unattached players, so Jewell began the thankless task of trying to bolster his squad from the rubble of has-beens, wannabes and journeymen who remained out of contract.

It was slim pickings.

Nevertheless, a story appeared in the *Daily Star Sunday* quoting Jewell as saying that he had been in talks to try and sign former Barcelona midfield star Josep Guardiola. The 34-year-old ex-Spanish international had rejected an offer from Manchester City and was a free agent, having left Qatar-based club Al-Ahli at the end of the previous season.

'I have spoken to Pep and I was very impressed that he knew so much about us,' Jewell was reported as saying. 'His experience would be a help to us.'

It transpired that Jewell made the remark at a League Managers Dinner… and was unaware he was within earshot of a reporter. But though true, talks vaporised as Jewell was passed from one advisor to the next.

The Wigan players, recharged and rejuvenated from their weekend off, began their preparations for their game at West Bromwich Albion. But Wigan did not escape the international weekend unscathed, with four on duty for their countries: Leighton Baines, Ryan Taylor (both England Under-21s), Josip Skoko (Australia) and Graham Kavanagh (Republic of Ireland). And with Henri Camara ruled out through injury, Jewell lamented that he could only assemble his squad for one training session before the match.

'It is a disruption,' he conceded. 'It's not the best situation for us to be in ahead of the game, but there's nothing we can do about it.'

Jewell paused, as if struck by a reality check, and allowed a grin to slowly creep across his face. 'I suppose we shouldn't complain about having international players in our squad,' he smiled.

Lee McCulloch was also battling a knee problem but, by Wednesday, the doctor told him he could play – but only if he had three pain-killing injections.

Problem. While McCulloch can lay claim to being one of fittest and bravest players at Wigan, he has always had one fear – needles.

'I faint at the sight of them,' he admitted. 'I shut my eyes and hold a cushion on my head when the doctor comes near me.'

Inevitably, Wigan's trip to the Hawthorns was rarely mentioned without Nathan Ellington being drawn into conversation. His £3 million defection to West Brom was proving the main focus of the game during all the pre-match publicity, and it played to Dave Whelan's sense of theatre and harmless mischief, with the Wigan chairman accusing the striker of not giving his all to the club during the closing stages of his career at the JJB Stadium.

Jason Roberts and Nathan Ellington before the start of the match.

'I have no regrets over allowing Nathan to leave Wigan,' Whelan wrote in his *Manchester Evening News* column. 'I can honestly say we were disappointed with Nathan's performances and his commitment to the club during the second half of last season. I started to question his commitment when he surprised everyone at the club by getting married on the Friday before we played Watford at home the following day. When it came to contract talks, I believe Nathan was poorly advised. His agent was aggressive.'

Incredibly, ironically, he added, 'We wish him well.'

Both Jewell and Ellington were more diplomatic about the split, though the Wigan manager was still puzzled about Ellington's motives for leaving. 'We made Nathan two great offers to stay here and he told me he didn't want to leave,' said Jewell. 'But then West Brom bid £3 million and we had to let him talk to them. Then he comes out and says he wants to leave and go and play for Bryan Robson because he had played with Manchester United. In the end I didn't know what to believe.'

Ellington was grilled about his decision but the softly-spoken 24-year-old

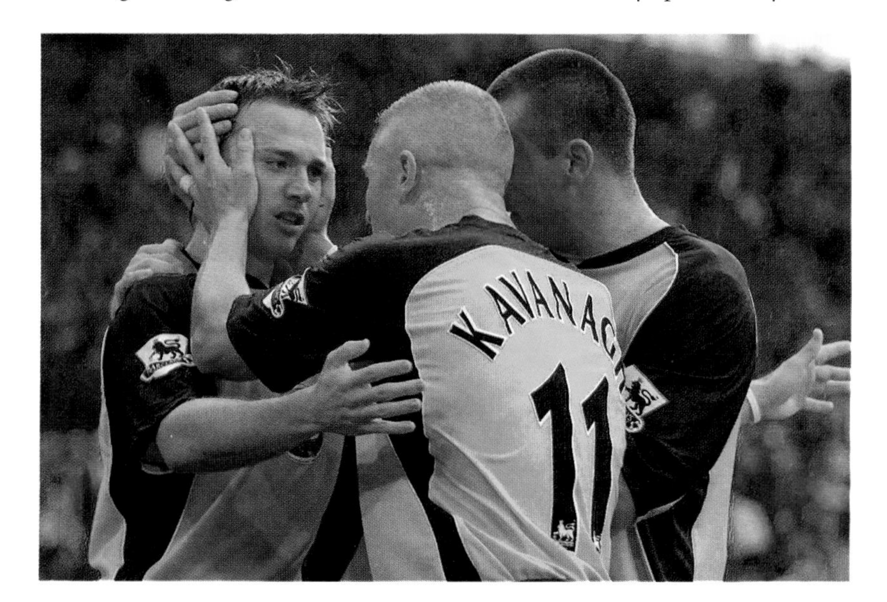

Graham Kavanagh congratulates David Connolly on Wigan's first ever away goal and their first in open play in the Premiership.

Saturday 10 September 2005

West Bromwich Albion 1 Wigan Athletic 2

WEST BROM: Kirkland 7, Albrechtsen 6, Gaardsoe 7, Clement 7, Robinson 6, Watson 7, Greening 7, Carter (Chaplow 57) 6, Wallwork (Campbell 71), 6 Horsfield 6, Ellington (Earnshaw 71) 5.

WIGAN: Pollitt 6, Chimbonda 6, Henchoz 7, De Zeeuw 8, Baines 6, Bullard 8, Kavanagh (Taylor 79) 7, Francis (Skoko 89) 6, McCulloch 6, Roberts 6, Connolly 9. Wigan star man: Connolly.

Goals: Greening (26), Connolly (40), Bullard (90)
Half-time: 1–1
Referee: Mark Clattenburg
Attendance: 25,617

replied simply: 'I made the decision to leave Wigan to further my career and I've no regrets.'

The fixture was given more spice when Jason Roberts, a close friend of Ellington's, reopened his disagreement with the Baggies' former manager Gary Megson in his BBC website column. 'In any walk of life, no matter what the rewards are, your boss can only push you so far,' he wrote. 'If they overstep that mark you have to make a decision and mine was to leave the club. You have a threshold and a limit and he overstepped the mark.'

Latics' game at West Brom proved historic, and few could have asked for a more dramatic way of recording their first away win in the Premier League. Jimmy Bullard's injury-time goal saw Wigan edge out the Baggies 2–1, and it proved sweet revenge for Hernan Crespo's wonder strike on the opening day of the season, when Chelsea denied them a memorable 0–0 draw.

But claiming their second successive win did little to convince sceptics and even some opponents that Latics deserved their place in the top flight.

'How the hell did that lot just beat us?' Geoff Horsfield raged as he stormed back into the home dressing room. Respect? There was no sign of it from the man who decided to stop all of three months at the JJB Stadium before pleading for a move to the Hawthorns.

As for Ellington, he had little to smile about after a – dispensing with diplomacy – woeful 71 minutes. By contrast, the Duke's replacement at Latics, Connolly, shone on his debut. He might never have had the opportunity to grace the Premiership stage before, but the 28-year-old produced a Premier League-style finish to score Wigan's first goal from open play in the top flight five minutes before the break.

Afterwards, Connolly admitted that their opponents had under-estimated Wigan's capabilities. 'We respect all teams in this division, but I don't think other

Jimmy Bullard celebrates after scoring in stoppage time against West Brom.

clubs respect us,' Connolly said. 'We're everyone's favourites to go straight back down. But we've got six points on the board and maybe teams' opinions might quickly change now.'

Jewell also made clear his feelings of discontent, but celebrated like his six numbers had come up when Bullard netted the winner a minute into stoppage time.

This was only the fifth time under Jewell's reign that Latics had come from behind to win. The last was at home to Stoke in October 2003 in a 2–1 win. Ironically, the scorer of both goals was a certain Geoffrey Horsfield.

'I read in the programme before the game that West Brom said they should really be getting three points against teams like Wigan,' Jewell said. 'But we won't be a pushover for anyone this season. People have been writing us off from day one saying we can't do this and we can't do that. It's nice to shut a few people up and we will build on this.'

Wigan's performance mirrored that of their first victory against the Black Cats. They frustrated their opponents, worked tirelessly and though their attack was not polished, they got the result that counted. Mike Pollitt hadn't put a foot or a glove wrong since being thrust onto the big stage against Chelsea, and his error, which gifted Jonathan Greening the 26th-minute opener, did little to dent his confidence.

Damien Francis's defence-splitting pass to set up the equaliser was worthy of a much better standard. And so was Connolly's finish, as he raced on and sent a first-time left-footed strike into the top left corner of the net.

'To score Wigan's first goal from open play in the Premiership is amazing, and something I'll never forget,' Connolly added.

As Ellington trundled off to cries of 'what a waste of money' from sections of the 2,700 travelling support, Wigan finished the game in firm control, but any sense they were going to settle for a draw was thrown out of the window in the 91st minute.

McCulloch won the ball on the left and played it into the middle, where ex-Baggies striker Roberts, with his back to goal, was met by a chorus of boos for what seemed like the hundredth time. Bullard arrived right on cue on the edge of the box

What the opposition said...

'We have gone back to square one as far as I'm concerned. The frailty in the way we give goals away is shocking. Yes, there were a few harsh words said. This was a bad one to lose because we have now given Wigan all three points. No matter which club you are in the Premier League, if you lose to a newly-promoted club like Wigan then you will be booed.' – Bryan Robson, West Brom manager.

What the fan said...

'I've seen better but both sides did battle well in the middle of the park with chances limited to a handful of long-range efforts. I didn't get involved in barracking Ellington but boy did he get some abuse from the Wigan section of the ground every time he got anywhere near the ball.' – John Heeley, editor *Cockney Latic.*

	P	W	D	L	F	A	Pts
Chelsea	5	5	0	0	10	0	15
Charlton	4	4	0	0	8	1	12
Man City	5	3	2	0	7	4	11
Man Utd	4	3	1	0	6	1	10
Bolton	5	2	2	1	6	4	8
Tottenham	5	2	2	1	4	2	8
Middlesb'h	5	2	1	2	5	6	7
Arsenal	4	2	0	2	7	4	6
Wigan	4	2	0	2	3	3	6
Liverpool	3	1	2	0	1	0	5
Aston Villa	4	1	2	1	4	4	5
Blackburn	5	1	2	2	3	5	5
Fulham	5	1	2	2	4	7	5
West Ham	3	1	1	1	4	3	4
Portsm'th	5	1	1	3	4	7	4
Birm'ham	5	1	1	3	4	8	4
West Br'm	5	1	1	3	5	10	4
Everton	4	1	0	3	1	4	3
Newcastle	5	0	2	3	1	7	2
Sunderl'd	5	0	0	5	2	9	0

David Connolly, jubilant after scoring on his debut.

to arrow his shot right into the corner, sparking scenes of wild celebration among the players, travelling fans and the coaching staff alike.

As he celebrated, a jubilant Bullard urged referee Mark Clattenburg – the official who added three minutes of injury-time in the opening clash with Chelsea – to blow for full-time. The Geordie official had signalled three minutes more at the Hawthorns, but Bullard's intervention saw him call time early. 'I asked the ref how long to go after I scored and he said "30 seconds" so I said "you better blow up now, you owe us one" and then he did,' the midfield dynamo grinned. 'It makes it extra sweet after what happened to us against Chelsea.'

Asked about Ellington's contribution, Bullard replied, 'I can't honestly remember what he did in the game.'

Elevated into the top half of the table, sandwiched snugly between Arsenal and Liverpool, Wigan were buoyed and encouraged after two consecutive achievements. Jewell gave his players the Sunday off but, by Monday, they were arriving at Christopher Park to prepare for their home game against Middlesbrough the following Sunday.

Meanwhile, Pascal Chimbonda had his first English lesson with Wigan programme editor Ed Jones, who was raised in Geneva and is fluent in French. Senegal international Camara, who only spoke broken English when he arrived, was offered the chance to join his French-speaking teammate in class, but declined (his decision only fuelled Steve McMillan's suspicions that he knew English already but was playing dumb).

The mood in the camp was bubbling. And for Graham Kavanagh, the tie with Middlesbrough was providing the source of reflection on his well-worn, snaking career.

'The last time I played in the Premier League with Middlesbrough was against Wimbledon at home in 1996,' he recalled. 'I never thought walking off the pitch that day that I wouldn't be back in the Premiership for nine years with Wigan coming up against them. I've never doubted that I had the ability to play at this level – it would be great to get one over them.

Graham Kavanagh looked forward to facing his old club, Middlesbrough.

'They gave me my first chance in England. I was playing in a tournament called the Milk Cup over in Northern Ireland with Home Park. The first club that were interested in me were Middlesbrough so I ended up signing for them under Colin Todd in the second division.

'Liverpool and Leeds offered me more money and an extra year. I'm a Liverpool fan, but I had a mate who had gone there from Home Park and he didn't get a chance. I didn't want to be a player who got forgotten about – I wanted to go to Middlesbrough and make a reputation. I was at Home Farm from their Under-13s until I was 17. I more or less agreed to move to Middlesbrough on my own even though I was still at school doing the equivalent of my A-Levels. I decided to give my studies up and rang the school and told them I'd left. My mum rang them back and told them I hadn't quit, but I told her I wasn't going back and was off to Middlesbrough. I knew I had the world at my feet and lucky enough it's worked out.'

Kavanagh played 10 times for 'Boro in the top flight but found his career path blocked when Bryan Robson brought in Juninho, Emerson and Ravanelli. 'I didn't feel part of the whole set-up,' says Kavanagh, who had impressive spells at Stoke and Cardiff before arriving at Wigan.

The first-team squad was joined on the Christopher Park pitches by John Filan, who resumed training after recovering from hernia and ligament surgery, though the 35-year-old Australian conceded he was now second choice behind Mike Pollitt.

With six points under their belt, the emphasis in training was on collecting more points as soon as possible, and it was an issue Jewell highlighted with the example of West Brom, who 'only got their second win of the season in their 24th game last year'. And they still managed to survive.

'Getting points on the board as early as possible is so important at this level,' added Jewell, who outlined plans to make a new move for Brondby frontman Johan Elmander in January.

In analysing their opponents, Jason Roberts warned his teammates about the dangers of his former Portsmouth colleague Yakubu, who had joined 'Boro in the summer for £7.5 million and netted their opener in their previous week's 2–1 win over Arsenal.

'He's really strong and is a good goalscorer who is very single-minded,' he said. 'Our defenders are going to have to be at their best to keep him quiet.'

The defenders, it transpired, were not far off their best, though they still weren't able to contain Nigerian Yakubu, who opened the scoring for the visitors before Wigan clawed a point back through a fit-again Camara.

The Middlesbrough entourage appeared dejected by the draw, seeing it as two points lost rather than a point gained. They seemed stunned by Wigan's guile and endeavour and Steve McClaren's body language spoke volumes as he laboriously trudged around the corridors of the JJB Stadium trying to explain his side's performance.

'Wigan really gave us a tough game,' said England's then assistant coach. 'They are going to fight and scrap and will never stop working.'

Despite the praise, his tone carried a tinge of regret and a certain embarrassment. Once again, a side had underestimated Wigan.

'To be honest, I think that's as well as we've played,' said Jewell. 'They are a top-six side, they are full of international players, real good players, and for us to push them all the way is a credit to us.'

Camara celebrates his goal against Middlesbrough.

Stephane Henchoz blocks a Emanuel Pogatetz shot.

Sunday 18 September 2005

Wigan 1 Middlesbrough 1

WIGAN: Pollitt 6, Chimbonda 8, Henchoz 7, De Zeeuw 7, Baines 6, Bullard 8, Francis 6, Kavanagh 8, McCulloch 7, Roberts 7, Connolly 6. Subs: Camara (64 for Connolly) 8. Wigan star man: Kavanagh.

MIDDLESBROUGH: Schwarzer 7, Xavier 7, Queudrue 6, Ehiogu 6, Southgate 7, Boateng 6, Rochemback 8, Morrison 7, Pogatetz 7, Yakubu 7, Viduka 6. Subs: Doriva 6 (for Morrison 44), Maccarone 6 (for Viduka 61).

Goals: Yakubu 14, Camara 68
Half-time: 0–1
Referee: Uriah Rennie
Attendance: 16,641

What the opposition said...

'Our performance wasn't quite at the level it should be. I thought we would control the game. To be fair Wigan made it really tough for us but we're disappointed because we started the game well and when we went a goal up we didn't take advantage. Wigan got stronger as the game went on and, but for the character of our team, we might have lost the game.' – Middlesbrough manager Steve McClaren.

What the fan said...

'The defence was solid but we didn't create enough up front. In the second half I thought we were much better, especially when Camara came on and Pascal Chimbonda and Bullard were outstanding. I thought Wigan could have won it in the end.' – season-ticket holder Tom Humphreys.

After a bright start Latics were pegged back by 'Boro and as the first goal went in there was a fear that the visitors could run riot.

But Jewell's side, instilled with scouse grit and with the ferocious Kavanagh dominating the midfield, slowly got back into the contest. The Irishman's intentions were clear from his first biting tackle and he was thrilled after seeing Camara's goal earn a point.

'It was a great team effort,' smiled Kavanagh. 'It's really pleasing when you go a goal behind, albeit against the run of play, to show great character and bounce back in the manner that we did. We never dropped our heads, we kept passing the ball, creating chances and Henri came off the bench and got a great goal, so we are very pleased.'

Kavanagh's approach certainly set the benchmark for the rest of the side and he was central to everything good that the hosts did. The midfielder raised his game against his former club and Jewell later urged his roving general to show that level of performance consistently.

'Hopefully he can think we are playing Middlesbrough every week because I thought that was probably his best game for Wigan since he has been here,' said the manager.

'I thought he was outstanding. He was snapping in the tackle, he was passing it crisply and he played well. He is a good player and he knows – and he's not the only one – that there is competition and people are waiting to take players' places. That can only be good for the club.'

Wigan were unlucky to fall behind to a classy finish from Nigerian striker Yakubu but they were also lucky not to be 2–0 down shortly before the break, with Pollitt left clutching the cool autumn air as Emanuel Pogatetz headed a Fabio Rochemback free-kick on to the bar.

Graham Kavanagh and Lee McCulloch… job well done!

Earlier Wigan's best chance fell to Jason Roberts, who scuffed his shot following excellent link-up play from Pascal Chimbonda – sporting his infamous woolly gloves as early as September – and Jimmy Bullard.

Former Barcelona midfielder Rochemback continued to threaten for 'Boro, who switched to a 4–5–1 formation with the introduction of Massio Maccarone. But Wigan's grit earned them a thoroughly deserved equaliser when, with 22 minutes to go, Camara, who had been on the pitch for just four minutes, took advantage of some sloppy defending.

A hopeful ball from Leighton Baines was hooked on to the chest of the Senegalese forward and he eluded Gareth Southgate to prod the ball past Mark Schwarzer.

The shouts for handball were of little concern to the substitute as he embarked on a celebratory jig with Chimbonda in front of a rampant East Stand.

After the game it emerged that the real hero had been Jimmy Bullard, who refused to leave the pitch for treatment despite suffering a nasty leg injury close to half-time. The energetic midfielder did not just survive the match, he helped control it, and his performance earned him a glowing appraisal from his manager.

'Jimmy is a bit of an irritant at times but one thing he is, he's as brave as a lion,' Jewell said. 'He is only small and he drives you mad, but he has got good spirit and he wants the ball all the time. He needs to learn the game a little bit more, when to play and when not to play, but you can never knock his enthusiasm and endeavour.

'He got a nasty knock on his leg but he wouldn't come off. He was on a bike at half-time in the dressing room trying to keep it moving and I can think of a lot of players, 1–0 down against a good side, might have just come off with that. He epitomises our grit and determination.'

	P	W	D	L	F	A	Pts
Chelsea	6	6	0	0	12	0	18
Charlton	5	4	0	1	8	3	12
Man Utd	5	3	2	0	6	1	11
Bolton	6	3	2	1	7	4	11
Man City	6	3	2	1	7	5	11
West Ham	5	3	1	1	10	4	10
Tottenham	6	2	3	1	5	3	9
Middlesb'h	6	2	2	2	6	7	8
Wigan	5	2	1	2	4	4	7
Arsenal	4	2	0	2	7	4	6
Liverpool	4	1	3	0	1	0	6
Aston Villa	6	1	3	2	5	9	6
Portsm'th	6	1	2	3	5	8	5
Newcastle	6	1	2	3	4	7	5
Birm'ham	6	1	2	3	5	9	5
Fulham	6	1	2	3	5	9	5
West Brom	6	1	2	3	6	11	5
Blackburn	6	1	2	3	3	8	5
Everton	4	1	0	3	1	4	3
Sunderl'd	6	0	1	5	3	10	1

Dave and Pat Whelan applaud the team at Goodison.

Bullard was added to Jewell's mounting casualty list, with Arjan De Zeeuw, Lee McCulloch and Matt Jackson all struggling with injuries. But when asked about a bandage on Henri Camara's leg, Jewell smiled and added: 'I think that's one for the crowd – "look at me I'm playing with a sore leg". He is okay.'

The draw kept Wigan in the top half of the table but Wigan refused to accept they faced anything but a scrap against relegation.

Meanwhile, Jewell stepped into the nationwide row over whether the Premiership was losing interest by admitting the fickle nature of hiring and firing managers was the root of the problem. 'The Premiership is boring and it's because of a fear factor,' he offered. 'Too many managers are scared of getting sacked. No wonder we're seeing so many empty seats at games.'

A miserable, Tuesday night 1–0 win over Bournemouth in the second round of the Carling Cup provided little evidence that Wigan's impregnable run would continue at the Goodison cauldron. The match was hotly anticipated by fans – it was only Wigan's second-ever visit to Everton, having lost 3–0 in an FA Cup fourth-round match 25 years earlier when Wigan were in the lowest echelons of League football.

David Moyes and Paul Jewell.

Former midfielder Tommy Gore played in that game under Ian McNeill's stewardship – Gore had netted the winner in a 1–0 victory over Chelsea at Stamford Bridge in the previous round – and confidently predicted an upset. 'Everton are

Graham Kavanagh closes down on Tim Cahill.

under pressure after three defeats. Now's as good a time to play them as any,' he said.

For Jewell himself, it was a game for the fan inside of him. A game for the child in him.

Had he been offered the choice, at the start of the season, of a victory at any ground, he would no doubt have chosen Everton. Naturally, his delight with Wigan's 1–0 victory was uncontainable.

The former Liverpool FC trainee had spent the entire 90 minutes on his feet; playing every ball and tackle from the edge of the technical area, while the home fans reminded him of his formative years across Stanley Park. This victory meant everything to him, a point evident as he marched across the Goodison Park pitch to acknowledge the 3,000 jubilant visiting fans, and then thrust his clenched left fist towards them before retreating down the tunnel.

Out-of-breath after clambering up three flights of stairs to the cramped Everton press lounge, Jewell reflected on another momentous day at the office.

'It's a local derby for us coming to Everton, who were Champions League last year and are a great, great club,' he said. 'It doesn't matter if it's Liverpool or Everton, three points in this League are very hard fought. It was quite nice for the people next to the dug-out mind – some people have got long memories!'

However, the Liverpudlian wasn't quite as pleased during the interval. It was David Moyes's men who edged a first half throughout which Jewell barked out incessant instructions. 'I thought we were rubbish in the first half to be perfectly honest and I couldn't wait to get in at half-time and get among them,' he said. 'We didn't show anything that we'd been working on.

'I thought that all over the pitch; tackles, second balls, passing, we didn't play anything like we can do and I was glad to get in at half-time with no score.'

Despite holding out against last season's fourth-placed finishers during a lively first half, Jewell typically wanted more from his side. Damien Francis still had his

Jimmy Bullard and Damien Francis celebrate the winning goal against Everton to crown a fine month.

manager's angry scouse tones ringing in his ears when he slotted in what turned out to be Wigan's winner.

The visitors, who had mustered only one goal-bound effort in the first half, rattled in five shots on target and two off target within 15 minutes of the restart.

Everton switched from the expected 4–5–1 formation and started with James McFadden up front supported by Up Hollander Leon Osman. The change in ploy and personnel initially paid off for Moyes as Osman was allowed to pick up the scraps and feed Tim Cahill, Simon Davies and Kevin Kilbane. The Merseysiders could have become the first side to beat all 38 Premiership clubs with a win, but, as ever, Latics had other ideas.

Kilbane flicked a header on to the bar and John Filan, making his long-awaited return to the Premier League he had graced while with Blackburn, uncharacteristically fumbled a trio of crosses in the afternoon sun, while Tim Cahill headed tamely into the Aussie's arms. Stephane Henchoz and Pascal Chimbonda both had penalty shouts against them turned down before, in added time, Davies wasted a chance superbly set up by McFadden.

At the other end Chimbonda had a header cleared off the line by Nuno Valente and saw a dangerous cross frantically cleared by Phil Neville, while Henri Camara went close. Many of the supporters were still under the stands of the old ground devouring their half-time grub when Latics struck the killer blow.

The visitors flashed a cross in front of Nigel Martyn straight after the restart, but sleepy Everton failed to clear the danger and the ball was eventually sent back in by Chimbonda. Camara knocked the ball down to Roberts, who returned the favour for the Senegalese striker to shoot and Francis reacted first to Martyn's spill.

Roberts, who was a constant threat along with Camara, should have converted a great inside ball from Francis to double the lead.

Later on Filan pulled off a great reflex save from a McFadden cross-come-shot and Wigan were slightly fortuitous to see the whistle-happy Rob Styles disallow a Marcus Bent strike. But what David Moyes described as a crazy five minutes ultimately proved to be the undoing of rock-bottom Everton and the making of another three points for high-flying Wigan.

The euphoria was a feeling mixed with surprise for Filan, who was reinstated to the side ahead of Mike Pollitt despite the former Rotherham 'keeper's starring performances in the opening five League games. Jewell even admitted that Pollitt did not deserve to be dropped, but justified his selection because he predicted Everton would bombard Wigan with crosses and Filan was more experienced.

'It was the gaffer's decision and I was delighted when he said I was playing,' said Sydney-born Filan, who started his professional career at Coventry before moving to Blackburn and then Wigan.

'Every player in this game has got the desire to win and that's what has kept me going as long as I have done. Even when I'm playing table tennis or head tennis after training I really want to win. People say it's because of my roots and Australian nature. We are a sporting nation and everyone has been brought up on it.

'In Australia winning is the most important thing, no-one wants to come second.'

Understandably, Pollitt was upset by the decision and didn't celebrate his manager's 41st birthday. 'I didn't get a birthday card from Mike,' Jewell admitted. 'Mike is not very happy with me and I don't expect him to be. But I expect him to get on with his job and I'm sure he will.'

Jewell, meanwhile, was swift to leap to the defence of Sven-Goran Eriksson after England lost 1–0 to Northern Ireland, a defeat which fuelled calls for the national coach to be sacked. 'Sven shouldn't be judged on one result,' Jewell offered. 'They need to find their best system and quickly. I don't think you can play all the best players – you have to play your best team. Sometimes that means one of your best players has to miss out.'

Nevertheless, that did not stop the tabloids speculating on a natural successor to Sven, though Jewell was quick to rule himself out.

Saturday 24 September 2005

Everton 0 Wigan 1

EVERTON: Martyn 6, Neville 6, Yobo 6, Weir 6, Valente 5, Davies 5, Arteta 5, Cahill 7, Kilbane 5, Osman 7, McFadden 7.

WIGAN: Filan 7, Chimbonda 7, Henchoz 6, De Zeeuw 7, Baines 7, Bullard 6, Francis 7, Kavanagh 7, McCulloch 6, Roberts 7, Camara 7. Subs: Connolly 6. Wigan star man: Francis.

Goal: Francis (47)
Half-time: 0–0
Referee: Rob Styles
Attendance: 37,189

What the opposition said...

'I thought it was a goal we scored. But we shouldn't be relying on a referee's decisions to win games, so that isn't the reason we have lost. I'm disappointed that I'm even saying we were worth a point, we should be winning games like that. If it wasn't for a crazy five minutes after half-time when we let ourselves slip we were going okay. Then we were chasing it.' – Everton manager David Moyes.

What the fan said...

'In the second half, for 15 minutes we battered them and played some really good football. Good to see Chimbonda's ski gloves making another appearance, Wigan's very own Eddie the Eagle! Goodison is a proper football ground and it's got bags of character.' – East stand season-ticket holder John Davies.

	P	W	D	L	F	A	Pts
Chelsea	7	7	0	0	14	1	21
Charlton	6	5	0	1	10	4	15
Bolton	7	4	2	1	8	4	14
Tottenham	7	3	3	1	6	3	12
West Ham	6	3	2	1	10	4	11
Man Utd	6	3	2	1	7	3	11
Man City	7	3	2	2	7	6	11
Arsenal	6	3	1	2	9	4	10
Wigan	6	3	1	2	5	4	10
Newcastle	7	2	2	3	5	7	8
Middlesb'h	7	2	2	3	6	9	8
Blackburn	7	2	2	3	5	9	8
Liverpool	5	1	4	0	3	2	7
Birm'ham	7	1	3	3	7	11	6
Aston Villa	7	1	3	3	6	11	6
Fulham	7	1	2	4	5	10	5
Portsm'th	7	1	2	4	5	9	5
West Brom	7	1	2	4	7	13	5
Sunderl'd	7	1	1	5	5	10	4
Everton	6	1	0	5	1	7	3

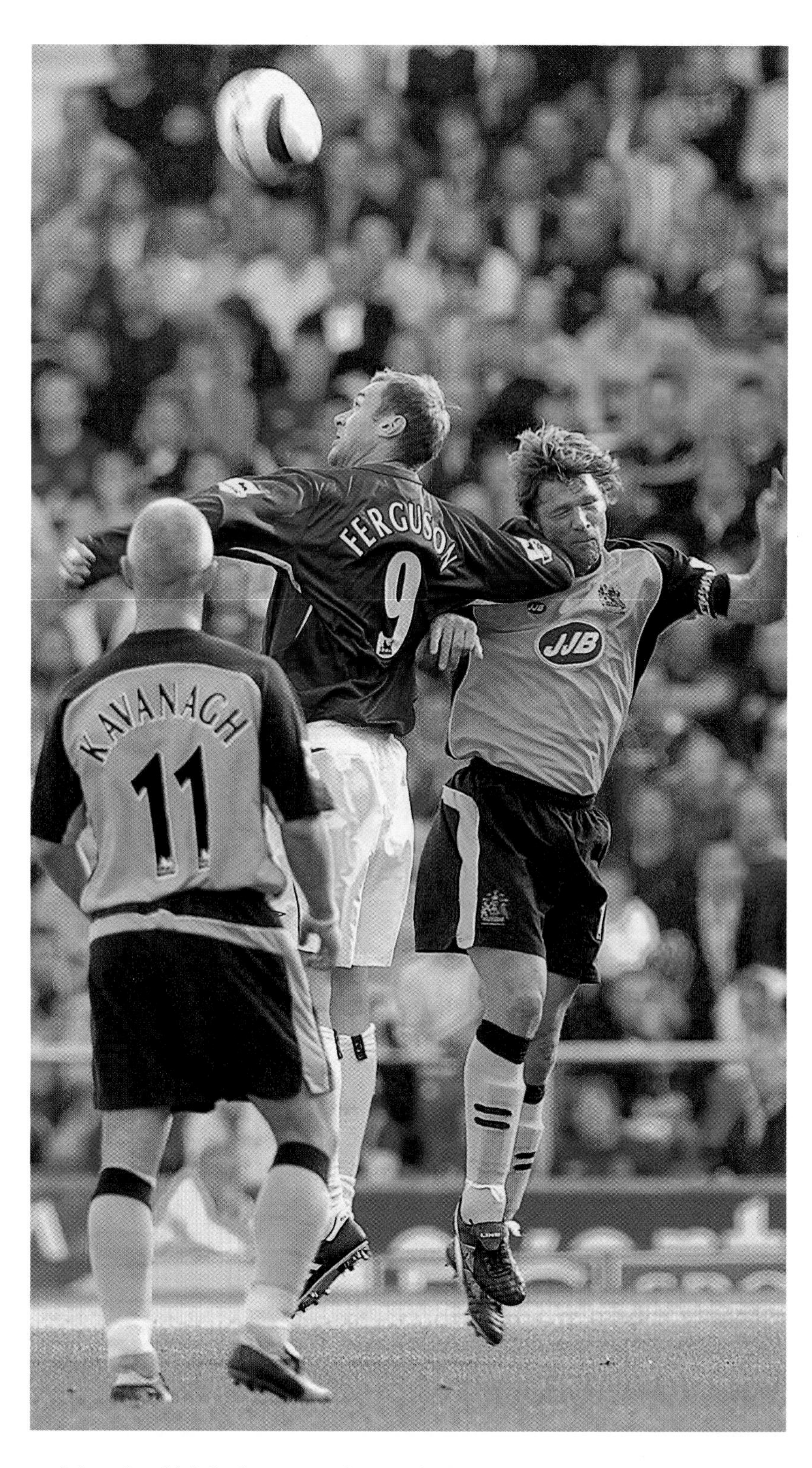

Arjan De Zeeuw loved this picture of Duncan Ferguson elbowing him in the face – he requested a copy!

'They shouldn't look at me – I've got far too many skeletons in my closet,' he laughed. 'That's me officially ruled out now!'

September ended with Matt McCann on the phone to the *Wigan Observer* sportsdesk with a small favour on Arjan De Zeeuw's behalf. 'Arry loved the picture in the paper of Duncan Ferguson elbowing him in the face,' he chuckled. 'Can he get a copy?'

DIXIE BAINES knew a professional footballer when he saw one... and he was the first to tell his young grandson he had all the tools and ability to make it to the very top. Leighton, Wigan Athletic's brilliant left-back, didn't let his late granddad down.

While his friends were doing what most do during their formative teenage years, the Kirkby youngster was sharpening his skills behind the scenes with his grandfather as he took the first steps on the steep footballing ladder where only the very best survive.

Dixie had played the game for the army in Australia and America and he took a keen interest in his grandson's game. But tragedy struck in the Baines household when he sadly passed away. Leighton was just 15 years old.

'My grandad was a very special man who will always have a special place in my life,' said Baines, who fulfilled his promise to his grandfather that nothing was going to stop him reaching his destiny. 'He loved football and he gave up so much of his time to help me, taking me to games and offering advice. He always said I would make it in professional football if I worked hard, gave 100 percent and made sacrifices. I even lived at my grandad's house one year in the summer holidays.'

Baines is more than a fearless defender. He has maturity that defies his age and he likes to surge forward into the attack, a quality he attibutes to his grandad.

'He would talk to me about the game's finer points, the need to make penetrating runs,' says Baines. 'It would go over my head, but it eventually sunk in and it has served me well. We'd have a kick-about in the garden. I have always been predominantly left-footed so he'd work on playing the ball against the wall with my right foot.'

Baines started out on his road to stardom with the Keyways Junior Club on Merseyside. Everton and Liverpool both showed an interest in the young defender, but it was Wigan who snapped up the full-back, who progressed through the youth system under the eye of coach David Lee before making his first team debut in a 2–0 win at Oldham in December 2002.

England Under-21 honours eventually followed and Baines admits, 'Seeing me called up by England would have meant so much to my grandad and he would have been so proud to see what has happened to me with Wigan.'

Baines played a key role in the club achieving its top-flight status and scored one of the most memorable goals ever by a Wigan player. Against Ipswich, in December 2004, he picked up the ball in the opposition half and, seeing no obvious pass, he struck a rocket from 40 yards out with a shot that flew like a missile into the top right corner. Video analysis later revealed the shot reached a speed of close to 70mph.

In his maiden Premiership season, Baines made more than a mark against some of the world's finest players. He was given the hardest task of all in Wigan's first Premiership game as he came up against Chelsea superstars Arjan Robben, Damien Duff and Shaun Wright-Phillips. But from the first game of the season up until the last, Baines proved he had what it takes to live with the best.

'It's a totally different world,' Baines said. 'It's international quality right the way through the League. We've been playing against well-known players every week. It's a massive step and it is great to be a part of that standard of football. I wouldn't say I was really looking forward to coming up against them. But I knew it would be a good test. When you look at the likes of Damien Duff and Arjan Robben at Chelsea, Cristiano Ronaldo and Wayne Rooney at United, the Premiership has got some of the best talent in the world.'

Baines is continuing the family tradition by passing on tips to his own young son Reiss. He wouldn't swap his current position for anything else.

'It's what you dream of as a kid,' he says. 'We've all watched the Premiership every week growing up. It's the best League in the world and to be a part of it with Wigan is really special.'

5: Without Pier – how Latics became a worldwide phenomenon

Dave Whelan's rags to riches tale was retold countless times when Wigan got promoted.

WHEN REVEREND William Wickham arrived to take over a parish in 1878, he remarked that the name of Wigan conjured up images of 'colliery explosions and monster strikes.' These days, those words would be replaced by 'colossal exploits and monster strikers'.

The extraordinary rise of Wigan Athletic into the Premiership elevated the town into the national spotlight and onto the global stage. To coin the popular phrase, it put Wigan on the map.

The presence of some of the world's leading players in England makes the Premiership popular viewing abroad, much more than La Liga or Serie A is on these shores, while countries with large numbers of British ex-patriots – including Australia, New Zealand, Spain and Canada – have an added reason to follow the competition keenly.

In England, it seemed newspapers and television programmes couldn't get enough of Latics and in the weeks leading up to their opening Premiership game with Chelsea, the *Wigan Observer* office fielded calls from newspapers and radio stations across Europe, asking for background information on this 'new team called Wigan Athletic'.

In the months that followed, more headlines appeared, while prestigious titles such as *The Sydney Morning Herald* and *New York Times* ran features about their remarkable journey. Wigan's international appeal was confirmed when Al-Jazeera TV sent a crew to the JJB Stadium to report on their progress.

'I have no doubt whatsoever that Wigan has never experienced such publicity before – not only in this country but worldwide,' admitted Dave Mather, in a perfect position to comment as Wigan council's long-serving Head of Public Relations. 'There have been features in all the British papers and across the globe.'

Wigan was, of course, already well known throughout the country as England's most northern – not northernmost – town. *The Guardian*'s Simon Hoggart said that when the Uncle Joe's sign is glimpsed from a northbound train, the traveller knows he has just entered the 'real' north-west.

'It seems to exist in southern imaginations as an almost fictional distillation of all things northern, a bit like *Brigadoon* with cobbles and whippets,' wrote Paul Wilson – a resident of the town – in *The Observer*. Those associations were easily traced.

Wigan's earliest, and until now arguably its strongest, claim to fame was George Orwell's book *The Road to Wigan Pier*. Orwell came to stay in Wigan, wrote a book exaggerating the state of the place and used the pier in the title. His examination of the social deprivation of 1930s Britain invariably linked the town with poverty and, as such, he was reviled for fashioning Wigan's image.

But while the council has embraced the fame of Wigan Pier – they invented the Wigan Pier Experience with museums, a heritage centre and waterbuses and are rightly proud of their award-winning attraction – they have worked hard to shed the town's association with terraced houses and smoky chimneys.

It's been a losing battle, and Wigan's image has always sat uncomfortably with the majority of the town's 180,000 residents (that figure does not include those in Leigh, who begrudgingly accept the fact they fall under the 'Wigan borough' umbrella).

These days, there is little evidence left of the once booming coal and cotton industries, the two pillars of prosperity during the Victorian era. The council is the biggest employer in town – followed by the NHS, JJB and Heinz – and there is not a single colliery left, while go-karts race around inside the shell of a building which was once a cotton mill.

The incredible success of Wigan's rugby league team in the mid-1980s and early 1990s, when they trampled over opponents to win a staggering 43 trophies, helped

Wallace and Gromit, two of Wigan's most famous residents.

Wigan is famous for its pies and, following Latics' success, Edwards Bakery was among those to join in the celebrations with a special blue pie.

make the town known outside the traditional northern heartland of the sport, and in Australia, New Zealand and Papua New Guinea the word 'Wigan' is still a by-word for success.

But Wigan's association with rugby league only strengthened the image of a gloomy town with cobbled streets. And it came as little surprise during Latics' swift rise through the Championship that national newspaper sports writers continually reached for the same stereotypes. Martin Tarbuck and Andrew Vaughan, in their book, *Pies and Prejudice*, which traced Wigan's successful Championship season, compiled a list of clichés that sports writers had to include in each match report.

'Just insert the following, join the letters up,' they wrote, 'and hey presto, an article.'

1. It's grim up north.
2. Refer to Wigan Pier.
3. Refer to George Orwell.
4. Mention pies.
5. It's a rugby town.
6. Point out that the crowds are the lowest in the world (bonus points for this).
7. Add that the stadium is in a retail park.
8. Insert Dave Whelan's rags-to-riches story.
9. Spend 90 percent of your article talking about the other team.
10. Finally, don't forget to mention it's a rugby town.

When Wigan were promoted to the Premiership, the same tired and dated stereotypes were reaffirmed and repeated in force by the national press. It seemed the story about a football team going from the Cheshire League to the Premier League wasn't remarkable enough to satisfy some.

The articles ranged from the ludicrous to the humorous, with Rod Liddle's assassination of Wigan – the town and the football club – in the *Sunday Times* one of the most colourful contributions. He wrote, tongue surely placed firmly in cheek, 'Everybody loves Wigan, homely little Wigan, with their hally-go-lucky handful of honest fans battling through the grim northern weather from the mill to the little football ground, via the pie shop, their grim northern trousers alive with the squealing of ferrets.

'Wigan, the team that brought the whiff of romance back to the Premiership, together with the idea that any club can do it if only they would really, really, try.

'Much as I can't stand Chelsea, I don't have much time for Wigan either. I'd settle for a nil-nil draw [on the opening day] with Wigan having three points deducted for some technical infringement of Fifa rules, fielding an unregistered whippet or something. If your principle objection to Chelsea is that they have merely bought their way to success, then your approbation should be tenfold for Wigan.'

Thanks to George Orwell, Wigan Pier is world famous.

Such features came as little surprise to Dave Calderbank, who has been covering both Wigan Athletic and Wigan rugby league club for the local Barnes News Agency for decades.

'Latics have always had the ability to attract attention,' says Calderbank. 'Back in the old days, it seemed every time they got a glamour tie in the Cup the national newspapers would roll out the predictable clichés – pies, flat caps and ferrets. In that respect, not much has changed.'

Across the country, it seemed everyone had heard of Wigan, but few knew much about the town, and in trying to cut through the myths and hyperbole some uncovered more quirky insights into the place which generated even more smiles.

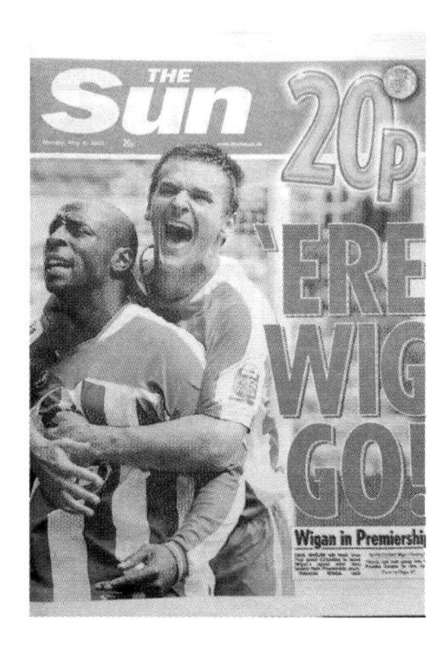
THE Sun
20p
'ERE WIG GO!
Wigan in Premiership

Wigan Athletic made it onto the front pages of the national newspapers for the first time in their history when they won promotion to the Premiership.

The Independent informed its readers that, 'For £1.25, visiting fans pouring out of the station will be able to sample a chip barm (buttie) from Ray's Chippy', while *The Times* compiled a list of 'Road to Wigan souvenirs' that included a Wigan kebab, the Verve CD, Uncle Joe's Mint Balls, pants (M&S was launched in Wigan), Plasticine (Wallace and Gromit live at 62 West Wallaby Street, Wigan) and a bin (because Wigan is home to the Keep Britain Tidy campaign).

'The phones have never stopped ringing this season, with reporters from all over the globe wanting factual information about the borough,' admitted Chris Dunbar, spokesman for the Wigan Leisure and Culture Trust.

For the record, George Formby Snr, father of the ukulele strummer and a music hall performer, made up the title Wigan Pier as a joke about bathing off the coal jetty on the Liverpool–Leeds canal and, as *The Independent* said, 'This Lancashire town is the sort of can-do place where people take a joke and turn it into an astonishing success. The latest, most dramatic example of that, is the football team.'

The football team changed Wigan's image. Out went the dusty image of cobbled streets, in came the picture of a modern, sporting town where the most daring dreams can come true.

'People saw Wigan as being pies, rugby and Uncle Joe's Mint Balls,' admitted Paul Jewell, who first served Latics as a player before returning as a manager. 'We wanted to change that.'

An estimated additional 200,000 visitors came to watch 19 home games this season, bringing an estimated £10 million boost to the economy of the town, and Wigan council jumped on the back of Latics' success and used the opportunity to create an improved, fairer image of the town.

Last summer, new road signs sprung up welcoming visitors to 'Wigan – Home of Premiership Football' and the metro rebranded the place as 'Wigan Premier Town'.

The television images of Jose Mourinho consoling Paul Jewell after the opening 1–0 defeat were beamed across the world.

Wigan tried to spice up their image with cheerleaders.

'The council is trying to rebuild the image of Wigan nationally and this has been heaven sent – we couldn't buy this amount of coverage,' admitted Mather. 'Sometimes it's a bit patronising but we can handle that because generally it has been positive.'

Other promoted teams never enjoyed so much publicity. They never basked in the spotlight like Wigan. But no other promoted team captured the imagination like Wigan Athletic, a team whose rags-to-riches story transcended cultures, borders and even language barriers, judging by the amount of international coverage.

'It's a one-off – there will never be a repeat of this,' added Mather. 'No matter how well Wigan do in the future there will never be the same surprise factor as this year. It's a unique tale.'

As Wigan's rise continued the media interest in them shot through the roof. The BBC's Gordon Burns talks to Paul Jewell at the JJB Stadium.

The BBC quickly gauged the extraordinary level of interest in the club. Their news department adopted the team as their own, and decided to follow Wigan throughout the campaign with a series of features.

'On the Monday morning after Wigan were promoted to the Premiership, when the *Six* team came into work it was literally all we could talk about,' revealed Amanda Farnsworth, Editor of BBC Daytime News. 'It just seemed such a tremendous achievement – a sort of soccer rags-to-riches tale that viewers up and down the country could appreciate. The team of a town known much more for rugby than football was about to start rubbing shoulders with the likes of Manchester United and Chelsea. My assistant editor immediately came up with the idea of following the players and fans through the season and I agreed at once.'

She added, 'I must admit I didn't expect Wigan to do so well so quickly this season – and coming from a West Ham fan like myself, readers may understand why my outlook was a little less optimistic than it perhaps should have been – but the team has performed way beyond expectations and it's been a pleasure to record their achievement.'

What the BBC found was a team living in the clouds but with their feet firmly on the ground, and such a humble approach – instilled by Jewell – allowed fans to relate to the players on a basic, human level as people, rather than superstars. They were the real deal – not pretenders, and not pretentious either.

'An overpowering stench of sweat and champagne greeted me in the changing room of Wigan Athletic on the morning after the club made it to the Premiership,' admitted Catherine Marston, the BBC's North of England correspondent. 'That and puddles of alcohol and shin pads. As I stood interviewing the captain in there I thought: "What other premiership team would let me see all this?"

'They'd certainly had quite a bash. There's a spirit of fun and excitement at Wigan Athletic and it's made following their progress for the *Six O'Clock News* a real pleasure. It's been astonishing to see the impact it's had on the town, too. The investment it's bringing and the pride people feel.'

Latics' Head of Communications Matt McCann was inundated with media requests from across the world.

Wigan's Carling Cup semi-final heroics at Highbury were splashed across the back pages of the national newspapers.

As well as featuring in *FHM* and many other publications, Wigan Athletic supporter Lianne McNally was *Nuts* magazine's 'Fittest Fan of the Year'.

Dave Whelan has handled more media requests then ever before.

Wigan's blistering start to the campaign sent interest in the team, and the town, into a frenzy.

'Everyone says, "Where's Wigan?"' Dave Whelan revealed last August. Whelan grew up in Chadwick Street and confronted prejudices about the town all his life. 'And now we're playing Chelsea in a match that will be broadcast worldwide.'

Their heroic performance in that defeat earned Wigan widespread praise and their win over Sunderland two weeks later sparked an unbeaten nine-game run that elevated them to second in the League behind only Chelsea. Sky Sports News filmed at the *Wigan Observer* offices, Dave Whelan's remarks and Paul Jewell's side's exploits were making the back pages of the tabloids and newspapers in France, South Africa, Canada, Hungary and Austria.

Even Budweiser used Wigan in their advertising campaign. As the official beer of the Premier League, the American corporation used a TV and print campaign mocking their own lack of knowledge about 'soccer' with the slogan, 'You do the football, we'll do the beer.' A full-page advertisement appeared in the leading men's title, *FHM*, depicting Wigan Athletic's logo as a baseball club, 'Wigan A's'. Such coverage was unprecedented.

'Wigan is still a big name in rugby league circles,' added Calderbank. 'But football is a much, much bigger game worldwide and that has helped make the town a name in Europe, South America and Asia. Certainly, the number of visitors to the stadium suggests that.'

Wigan Leisure and Culture Trust monitored the levels of interest from film companies and TV stations and say the rise in interest reflected that of Wigan Athletic. Living TV, BBC, Granada and Channel 5 used Haigh Hall and Wigan Pier as backdrops for programmes and club captain Arjan De Zeeuw presented a documentary about Wigan's industrial heritage for a Dutch TV station.

Latics even made the Carling Cup competition popular. Usually largely ignored until the later rounds, Wigan's defeat of a full-strength Newcastle made people sit up and they followed that up by sweeping past Bolton and Arsenal to reach the Final.

The fact that they met Manchester United in the Cardiff showcase almost epitomised the Wigan Athletic story as it stood as a benchmark for how far they had travelled. When United won their first European Cup in 1968, Wigan were in the Northern Premier League. When United won the treble in 1999, Wigan were two divisions behind, and on their way to winning the Auto Windscreens Shield.

Such romance tugged on heart strings and drove the phenomenon of Wigan Athletic. Their media manager, Matt McCann, worked tirelessly to meet the demands of an endless list of broadcasters and publications. 'It was crazy, absolutely crazy,' admitted McCann.

The day before Wigan journeyed to Wales, they were beseiged by press calls, with manager Paul Jewell and three players, De Zeeuw, Jason Roberts and Graham Kavanagh, all fulfilling their media duties with radio, press and TV interviews at the ground.

'The whole story has captured a lot of imaginations and a lot of people across the world have bought into this story,' said Kavanagh.

As the curtain came down on an historic campaign, Wigan ensured their match on the final day was the one everyone was talking about. In fairness, the coverage belonged to Arsenal as it was their final game at Highbury, but Latics didn't complain at taking the back seat for once. They had been up on a pedestal for the best part of nine months and in doing so they changed the way Wigan was perceived across the country and, indeed, the world.

'The BBC interviewed people in the street in Birmingham last summer and they asked them what they knew of Wigan,' added Mather. 'Almost to a man they said something along the lines of, "It's somewhere up north", "They have a rugby team", "Isn't it a gloomy town"… If they did it now, I'm confident it wouldn't be like that, and that's all because of Wigan Athletic and the coverage they have had.

'In the past, people have gone on holiday and had to explain that Wigan is a town roughly halfway between Manchester and Liverpool. They won't have to do that now.'

AMERICAN documentary maker Paul Doyle was sitting on his bed in his Chelsea hotel room, flicking the buttons on the television's remote control as he scanned the channels for something entertaining to watch. He settled on channel 401. Sky Sports. And straight away he knew he had to get involved in the Wigan Athletic story.

'I was watching the second Carling Cup semi-final and I just couldn't stop thinking how incredible it was that this side had even got to Highbury,' recalled Doyle, a laid-back 44-year-old from New York. 'I watched Wigan in a trance and as soon as the game finished I sent a text to my partner in the States saying, 'We have to do this one about Wigan'.

That text message spawned a documentary about Wigan Athletic's incredible debut season in the Premiership. Early 'footage' captured the Wigan players in a new light – playing golf, and kicking back in the cafeteria at the Christopher Park training ground. The presence of Doyle's locally-hired crew sparked rumours of a Hollywood-style film though, unfortunately, the finished product is unlikely ever to be screened in America.

As he spoke to *Season of Dreams*, Doyle was confident the finished documentary would be broadcast on British television and then released on DVD. He acknowledged that making a documentary about Wigan was more of a risk than, say, Chelsea's Championship season or Arsenal's final campaign at Highbury, but believes it may ultimately prove more popular.

'I think the story plays to people outside of Wigan more than, say, the Chelsea story does to non-Chelsea fans,' says Doyle, who has been making films 'since I got out of school'. 'The interesting thing about Wigan is that for a lot of the players they are seeing it through new eyes – in a way they're experiencing it like the fans are. Everything is an experience for them, it's not like they've been doing it at this level all their life.

'Wigan doesn't have the fan base of Man U but it's a great story. I wish we had this in the States with relegation and promotion, rather than the franchise system. In baseball, smaller clubs in the minor league are feeder clubs to the major league sides – they don't go up or down. I explain it to my friends in America and say, 'Imagine if the New York Mets had a bad season and were in danger of being dropped to the minor league, and were being replaced by the Toledo Mudhens'. They think, "Whoa, that would be amazing"... you have that here in England with football.'

And it is that sense of adventure, as well as the freshness and naivety of the players to the big-time of the Premiership, that Doyle believes will help an audience relate to the Wigan players. He continues, 'You see players here who have been asked by their friends and families to get autographs from some of the Man U players after they play them. How weird is that? Imagine anyone else going into a work place and asking for a co-worker's autograph!

Paul Doyle, executive producer and partner of Bamboo Sports and Entertainment, during the making of a behind-the-scenes documentary on Wigan Athletic with cameraman Robert Foster and sound recorder Brian Davies.

'These people aren't superstars and so people can relate to them. Look at Arjan De Zeeuw, he's already thinking about work after football with his medical career – he's got three kids and one on the way. Jimmy Bullard and Jason Roberts worked 40-hour-a-week jobs before turning professional and I think they'd say they're better for it.

'It's healthier and more interesting that way. I'm not blaming the big-name players who were groomed from when they were 14 for stardom because it's not their fault, but they're probably not as grounded as some of the Wigan guys and that's why the guys here have interesting stories to tell.'

Doyle's track record with Bamboo Sports and Entertainment is impressive. He has made football documentaries with the co-operation of Manchester United, Liverpool, England Rugby Union and Chelsea in recent years and has worked with a variety of American sports stars such as golfer Tiger Woods and NBA basketballer Shaquille O'Neal.

'We're small fish to them,' smiled Irish midfielder Graham Kavanagh. 'They've done Tiger Woods, Shaq and now Graham Kavanagh! But they're good lads. A few of the lads went playing golf and they came around so hopefully they got some good shots on film!'

Doyle admits his track record helped convince Paul Jewell and Dave Whelan to allow cameras to follow their every move in the closing months of the season. 'We've got a reputation so if Paul wanted to check up on us he could do by phoning Mourinho or Fergie,' Doyle says. 'We're trusted. We got in touch with Wigan and what helped is that it's a smaller club. You can go to Dave Whelan and present your idea and he can talk to Paul and they can say yes or no. You don't have to go through 15 people just to speak to the decision maker, like at a big club.'

Doyle also won the support of the players by using his worldwide contacts for favours. Gary Teale and Kavanagh are self-confessed fans of Ultimate Fighting and, after learning that Doyle had recently worked with champion Andre Arlovsky, they asked could he get his autograph.

Dave Whelan, pictured after breaking his leg in the 1960 FA Cup Final, has seen Wigan grow and grow over the decades.

'I contacted his agent and asked for 10 autographs each, five addressed to Gary and five addressed to Kav,' Doyle explains. 'A few days later a FedEx parcel arrived and I opened it and there were five to Gary... then I flicked through and the others were addressed to 'Pav'! I tried getting a marker and changing the P into a K, but I couldn't. I gave them to him anyway and he seemed happy.'

Doyle had heard of Wigan Athletic before. Last autumn, he was in a brainstorm session for new ideas for English sports documentaries when Wigan were brought up as a possible contender. But it was Latics' heroics in their semi-final at Highbury, when Jason Roberts sent them through to the Carling Cup Final with a stunning goal in the 120th minute of an epic game, that convinced him to get involved.

'The players have been great,' he reports. 'None have really been shy, they've all been good. They've given me a free rein except they want to be protected from being embarrassed, and that's fair enough. We're not curing cancer here – it's a sports film, it's entertainment.

'We're storytellers, not journalists. We didn't discover this story – everyone knows how good this story is. I guess we're just telling a story from a different perspective.'

6: October: You dipstick, Rodney

IF SEPTEMBER ended with an elbow, then October opened with an old-fashioned 'umdinger. Emulating nearby neighbours Bolton was Latics' recognised ambition before the season started – even if no one in the town was prepared to accept it. Ploughing the same furrow as their fellow Lancastrians would have suited Wigan's top brass just fine, and they at least were conceding 'yes, we want to be like Bolton' – an unfashionable northern upstart, who had moved to a state-of-the-art ground rekindling latent support, and battled against relegation for a few seasons before becoming a force in the top flight.

Paul Jewell celebrates Wigan's win over Bolton, which left rival boss Sam Allardyce deflated.

'Bolton are the closest team to us and there's been a fierce rivalry when we've played them over the years,' said Paul Jewell, before admitting what many die-hard supporters never could. 'They have established themselves in the Premiership and are playing in Europe this season. That's the aim for us. We want to establish ourselves at this level and then push on. When they first came up into the Premiership, people said they would struggle to survive – just like they have about us. But these days no one ever talks about Bolton being relegation candidates. They are part of the Premier League furniture now. That's our goal here.'

Going into the game, Latics had won three of their previous four League games, and could become early contenders for a European place if they managed to topple the Trotters. Confidence among the squad, never low, was on the rise. A worry for Wigan was the fitness of Lee McCulloch, still battling through the pain barrier, yet still frightening Premier League full-backs witless with his battering performances on the field.

'The pressure is on Bolton,' he claimed. 'People like talking about it being a big local derby, but we can't afford to get caught up in all that. I've played in quite a few derbies, Wigan against Preston and Motherwell against Hibs. To be honest, the players all just knuckle down and get on with it.'

A sub-plot to the game was David Connolly's last chance to impress his international manager, and stake a claim for Ireland's World Cup squad. The Latics striker was dropped to the bench in favour of Henri Camara the previous Saturday and was sidelined again as Paul Jewell stuck with the same team against Bolton. But Connolly, who came on for the last five minutes against Everton, knew the clock was against him in his bid to relaunch his international career.

Sam Allardyce.

Wigan's game against the Trotters was the last before the World Cup qualifiers resumed. Connolly may have earned 40 caps for his country, but hadn't played for Ireland for two years. But after making a sparkling start to his Wigan career – he scored against West Brom on his debut – he was being tipped to reclaim his international place alongside club and international teammate Graham Kavanagh. 'I was out of the international picture for a while and I thought I was good enough,' sympathised the tough tackling midfielder. 'All he can do is try and stay in the Wigan team and score some goals. If he keeps scoring the goals for us it will be strange if he gets omitted. He's now on the right platform and on the stage to try and get back in.'

And so, to the game itself. By way of introduction, Latics hadn't beaten the Trotters in 15 years. When the sides last met, 12 years earlier, Bruce Rioch guided Wanderers to two victories. Bolton were also buoyed by their third place in the table, having lost only one in 11, and were unbeaten on the road.

The previous day Paul Jewell told the press: 'My worst nightmare is having to go to Highbury on the last game of the season needing one point to get into Europe.' No one thought he was serious.

Henri Camara celebrates his goal with the injured Pascal Chimbonda.

Sunday 2 October 2005

Wigan 2
Bolton 1

WIGAN: Filan 6, Chimbonda 6, Henchoz 7, De Zeeuw 9, Baines 7, Bullard 8, Francis 6, Kavanagh 7, McCulloch 8, Roberts 8, Camara 9. Subs: Taylor (for Chimbonda 22) 8, Connolly (for Camara 90). Wigan star man: Camara.

BOLTON: Jaaskelainen 7, Haim 6, Jaidi 6, N'Gotty 5, Pedersen 7, Nolan 7, Okocha 7, Speed 7, Nakata 7, Gardner 7, Davies 7. Subs: Giannakopoulos 7 (for Okocha 54), Diouf 6 (for Gardner 58), Borgetti (for Nakata 84).

Goals: Camara (48), McCulloch (63), Jaidi (68)
Half-time: 0–0
Referee: Alan Wiley
Attendance: 20,553

	P	W	D	L	F	A	Pts
Chelsea	8	8	0	0	18	2	24
Charlton	7	5	0	2	12	7	15
Tottenham	8	4	3	1	9	5	15
Man Utd	7	4	2	1	10	5	14
Bolton	8	4	2	2	9	6	14
Man City	8	4	2	2	9	6	14
Arsenal	7	4	1	2	10	4	13
Wigan	7	4	1	2	7	5	13
West Ham	7	3	3	1	11	5	12
Middlesb'h	8	3	2	3	9	11	11
Blackburn	8	3	2	3	7	9	11
Newcastle	8	2	3	3	5	7	9
Liverpool	6	1	4	1	4	6	7
Portsm'th	8	1	3	4	5	9	6
Birm'ham	8	1	3	4	7	12	6
Aston Villa	8	1	3	4	8	14	6
Sunderl'd	8	1	2	5	6	11	5
Fulham	8	1	2	5	7	13	5
West Brom	8	1	2	5	7	15	5
Everton	7	1	0	6	1	9	3

The Trotters arrived three days after a long and draining European trip to Bulgaria – there would never be a better time for Wigan to face them. Latics had the better of the opening exchanges, but lost their tempo as the first half wore on. Lee McCulloch and Jason Roberts saw early sights of goal, but left their shooting boots in the changing room. Pascal Chimbonda's 23rd-minute exit with a dead leg was hardly met with cheers, but Ryan Taylor proved a more than able deputy in his absence.

Bolton stepped up a gear after the half-hour mark and were almost rewarded when Kevin Nolan got in behind, but saw an attempted lob sail just wide. Camara's pace at the other end was Wigan's outlet. He laid a free header on for Jimmy Bullard, who could only direct it straight at Jussi Jaaskelainen.

As the interval approached McCulloch had his head in his hands with embarrassment when he fluffed an eight-yard left-footed shot, which neatly underlined the problem of playing a right-footer on the left. A typical Liverpudlian rant from Jewell at half-time saw his men come out with their ears ringing. They responded just three minutes into the second half.

Camara broke clear and played in Bullard on the right. His cross was suicidally headed back into Camara's path by Bruno N'Gotty and the striker's chip went in via the bar. The Senegal striker bagged his second of the campaign to open the scoring and was displaying all the attributes of an Olympic sprinter. 'I wouldn't like to face him in this kind of form,' admitted Latics colossus Arjan De Zeeuw.

Taylor headed off the line from Kevin Davies before McCulloch made amends for his earlier miss. Camara went into a challenge with Henrik Pedersen and the loose ball was thrashed superbly into the bottom corner by the Scot.

A second goal looked to have killed Bolton off, but with 22 minutes left to play, Jaidi threw a spanner in the works, nodding in Stelios Giannakopoulos's cross. The two sides slugged it out like heavyweight boxers until the death. Jaaskelainen kept out Damien Francis's 20-yard volley with a great stop and saved from Roberts before Giannakopoulos wasted another glorious opening right in front of the sticks.

De Zeeuw had the last laugh when he saw old foe El-Hadji Diouf – who caused uproar when he spat in the defender's face the previous season – put a late free

Latics fans celebrate victory over Bolton.

header wide from all of five yards. 'I had to smile when that happened,' De Zeeuw admitted.

As the final whistle confirmed the 2–1 scoreline, Latics fans were pinching themselves. The side had won their fourth league game in five outings to move up to eighth. 'You should have heard the lads in the shower – they think we can win the League now,' Jewell said. De Zeeuw revealed one of the secrets to Wigan's unimaginable early success. 'I keep thinking of what Rodney Marsh said at the start of the season,' he said. 'He said we wouldn't win six games all season and I'm really grateful for him saying that. We've got four wins now and definitely look like getting a lot more.

'It's great when people say nice things about you, but it's also good when they say something which isn't so nice because you want to prove them wrong. He's helped to push us on to bigger things.

'We were always confident of getting the victory. It was a good September for us and we've started this month well.

'If you average a point a game at this level you should stay up.

'Every point we get now is so vital because we've got it really tough over Christmas against the top sides in a short space of time.'

The players got a well deserved day off after their victory over Bolton, although it soon became clear that Jewell also benefited from his grand gesture – he got a chance to pursue his other love: golf. And he wasn't just relaxing on a course – ever the competitor, Jewell had an amateur golf championship in his sights. He was

What the opposition said...

'Wigan showed what a good side they are and you can't underestimate them. We would have settled for a point. Wigan work really hard and deserve to be where they are in the table. But I must say we had enough chances to win two games. We gave them too much space and time at the back and then wasted a lot of chances at the other end.' – Sam Allardyce, Bolton manager.

What the Wigan fan said...

'I thought we had the most clear chances on goal and could have been two up by half-time. Camara is showing his worth up-front, his pace and quick feet scare defences. The rivalry between the fans goes back a long way and I remember well their visits to Springfield Park.' – Dave Webster.

Eugene and Sean O'Reegan from Marus Bridge before the game.

On the eve of the game against Newcastle Henri Camara revealed he turned down a move to the Toon in favour of Wigan.

taking part in the International Pairs, the largest golf competition for club golfers in the world. The 12-handicapper took his place alongside more than 500 other club golfers in six UK semi-finals in Scotland after two earlier qualifying events at his home club of Bradford.

'For a start I didn't think we'd win our qualifier because my partner's rubbish,' he laughed. 'And when we did, I didn't think I'd be able to take it up, but with it being an international week we were able to take part.'

But Jewell, who describes himself as having 'played on and off for the last 15 years', and his partner John Bedford didn't make it through to the final at five-star St Andrews Bay Golf Resort and Spa. Having scored a total of 33 Stableford points he and Bedford were soon heading back south. 'We didn't play very well,' admitted Jewell. 'And we were disappointed to miss out on the trip to St Andrews.'

The day off came during international week. Latics had four players on duty: Lee McCulloch joined up with the Scotland squad, Henri Camara trotted off to Senegal and Graham Kavanagh was one of two Latics lads playing for the Republic of Ireland. And, as previously mentioned, another Latics player regained international honours riding on the coat-tails of his club's success. David Connolly was over the moon to receive the call from the then Ireland boss Brian Kerr. He had won his 40th cap in September 2003 before being axed from the squad.

'Everyone loves playing for their country and I'm no different,' he said. 'I've always said that players stand more of a chance playing for their country if they are in the Premiership.'

In the event, Connolly came on as sub for Roy Keane in the first of their two games that week, a 1–0 victory against Cyprus. But luck wasn't with the Irish. They couldn't find a way past the Swiss at Lansdowne Road and were left rueing missed opportunities as they finished fourth in the group and out of the World Cup.

Although the time off was great for the lads, and well deserved of course, it was a pain in the neck for sports writers who had acres of white space to fill on the back pages during international week.

It goes like that sometimes on a local newspaper sportsdesk. Yet Henri Camara provided relief for the drought when he revealed he had snubbed summer moves to Premiership giants Newcastle and Aston Villa – in favour of a switch to Wigan. What a filip for the club and its manager, who had been under fire before the start of the season for his transfer policies.

'There were bigger clubs than Wigan who wanted to sign me in the summer,' Camara admitted. 'Newcastle and Aston Villa both came in for me. But I chose to come to Wigan because I know I can achieve my ambitions here. I've got no regrets over coming here.'

High-flying Latics had made the best start to a Premiership season by a promoted club since 1994. A total of 13 points from their opening seven fixtures bettered any of the previous clubs who have gone up to the top flight in more than a decade.

Wigan were now level on points with Arsenal and just two points behind second-placed Charlton. But could it get any better? Paul Jewell certainly thought so. He said: 'To be eighth in the table at this stage is a great effort by the players. We are there on merit and I know there's still a lot we can improve on. We would have all settled for 13 points after seven games – I don't think many people would have had us level with Arsenal at the start of October. But we're not going to sit around here thinking to ourselves "haven't we done well". We're going to try and push on even further and keep this run going.'

Only Nottingham Forest in 1994 and Blackburn in 1992 went up to the Premiership and had better starts. Both clubs had 17 points at the same stage. Forest went on to finish third in the table and Blackburn ended fourth. Only Middlesbrough could match Wigan's achievement – they arrived in the top flight in 1992 and also had 13 points just seven games in. This time the previous year, Premiership new boys Norwich, West Brom and Crystal Palace hadn't won a game between them after seven outings. They occupied the bottom three places – the Baggies having made the best start with four points from four draws, to sit in 18th place.

Cheeky chappie Jimmy Bullard had played every minute in the Premiership – and he was still bouncing around like he had thoroughly enjoyed each and every

Pascal Chimbonda beats Alan Shearer to the ball.

one of them. He said: 'A lot of people wrote us off after we lost the first two games against Chelsea and Charlton. But those were two really difficult games – they are first and second in the table. We know we're a good team and it's no surprise to me to see us eighth in the table.'

New recruit Pascal Chimbonda was fast becoming part of Wigan folklore – the faithful warmed to the right-back's tireless energy and now famous woolly gloves. But as he reflected on his first three months at the club in a changing room at Christopher Park – donning a Tupac and Biggy Smalls t-shirt – the instantly likeable defender couldn't wait to be back against the Toon Army after picking up a dead leg against Bolton.

'I want to be a favourite with the Wigan fans,' he admitted. 'There is a lot stronger bond and loyalty between the English supporters and players. The fans here cheer for you whether you are winning, losing or drawing. In France when I was with Bastia, the fans are a lot more fickle and will boo you a lot quicker. It's one of the reasons I turned down Marseille in the summer and came to England.'

But the 26-year-old, who had played every League game so far, didn't need to stop for breath when asked if there was one aspect he'd change about his new home. 'The weather,' he smiled. 'As soon as September came I knew I would have to start wearing gloves. When it gets even colder I'll be putting two pairs on. I'm going to be putting a hat on soon as well in training. I can't believe that some people find this weather warm.'

Paul Jewell was also pleased to see two of his foreign legion recruits – 'Chimmy' and Henri Camara – settling in well. Jewell said: 'Pascal has started having English lessons and Henri will as well – if we can pin him down. They just shrug their shoulders at most things I say so I just tend to shout at them a bit louder. It's funny though, they seem to understand me when I tell them they're getting a day off. I think we need to get Henri a watch – I'd love to know what the French words are for "lazy bastard".'

(For future reference, the phrase Jewell was looking for was: 'Tu est un sale paresseux').

Club chairman Dave Whelan had been 'bigging up' his manager in recent weeks, saying he was good enough for England and that he wouldn't stand in his way if either the country or one of the country's famous clubs came a-knocking. The next big club to take a knocking was on its way to Wigan.

Newcastle United – although that should really read Newcastle Divided, such were their troubles in the early part of the season under Graeme Souness's soon to be terminated stewardship – visited the JJB on 15 October. The game was a chance to settle a few scores.

Old teammates Stephane Henchoz and Michael Owen would meet. Even older (age-wise) teammates Roy Tunks and Paul Jewell would be up against one another. Latics' legendary 'keeper was now part of the backroom staff at St James' Park. And the oldest score of all was the chance to settle a bad-tempered Cup tie between the sides.

Fifty-one years ago the two sides had slugged it out over two FA Cup third-round ties, the Magpies eventually winning the replay after an epic battle. In the 1953–54 season, another successful Latics side had retained the Lancashire Combination championship for the third time in four years, won the Lancashire Junior Cup and completed a treble with the Lancashire Combination Cup.

Stephane Henchoz in the air with Alan Shearer.

Their FA Cup run started when they beat Burscough 2–1 in the fourth qualifying round, which was followed by a 4–0 win against Scarborough at Springfield Park in the first round proper. In the second round they saw off Hereford United 4–1 at home in front of a gate of 27,562 – a crowd that remains a record between two non-League teams outside Wembley. The draw for the third round took them up to St James' Park to face Stan Seymour's side on Saturday 9 January 1954. Latics were only the second non-League team to ever visit Newcastle.

The Toon Army had won the Cup in 1951 and 1952. Their team contained six internationals, including household names Jimmy Scoular, Ivor Broadis... and Jackie Milburn. Newcastle's Ivor Broadis scored after 27 minutes, but Jackie Lyon equalised seven minutes into the second half. Jackie Livesey put Latics ahead in the 75th minute, but Milburn hit back straight away for the home side. A replay was swiftly arranged for 13 January.

Here the controversy began. Newcastle refused to change in Latics' makeshift changing rooms at Springfield Park after a fire the previous year had destroyed the main stand. Newcastle insisted on using the Corporation Baths. Latics fielded the same team in front of a crowd of 26,000. Vic Keeble put Newcastle ahead in the 13th minute and White doubled the lead 21 minutes later, but Billy Lomax hit back before the break.

Graeme Souness couldn't believe his side went a goal down.

Within minutes of the second half beginning Jackie Lyon lobbed the ball high into the area, Newcastle 'keeper Ronnie Simpson caught the ball and his momentum carried him at least a foot over the goal-line. Referee, Mr Williams, waved 'play on'. Broadis headed in Newcastle's third and although Latics managed to score another through Lomax, their magical Cup run came to an end.

The only man old enough to remember that performance was Dave Whelan, a 17-year-old trombonist with Wigan boys' band who played a fanfare welcoming the teams to the field on that day. 'I remember it well, it was freezing,' he said. 'The crowd were fantastic, some 26,000 and it was quite daunting being out there as a 17-year-old. I remember watching an outside-left called Bobby Mitchell and he was mesmerising.'

Days later Whelan signed professional terms with Blackburn and his own career started in earnest. Now chairman of one of the Premiership's youngest clubs, Whelan reckoned his Latics had changed opinions across the globe. 'We have surprised the whole nation and everyone who follows the Premiership around the world. We have forced people to sit up and say "look at Wigan Athletic". The town of Wigan has a football team to be proud of. We are a decent side – that's why we're doing so well, there's no fear at this club. We were written off at the start of the season, but I think people's opinions have suddenly changed.'

He also thought Paul Jewell's men could beat the mighty Newcastle. In the event, a tough game produced few chances for either side. Latics could have gone ahead in the 10th minute when Roberts raced on to Jean-Alain Boumsong's weak back header, but saw his left-footed drive strike the outside of the post. Lee Bowyer repeated the feat at the other end when Stephane Henchoz totally missed the ball and allowed him through. The midfielder's shot trickled past John Filan, but thankfully bounced back off the upright and into the big Aussie's grateful arms.

Newcastle took the ascendancy in the first half, with Latics happy to sit and play on the counter-attack. Owen's only sight of goal saw him fire wide from seven yards from Andy Faye's cross. But the move which eventually settled the match was

Delight for Jimmy Bullard and Leighton Baines after beating Newcastle.

Saturday 15 October 2005

Wigan 1
Newcastle 0

WIGAN: Filan 7, Chimbonda 7, Henchoz 7, De Zeeuw 9, Baines 7, Bullard 8, Francis 7, Kavanagh 7, McCulloch 7, Roberts 7, Camara 7. Subs: Connolly (for Camara 76) 6, Taylor (for Bullard 82) 5. Wigan star man: De Zeeuw.

NEWCASTLE: Given 7, Carr 6, Taylor 6, Boumsong 6, Elliott 7, Bowyer 7, Parker 8, Faye 6, N'Zogbia 7, Shearer 6, Owen 6. Subs: Ameobi 6 (for Bowyer 37), Emre 8 (for Faye 45), Clark (for Elliott 88).

Goal: Roberts (40)
Half-time: 1–0
Referee: Phil Dowd
Attendance: 22,374

What the opposition said...

'Wigan worked exceptionally hard, we knew they would before the game. All credit to them, they scored a good goal, defended well and got the points. Wigan aren't where they are in the table by luck. Their players all work so hard for each other. But I'm deeply disappointed for a number of reasons. We didn't get going until the second half. It took the introduction of Emre to wake us up.' – Newcastle manager Graeme Souness.

straight off Christopher Park. Pascal Chimbonda found Henri Camara, his lay-off was picked up by Damien Francis and a defence-splitting ball saw Jason Roberts bursting through to slip the ball under Shay Given to make it 1–0.

Two incidents dominated the second period. With 10 minutes to go, Lee McCulloch was sent off after he brought down Emre, meaning it was backs to the walls for the boys in blue. But what got right up Newcastle's noses was a 'goal' that never was. Shearer rose highest after an Emre corner in the 65th minute to head goalwards, but it was booted away by Leighton Baines. Controversy.

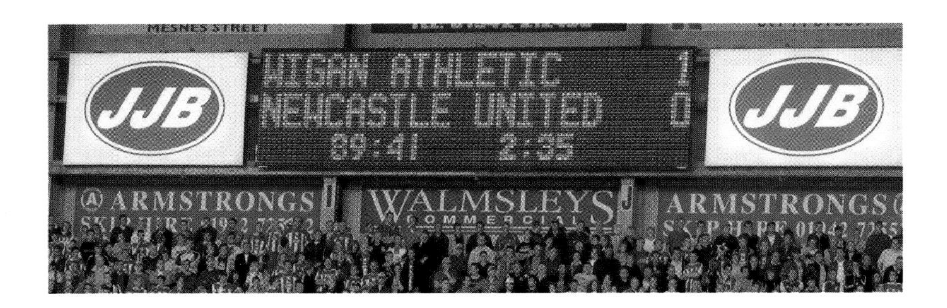

The final score.

'The defender was a yard and a half over the line when it hit him, so it had to be over the line,' said Shearer. Souness backed up his claim, saying: 'It was a goal. I don't know how the linesman didn't see it.'

Unlike his Newcastle side, the butties flew. Newcastle were plunging down the table, but the team's complimentary match day sarnies were airborne – winging their way toward the dressing room door. At a rate of knots.

And Souness wasn't done yet. 'This was the same assistant referee who allowed Gareth Taylor's goal to stand last season at Nottingham Forest, even though he was four yards offside. You owed us that one Mr (Andy) Williams.'

Match-winner Jason Roberts, clutching a bottle of bubbly to celebrate his third goal of the season, was happy to gloat in earshot of the visitors as they trundled off to catch their bus home. 'We deserved the three points,' he grinned. 'It's nice to be where we are in the table, but we're not getting carried away. We have to maintain these levels of performances. We're coming up against world-class players every week. But we're here to compete against them and we're beating them through sheer hard work.'

At least one Geordie kept his head in the wake of their defeat at Wigan. Ever level-headed, Alan Shearer tipped Latics to avoid relegation and fully establish themselves as a Premier League club. The Newcastle captain had fully expected the Toon Army to breeze past Paul Jewell's high-flyers, but the former England captain was forced to admit that Wigan were proving to be a force in the top flight. 'I think Wigan will do well for the rest of the season,' Shearer mused. 'I definitely think they are going to stay up. Wigan have had a great start to the season and that's continued against us. I'm sure they will beat a lot of other teams this year.'

As the dust settled on the Newcastle match, Wigan's star striker Henri Camara apologised for a bout of petulance; he stormed down the tunnel after being substituted. Jewell read him the riot act, accusing him of disrespecting his teammates, but Camara's reticence – 'I was tired and I'd had a bad week with Senegal missing out on the World Cup' – meant he avoided a club fine. Case closed and another example of Jewell's fine man-management.

Although he strives to be everyone's mate on the training pitch, Jewell, who was rapidly gaining the respect of national newspaper hacks for his wise-cracking persona, wanted his players to know who was boss and that he was deadly serious about this season in the Premier League. This was the perfect opportunity. Not too large an issue, not too big a problem, but Jewell stamped his authority all over it. In the end, it turned into a situation which could only help team bonding, as Camara professed his respect for his fellow pros.

An out-take from the following week's press conference, which, unusually, started bang on schedule at 12.30pm, is another great example of Jewell's nature.

What the Wigan fan said...

'It was a cracking game. It was an open, end to end match which never let up. Wigan played well in the first half and caused Newcastle a lot of problems. Maybe a draw would have been a fair result. Newcastle did have a lot of the ball and looked dangerous.' – West Stand season-ticket holder Len Marsden.

	P	W	D	L	F	A	Pts
Chelsea	9	9	0	0	23	3	27
Tottenham	9	5	3	1	11	5	18
Man Utd	8	5	2	1	13	6	17
Man City	9	5	2	2	11	7	17
Charlton	8	5	1	2	13	8	16
Wigan	8	5	1	2	8	5	16
Bolton	9	4	2	3	10	11	14
Arsenal	8	4	1	3	11	6	13
West Ham	8	3	3	2	12	7	12
Middlesb'h	9	3	3	3	10	12	12
Blackburn	9	3	2	4	7	10	11
Liverpool	7	2	4	1	5	6	10
Newcastle	9	2	3	4	5	8	9
Aston Villa	9	2	3	4	9	14	9
West Brom	9	2	2	5	9	16	8
Portsm'th	9	1	4	4	6	10	7
Fulham	9	1	3	5	8	14	6
Birm'ham	9	1	3	5	7	13	6
Sunderl'd	9	1	2	6	7	14	5
Everton	8	1	0	7	1	11	3

Henri Camara takes on Aston Villa.

Wigan's Alan Mahon in action against Villa.

John Filan punches away a Villa attempt.

Saturday 22 October 2005

Aston Villa 0 Wigan 2

ASTON VILLA: Sorensen 7, Hughes 6, Mellberg 6, Ridgewell 6, Samuel 6, Milner 7, Davies 6, Bakke 6, Barry 7, Phillips 6, Moore 6. Subs: Angel (for Moore 55) 6, Berger (for Bakke 70) 6.

WIGAN: Filan 9, Chimbonda 7, Henchoz 8, De Zeeuw 8, Baines 7, Bullard 8, Francis 7, Kavanagh 9, Mahon 6, Roberts 7, Camara 7. Subs: Teale (for Roberts 68) 6. Wigan star man: Filan.

Goals: Hughes (og, 32), Mahon (82)
Half-time: 0–1
Referee: Richard Beeby
Attendance: 32,294

The prompt start wasn't good news for *Daily Express* reporter Matt Dunn. Jewell was already in mid-flow when Dunn burst into the conference after a harrowing trip to Wigan over the Pennines. With a look of embarrassment, Dunn timidly walked over towards Jewell to place his dictaphone in front of the Wigan manager's nose.

A tray of bourbons occupied the table, surrounded by a dozen other tape recorders. Dunn smiled, waited for Jewell to finish his first answer, then whispered, 'I don't want a biscuit, thanks Paul.' Dunn hurriedly about-turned to find a seat, but the quick-witted scouser didn't let him get away with his late arrival. 'You don't look like you need one either pal,' Jewell quipped.

The mood in the Latics camp was, as ever, on the rise. And in what was to prove a record-breaking season for the team in so many ways, one of the club's most long-standing records went at Villa Park. Jimmy Bullard ran out to make his 117th consecutive League appearance for the club, to equal Colin Methven's 23-year all-time record.

'I never saw Colin play, but some Wigan fans who live on my road in Orrell have told me he was a complete legend at this club,' he said. 'It will mean a lot to me to equal the record. To be a part of Wigan's history is really special – one of the best moments of my career.'

Earlier in the season Bullard overtook Jeff Wright's total of 110 League games in a row at Charlton. He also surpassed John Filan's total of 109 consecutive League games, which came to an end in March the previous year when the 'keeper was sent off at West Brom. 'I never thought I'd play this many games in a row,' Bullard admitted. 'This is something I never dreamed about when I came here. It was only when I'd played 96 consecutive League games that I realised how many games I'd played. Ever since then I've just been desperate to stay in the team.'

Methven, born in India and raised in Scotland, joined Latics from East Fife in September 1979. The defender began his record number of games in March 1980 before his run came to an end in November 1982.

He made 353 appearances and scored 28 goals. Bullard, who signed from Peterborough in March 2003 for £275,000, says he'd had his fair share of luck to always be available for Paul Jewell, especially in the days of tight fixture lists and an ever mushrooming number of games every season.

'There's been a few times when I've been injured, but then managed to shake it off and be alright for the Saturday,' he says. 'I've had a great time since I've been at Wigan – these have been the best days of my career without a doubt.'

His 117th game against Aston Villa turned out to be a bit of a corker. He laid on the pass for the game-sealing goal. Releasing Alan Mahon down the left, the bit-part midfielder hit a wonder strike to send Paul Jewell's men to the dizzy heights of fourth in the Premiership.

The Irishman's low-backlift left-foot fizzer from outside the box flew past Thomas Sorensen even though the Villa 'keeper got the tips of his fingers to it, sparking scenes of wild celebration from the Latics faithful. An earlier own-goal from Aaron Hughes gave Wigan a comfortable 2–0 victory and another precious three points.

Mahon admitted he thought his time was up at Wigan following a lacklustre display at Charlton in August. 'It's always in the back of your mind that you may have to look elsewhere if you're not playing,' said the 27-year-old midfielder. 'But the gaffer has been straightforward and honest with me and you can't ask for no

Arjan De Zeeuw celebrates another win, which made Wigan the most in-form team in Europe behind Juventus.

What the opposition said...

'You can't take anything away from Wigan – they deserve everything they've had so far. Paul has got a set of really hungry players who are playing out of their skin. They've certainly surprised a lot of people so far. We had some decent chances in the first half and we really should have taken them. But Wigan have got a lot of pace going forward and they made us pay the price.' – Aston Villa manager David O'Leary.

What the Wigan fan said...

'In the first half Villa had most of the game, but in the second half Wigan came in to it more. Overall Wigan deserved to win. It was Jimmy Bullard's 118th straight game, and for every corner he received a standing ovation. An adopted Wiganer!' – Wigan Athletic Supporters' Club chairperson Caroline Molyneux.

	P	W	D	L	F	A	Pts
Chelsea	10	9	1	0	24	4	28
Charlton	9	6	1	2	15	9	19
Tottenham	10	5	4	1	12	6	19
Wigan	9	6	1	2	10	5	19
Man Utd	9	5	3	1	14	7	18
Man City	10	5	2	3	11	8	17
Bolton	10	5	2	3	12	11	17
Arsenal	9	5	1	3	12	6	16
West Ham	9	4	3	2	14	8	15
Blackburn	10	4	2	4	9	10	14
Newcastle	10	3	3	4	8	10	12
Middlesb'h	10	3	3	4	11	14	12
Liverpool	8	2	4	2	5	8	10
Fulham	10	2	3	5	10	14	9
Aston Villa	10	2	3	5	9	16	9
West Brom	10	2	2	6	9	18	8
Portsm'th	10	1	4	5	7	12	7
Birm'ham	10	1	3	6	7	15	6
Sunderl'd	10	1	2	7	9	17	5
Everton	9	1	1	7	2	12	4

more as a player. I didn't play well against Charlton, I accept that and he made changes. It's been really frustrating not playing. But the lads have been fantastic so far, so I can't really complain.'

Mahon, who joined Latics in February the previous year, insisted he hadn't been banging on Jewell's door demanding a chance. 'I'm not a disruptive player – I just want to play,' he said. 'I understand this is a squad game – it's not just about one player who isn't in the side.'

A quarter of the way into the season, Jewell's men had earned 19 points and sat comfortably above decorated and distinguished rivals Liverpool, Manchester United and Arsenal.

Saturday 29 October 2005

Wigan 1
Fulham 0

WIGAN: Filan 6, Chimbonda 8, Henchoz 9, De Zeeuw 7, Baines 6, Taylor 7, Francis 7, Kavanagh 7, Mahon 6, Bullard 6, Camara 7. Subs: Johansson (for Mahon 62) 6, McMillan (for Baines 74) 6. Wigan star man: Henchoz.

FULHAM: Warner 6, Volz 7, Goma 6, Bocanegra 7, Jensen 7, Malbranque 8, Diop 7, Jensen 7, Boa Morte 6, Radzinski 6, John 7. Subs: Elrich (for Jensen 82) 5, McBride (for John 82) 5, Rosenior (for Bocanegra 90).

Goal: Chimbonda (90)
Half-time: 0–0
Referee: Andre Marriner
Attendance: 17,266

Wigan Athletic's breathtaking run could now only be bettered by one team across Europe. Latics had stunned the football world with six wins and a draw. Only runaway leaders Chelsea could match that record – and they were nine points clear at the top of the Premiership. In Europe's elite divisions, Serie A giants Juventus were the only team with a better record than Wigan over the same seven-game period, having won all their matches to claim top spot. Latics' astonishing form saw them beat Sunderland, West Brom, Everton, Bolton, Newcastle and Aston Villa and draw with Middlesbrough. And the omens were good.

Recent history showed Latics were effectively safe from the drop with just a quarter of the campaign gone. This time the previous season Everton had 19 points after nine games, were third in the table and went on to qualify for the Champions League in fourth place. In 2003 Chelsea had 20 points at this stage and finished second. Leeds topped the table in 2001 with 19 points at the end of October and finished fifth. Manchester United and Arsenal had 18 points on the board after nine games in 2000 and ended in the top two spots.

The revelations breathed even more confidence into the Latics squad ahead of their home clash with Fulham this Saturday. 'We're going into games believing we can win them – that's the mentality here,' offered Damien Francis, a £1.5 million signing from Norwich and one of the few players with Premiership experience before the season started. 'A lot of my friends tried to talk me out of coming to Wigan in the summer, but I know my football and I knew Wigan could stay up.'

But the season was only going to get harder. Wigan's element of surprise – neither Newcastle captain Alan Shearer nor Aston Villa skipper Olof Mellberg thought Latics could beat their sides – would soon be lost. And the injuries would begin to take their toll. But for now, even the most curmudgeonly critics were heaping praise on the side.

Cue *Match of the Day* pundit Alan Hansen and his inimitable Scottish brogue. 'Wigan have had a dream start. After two games they had no points and if that run had continued they would have been in a bit of trouble. Wigan are halfway towards

Paul Jewell has a laugh with Henri Camara after the Fulham game.

Premiership survival already and that is unbelievable.' No one says 'un-be-lieve-able', quite like Hansen. But it's a good point, well made.

Wigan went into their next game, a televised home match with Fulham on 29 October, with only one recognised striker. Paul Jewell claimed his second successive manager of the month award after a last gasp victory. Jewell's record in the previous month matched Jose Mourinho's, but, as the popular theory stands, the FA decided to hand the award to the Wigan manager because it would be his only chance of the season.

Chimbonda popped up at the back post to head in a Graham Kavanagh free-kick in the 91st minute at the end of an otherwise drab affair. It sent Wigan spiralling to second in the table and inscribed the glove-wearing Frenchman, who took what felt like a 10-minute bow after the match, into Latics folklore.

Leighton Baines used the superlative of the moment to describe how the players were feeling. 'It's unbelievable – no one would have thought it,' admitted the left-back. 'To win five League games in a row is a great achievement, plus two Cup wins as well.'

The roof came off the ground when the livewire Chimbonda planted Kavanagh's free-kick past Tony Warner with just 90 seconds of injury time left. There could be no more popular match-winner. Jewell celebrated on the pitch, Whelan was in a scrum with his wife and directors, while the fans were in dreamland. Again. 'It happened to us on the first day of the season when we conceded a goal in the last minute, so we were owed that one,' Baines smiled.

Chimbonda was the last off the pitch as he revelled in the *Conga*, pumped around the ground through the loudspeakers. 'He's brave, strong and athletic and has become a cult hero with the fans,' concluded Jewell, who refused to reveal how he had come across the £500,000 steal.

'I'm ecstatic to have scored the winning goal in the last minute,' said Chimbonda, lapping up the press attention. 'It was a trick we had been working on in training. I was slightly fortunate because Diop was marking me, but I managed to roll him and he slipped and I got a great connection on the ball. It was great to go second in the League, but it's far too early to be looking at the table. Our primary objective is still survival.'

What the opposition said...

'It defies logic that we can come away from that game and not have anything to show for it. We cannot keep seeing referees getting major decisions wrong. My players were going nuts at half-time. It wasn't just one decision – it was four. I had to change my team talk at the break. Rather than saying "well done, keep going, you are doing well", I had to try and calm them down. – Fulham manager Chris Coleman.

What the Wigan fan said...

'It was a tough battle. Fulham missed some early chances and for most of the first half I thought we were going to struggle to get a result. Wigan came out and dominated the second half and I believe the final result was fair. Wigan's dogged determination clinched it.' – West Stand season-ticket holder Diane Walker.

	P	W	D	L	F	A	Pts
Chelsea	11	10	1	0	28	6	31
Wigan	10	7	1	2	11	5	22
Tottenham	11	5	5	1	13	7	20
Man City	11	6	2	3	14	9	20
Bolton	11	6	2	3	13	11	20
Charlton	10	6	1	3	15	10	19
Man Utd	10	5	3	2	15	11	18
Arsenal	10	5	2	3	13	7	17
West Ham	10	4	3	3	14	10	15
Newcastle	11	4	3	4	11	10	15
Middlesb'h	11	4	3	4	15	15	15
Blackburn	11	4	2	5	11	14	14
Liverpool	9	3	4	2	7	8	13
Portsm'th	11	2	4	5	11	13	10
Fulham	11	2	3	6	10	15	9
Aston Villa	11	2	3	6	10	19	9
West Brom	11	2	2	7	9	21	8
Everton	10	2	1	7	3	12	7
Birm'ham	11	1	3	7	7	16	6
Sunderl'd	11	1	2	8	10	21	5

Pascal Chimbonda, wearing his famous gloves (in October)... Latics' new cult hero.

Midfield battler Graham Kavanagh looks back on the historic debut Premiership season and talks Guinness, champagne, celebrities... and Chas and Dave

Which was the best final whistle of the season? **Arsenal away in the Carling Cup semi-final. Definitely. The feeling was incredible – no one gave us a chance and we felt on top of the world.**

What was the best ground to walk out on to? **Anfield, because I've always been a massive Liverpool fan so for me personally, that was the best ground to go to. But the City of Manchester Stadium was an impressive facility – the dressing rooms are so big you can have a kick about in them.**

Who were the best visiting fans to the JJB? **From the players' point of view it was Newcastle. They came down in force and even though they lost they never stopped cheering.**

What did you know about Wigan before you signed for the club? **I'd played them a few times throughout my career so I knew a bit about them. I knew the manager, not personally but I knew him in football circles. As for the town, I knew they had been a hugely successful rugby team over the years and what else? That they were a big pie eating place!**

Graham Kavanagh gives his insights on playing in the Premiership.

What was the best goal of the season? **From our team, Henri Camara's at Sunderland was pretty good. There have been so many crackers but Portsmouth's Matthew Taylor's against Sunderland when he saw the 'keeper out and kicked it from 40 yards... that was a really good goal.**

What's been your favourite game this season? **Arsenal away, no question. (Laughs) My favourite game and we lost! But the feeling of qualifying for the Final was the best feeling ever... I'll never forget that feeling.**

What's been the funniest moment of the season? **That was after the Arsenal semi-final. Arsenal gave us some champagne and the gaffer (Paul Jewell) let us drink for the first time on the coach home. I sang a couple of songs and then Jimmy (Bullard) put on a CD of Chas and Dave and the whole team was dancing and singing along. It was fantastic.**

What's been the worst, erm, telling off from Paul Jewell? **That would come two minutes after he read this if I answered it, so I'm not going to!**

Tell us three things about yourself that people don't know. **I'm probably the only Irishman who doesn't like Guinness. I can't stand the stuff. What else? I used to dye my hair black, until I was about 20 and then I got rumbled and called plumhead so I had to stop! I can't think of a third.**

Are your kids big Wigan fans? **Calum is. He's two-and-a-half and he watches us on TV. He comes into the kitchen saying, 'Quick, Dad, Bainesy's on TV' and he walks around the house singing 'Who needs Mourinho, we've got Paul Jewell-io'. My daughter, Megan, is a very outgoing person but it's not as big a deal to her. I'm just her dad and that's it.**

Have your kids or any of their friends asked you to collect autographs or shirts? **(Laughs) No, they've not but a lot of my mates have. One of my friends asked could I get Duncan Ferguson's jersey after we played Everton. I was suspended for that game and I thought, 'Not a problem', and then Ferguson got sent off! As he was walking off the pitch I sent a text to my friend saying, 'There's no way I'm asking for it... he'll kill me!'.**

Have any players asked for your autograph? **Yeah, a couple. James Collins at West Ham and Chris Brown at Sunderland. You don't think before a game I'll go and get a jersey or an autograph but it's nice afterwards sometimes to swap them.**

Who's the most famous person whose number you have stored in your mobile? **Mate there's loads of them, hundreds... but I'd have to say Jimmy Bullard.**

What's been the nicest compliment from a rival manager? **I couldn't tell you. It doesn't interest me because one thing I've learned this season is that they say nice things when they've beaten you. When they lose it's the referee's fault or they're critical of their own team – it seems they only pay us a compliment when they've beaten us.**

What's your other favourite sport? **Boxing, I love it. I've always been a big fan. Those guys are unreal, they've nowhere to hide.**

At what point did you feel safe from relegation? **Before Christmas, when we beat Charlton and got to 28 or 29 points. I thought, 'We've got here so quickly there's no way we could go the rest of the season and only get 11 points'. I knew we would stay up.**

Famous face, celebrity Jimmy Bullard.

A shamrock in a pint of Guinness but Kavanagh will give it a miss.

What's been the best thing Paul Jewell has said before a game? **He always says the same thing. He always tells us to be focussed and start well and to give 100 percent. If everyone played at five percent less than they're capable then straight away the team is 55 percent down on what you can be. We may not always play as well as we can do but you have to work as hard as you can do and that's what's given us the edge this year.**

If you could sign one player past or present who would it be? **Diego Maradona, he was a genius.**

If you could change any defeat this season into a win, which would it be? **Cardiff, without a doubt. I felt embarrassed about our performance in the Carling Cup Final because it wasn't Wigan, not the real Wigan. We showed the following week when we should have won what Wigan Athletic are all about. If I could go back and put one game right it would be that one.**

When was the last time you paid to watch a football game? **When I was playing at Cardiff I used to go to quite a few games at the Millennium Stadium and I paid for those tickets. The last would have been the Charity Shield between Liverpool and Man United.**

Who was the last man standing at the bar after the Carling Cup Final? **Ha, Mike Pollitt I think. It wasn't me... but I certainly wasn't the first one to bed.**

7: Paul Jewell: frankly, our Bill Shankly

Paul Jewell has created a glittering legacy at Wigan Athletic.

PAUL JEWELL will forever be remembered as Wigan's miracle maker – the man who took the club into the Premiership. He has built his own glorious legacy in the town and at the club – Wigan's equivalent of Bill Shankly or Sir Matt Busby – that will be continually celebrated. And never forgotten.

He arrived at Wigan on Monday 6 June 2001, and few would have envisaged what he would deliver in the following four years. 'I'm thrilled to be here,' Jewell said in his first press conference. 'I'm fiercely ambitious and I hope this club can match me in where I want to take them.' The rest, as they say, is history.

He has been asked many times for his secret, and replied each and every time: 'There is no secret. It is all down to hard work.' But there is so much more to Paul Jewell's armoury than working hard. Like so many success stories in management, his philosophies, habits and style can be traced to his upbringing. But where does Jewell's story start? What is the background to the man who made history with 'Little Old Wigan', taking them from the old Second Division to the Promised Land of the Premier League?

Paul Jewell was born in Liverpool on 28 September 1964. Immensely proud of his working-class roots, his late father Billy was an engineer and a trade unionist and his mother, Teresa, a housewife who worked part-time in the NHS.

The former Blessed Sacrament and De La Salle schoolboy was certainly brought up the right way and he was a good pupil, finishing with a stack of O-levels while spending nearly every available minute taking part in a sport that would change his life. There was only one ambition in Jewell's mind when he left school. He had always dreamed of pulling on the famous red shirt of his beloved Liverpool – and he was presented with the opportunity of a lifetime. 'I've always been a Liverpool fan, my dad was and most of my family are,' he says. 'My mum lives in West Derby now and although I don't get back to see her as often as she would like, I do try to as often as I can. I met my wife, Anne-Marie, when I was still at school – she was from Bootle and went to Everton Valley – and both of us have still got a lot of family in Liverpool. I've still got a lot of mates in the city and of course I'll always have a soft spot for Liverpool.'

Paul Jewell, here discussing tactics with Alex Cribley, traces his managerial style back to his days as a teenager at Liverpool.

Jewell was a regular at Anfield as he screamed his beloved team on to victory every other weekend from the terraces. Liverpool was in his blood and, like so many other fans at the time, his passion didn't stop with just the first team. 'When I was a young kid my dad used to take me to watch the reserves a lot on the Saturday afternoons when the first team were playing away,' he said. 'There used to be crowds of about 12,000 there in those days. I remember collecting lemonade bottles and getting the money back off them just so I could go across to Birkenhead for a League Cup tie against Tranmere. I would travel all over the country to watch Liverpool, mainly on the special trains they used to run back then. There was a lot of trouble in those days and many times I just used to sneak off to the match without telling my mum or dad.'

The Liverpool first team in those days was blessed with some of the finest talent these shores had ever seen. But there was only one player the young Jewell aspired to be when he was growing up with his pals on Merseyside. 'My boyhood hero was Kenny Dalglish – I'd always be him when I was scoring goals in the street as a kid,' he reflected. 'I always wanted to play for Liverpool. I was gutted that I never got the chance to do it for the first team, but I had the time of my life when I was there.'

Jewell thought all his Christmases had come at once when he got the opportunity to join the same club as his boyhood heroes. It only seems like yesterday that he got the call that all budding youngsters in the red half of the city wanted. Jewell said: 'A scout from Everton started showing an interest in me, but Mal Bates and Liverpool's youth team coach John Benninson came round to the house and asked me to start training at Melwood on Tuesday and Thursday nights. This was in the days before the Academy. The funny thing was my school, De La Salle, didn't allow this. They thought it was more important that their pupils concentrated on their studies. But I attended for two years without them knowing. I just wanted to play football all the time and eventually, at the time I was doing my O-levels, I was offered an apprenticeship.'

There were plenty of sleepless nights as he realised just what an opportunity had presented itself. Liverpool were the dominant force in English football throughout the 1970s and 1980s and Jewell was still pinching himself many months down the line. 'As an apprentice I used to get the number 68 bus, get off at Queens Drive and walk down to Melwood,' he said. 'I was like a kid with a new toy. When I went to bed at night I couldn't wait to wake up in the morning and get into training. I loved it so much I used to go training on Tuesday and Thursday nights as well with the schoolboys. I was only 16 or 17 and they were the happiest times of my life. I didn't have a care in the world. I felt like the luckiest kid in the world going to work, although my dad didn't call it work, he used to call it playing out!'

Jewell soon realised the extent of the new world he had entered as he made his way through the youth ranks before signing as a professional at the age of 18 in September 1982. He recalled: 'I played in the 'A' and 'B' teams then made my debut for the reserves when I was 16. It was a big thing for a 16-year-old to play for the reserves and it was a great moment for me. The side was full of internationals. Even the 'A' team at the time was full of quality players. Roy Evans said I was unlucky because I played in the wrong era, because I had the likes of Kenny and Rushie ahead of me. Maybe things would have been different had I played in another era. It was nice of Roy to say those things, but to be fair I don't know whether I was good enough to play for the Liverpool first team. It was sink or swim and you were very rarely praised. If you got a "well done" off Ronnie Moran you'd run home and tell your dad about it!'

Jewell was with the Liverpool squad when they qualified for the European Cup Final in 1984. He ranks it as one of his greatest footballing memories.

Jewell twice got selected for the first-team squad, but knew he had little chance of making it on to the pitch. 'I was in the squad for games at Arsenal and Newcastle,' he says. 'The 13th man it was known as in those days and you'd only ever be called upon if someone went down with food poisoning or something on the night before or day of the match. I remember we lost 3–1 at Highbury and won 2–0 up on Tyneside, a game that was shown live on the telly. Dinamo Bucharest away, though, was the best memory for me. Travelling with the squad to a foreign country was a great experience. In the first leg Graeme Souness had broken one of their players' jaws and everyone was out to get him. There was police everywhere at the airport when we arrived and on the day of the game the ground was packed two hours before kick-off, they were going mad.'

His lasting memories come from his time in the Reds' reserves side. 'I remember when I played against Sheffield Wednesday reserves,' he says. 'We were trailing 2–0 with 15 minutes to go but ended up winning 3–2 and I scored a hat-trick. I came off the pitch feeling great, only to be told by Roy Evans that I was the luckiest man in the world not to have been taken off and that I did nothing apart from score three goals! That was typical of Liverpool at that time.'

Jewell's time at Anfield came to an end in December 1984. Joe Fagan was reluctant to introduce him to the first team as his team were on the way to securing the treble. It was at that time when he first made acquaintances 20 miles down the road at Wigan Athletic. Tony Kelly spotted Jewell playing in the Liverpool reserves and went back with glowing reports to the late Latics manager Harry McNally, who wasted no time in inquiring about the services of the frontman.

Fagan allowed Jewell, 19, to join Latics on loan before a fee of £25,000 was agreed to make the move permanent. 'I loved my time at Liverpool and no one can take away the memories that I have,' Jewell says. 'To be in that dressing room after we'd just reached the Final of the European Cup in 1984 will live with me forever. I remember on the plane going home, Ronnie Moran was going around all the reserve lads, the likes of Steve Nicol, Jim Beglin, Phil Thompson and myself, and reminding us to be in early for training the next day because we had an important reserve game.

'That was typical Liverpool. We'd just won through the semi-final of the European Cup but uppermost in Ronnie's mind was this reserve game the next day. If I had been good enough, Liverpool wouldn't have let me go. Perhaps there are certain things I would do differently if I had my time again, like work harder, but no, I've no regrets.

'I learnt a lot from my time at Liverpool and enjoyed every minute of it. But that buzz got less and less as time went by, I must admit, and I got to the point when I needed to be playing first-team football. I went on loan to Wigan and that whetted my appetite. When I returned to Liverpool and played in the reserves again it just wasn't the same. I went to see the boss and asked if he could try and sort out a transfer for me. People may say I was a bit impetuous but I never look back.

'It was my decision to leave. I remember having to go and see Peter Robinson to sign a form at Anfield on a Saturday morning then driving out of the car park, looking back and thinking "I'm never going to come back here for work again". It was heartbreaking and really hit home to me what I was doing. It was a sad day for me but I had to move on to further my football career.'

Jewell signed for Wigan after failing to break into the Liverpool first team. 'It was heartbreaking leaving Anfield,' he says.

Jewell made an instant impression with the Wigan faithful, and remembers his time under McNally fondly. 'The first game I played for Wigan was a 3–3 draw against Rotherham,' says Jewell. 'I remember it because Harry got sent off from the dug-out and we had two others sent off and ended up with nine men and still managed to get a point. Harry was fantastic with me. He was a bit of a character, but he was his own man. He signed a lot of good players and we had a good group of lads with a good team spirit.'

It wasn't long though before McNally was replaced by Brian Hamilton and Jewell found himself on the substitutes' bench, battling for recognition with the limited chances thrown his way. Thankfully for Jewell, Hamilton's reign at the club only lasted a year. Ray Mathias succeeded him and, after describing Jewell as 'a striker in the Kenny Dalglish mould', he had no hesitation in putting him back in the side.

Jewell's spell at Latics then took off as himself and Bobby Campbell continued to find the net on a regular basis. 'I had my best run at the club under Ray Mathias,' Jewell says. 'He played me on a regular basis and I learned a lot from him.' Jewell's record at Wigan could not be questioned as he averaged a goal almost every three games, with 47 goals in 152 appearances. Most Latics fans will say his most important goal came against Norwich City in the fourth round of the FA Cup in 1987. That night, Jewell proposed to his wife-to-be Anne-Marie.

Surprisingly, Jewell never moved to Wigan during his time at the club and lived in Ainsdale, near Southport. When Bradford City came in for him in 1988 he realised it was time to move on. He said: 'My contract was up and we'd missed out on promotion to Division One and I wanted to play at a higher level. Other players left as well. We lost Mike Newell and David Lowe went to Ipswich and they got a decent bill for me at £80,000.'

Jewell finished his playing career at Valley Parade 10 years later and then hit the coaching scene. His passion for the game, thick skin and boundless enthusiasm made him a perfect candidate. 'I always wanted to be a coach,' he admits. 'I love football so much and wanted to stay in the game so it was the next stage to go.'

He was given the youth team job by Bantams boss Chris Kamara, but was quickly propelled up the ladder when chairman Geoffrey Richmond gave his

Jewell was a no-nonsense player for Wigan. In 2000, he attended a reunion with many of his former Latics teammates. Back row: Kevin Langley, Bobby Campbell, Graham Barrow, Mike Newell and David Lowe. Front row: Harry McNally, Barry Knowles, Jewell and Ray Mathias.

manager the bullet. Jewell takes up the story. 'I thought that was incredible. Richmond then called me into his office and I thought I was going to get sacked as well. But I had a player/coach contract and he told me to take over the first team at Stockport that weekend while he tried to find someone else. I changed the tactics, we played with a sweeper and we won 2–1, but our 'keeper Mark Prudhoe was brilliant that day. If we had lost that game that might have been the end for me.'

Jewell was appointed as the manager of Bradford in January 1998 and soon realised what he had let himself in for. 'It's a lonely job being a manager and any manager who says it isn't is telling fibs,' he says. 'You need to be able to turn to people for advice. It's impossible to switch off from the game – you can't get away from it. I've always been friends with Peter Reid and it's good to have people who have been in the same situation as you to be able to talk to.

'I can say from some of the courses I've been on that it's hogwash that you can do this job from a manual. I'm not against having badges because I suppose you've got to have them – it's like your driving licence. Adrian Boothroyd [Watford manager] has got as many badges as you can get. But you learn more whether you can do the job or you can't do it when you get the chance – not what any course has told you. There's nothing like being on the shop floor, the courses don't give you that.

'It's like learning to become a journalist. You can sit in front of a seminar and get told the theory, but you don't know if you could ask an awkward question to Sir Alex Ferguson until you're in that situation. All the badges in the world won't make you a great coach. I've seen some rubbish driving coming into work and all these people have passed their tests. But I know people who have been in the game a long time, but never had the chance. There are loads of potentially good managers who haven't been given a break.'

Jewell celebrates promotion to the Premiership with Bradford... in his now infamous purple shirt and brown jacket.

Jewell took charge of 21 games until the end of the campaign. 'I'd been no more than an average player there, and the supporters weren't too happy when I got the job,' he said.

With two games to go before the end of the season, Jewell took a call from Richmond one Friday night. The manager had only recorded six wins, but his chairman was struggling to find anyone who wanted the position full-time. Jewell said: 'The chairman called me one Friday night to say that he was giving me the job. We were playing Crewe the next day and he added, "provided we don't lose 5–0 tomorrow, of course". We both laughed. What happened? We were 4–0 down at half-time and I could see my chances of the job slipping away by the minute. I thought, "Jesus, what am I doing here?" I remember it was a hot day, so I chased the players out of the dressing room so they had to spend 15 minutes in the sun in front of our own fans. We still lost 5–0 but maybe that little thing showed the chairman that I could deal with the problems and wasn't frightened to make decisions. The chairman stuck with me, much to the annoyance of the supporters.'

Richmond's decision, however unpopular it may have been around the Yorkshire city, was soon vindicated. The fans were forced to change their minds when Jewell took the Bantams up in second place in his first full season in charge. They joined Sunderland in the automatic promotion positions, a 3–2 away win at Wolves on the last day booking their place. Jewell and his now infamous brown suit celebrated on the Molineux pitch at the full-time whistle.

Bradford were in England's top division for the first time in their history. Lee Mills, Robbie Blake and Peter Beagrie had rattled in more than 50 goals between them. Jewell, at the age of 34, was the youngest manager in the top flight – younger than some of his players. But he was learning the game fast and went on to enjoy even more success the following season when he kept them up on the final day as David Wetherall netted a famous header against Liverpool.

The majority thought Jewell had done a fantastic job. His side were labelled 'Dad's Army' because of their mature years. His make-do-and-mend squad included the archetypal journeyman Dean Windass – their leading scorer with 10 goals.

The celebrations, though, were short lived. Richmond wasn't happy. He told Jewell the club's season wasn't good enough and they'd need heavy investment and to bring in some 'fresh legs'. 'Me and the chairman didn't see eye to eye and I decided to leave,' Jewell says. 'He thought the answer was to go out and bring players in on crazy money. Benito Carbone came in on £40,000 a week, Dan Petrescu signed for £22,000 a week and Stan Collymore joined for £20,000. When it all started to go wrong for them, they had those players there stuck on those contracts and as a result they almost went out of business.'

Jewell wasn't out of work long. Three days later he thought he'd been rescued by Sheffield Wednesday. The Owls were in the old Division One, but Jewell soon realised he'd walked into a viper's nest of wily old pros, who were resistant to every change he wanted to implement. 'The day I walked in I knew the writing was on the wall,' Jewell reflects. 'There was a smell of death about the place. I didn't get on with the chairman, the players didn't want to be there – not all of them, but I knew I had no chance. In my first game against Wolves, our 'keeper Kevin Pressman was sent off after 13 seconds and it was downhill all the way after that.'

Jewell had an unhappy spell at Sheffield Wednesday. 'There was a smell of death about the place,' he says.

Jewell was out of the door, P45 in hand, just eight months down the line. 'In that eight months I learnt a lot about myself and other people,' Jewell said. 'That's when I realised you've got to be a strong person to do this job. A large majority of the players there had no soul and the team had no heartbeat. Look at the number of managers they've had there since: Peter Shreeves, Terry Yorath, Chris Turner and Paul Sturrock. Somewhere along the line they've got to realise that the problems extend further than the manager.

'I had the usual hurdle to get over. People wanted a big name. I was a young manager, in only my second year and I remember Carlton Palmer going on TV, saying I'd done all right at Bradford, but that Wednesday was too big for me. It's never nice to get the sack, but in the end it was a relief because I was banging my head against a brick wall every day.

'There was one international player there (Wim Jonk) on big money who played one-and-a-half games for me in the eight months I was there. He took his shin pads off one day, said he was sore and never played for me again. He had a big contract, part of which guaranteed him £5,000 a game, whether he played or not. I called it "disappearance money". Another player (Gilles De Bilde) came to me and said, "I want to play in the Premiership". I fixed him up with three months on loan at Aston Villa, but when I called him to tell him, he said "I've got a problem. I've got nobody to look after my dogs if I go there". I said "Give us your house keys, I'll feed the bloody dogs". That was the kind of thing I was up against.

Jewell worried for his future when Wigan were knocked out of the FA Cup by Canvey Island. But chairman Dave Whelan backed him and he never looked back.

'When I speak to a lot of older managers now they say they wouldn't like to do the job now because of player power. Supporters want instant change and instant success. Every manager is so many games away from the sack. It's just that some get longer than others. Chairmen have got to be strong.'

Jewell started to wonder where his next opportunity was going to come from when he was shown the door at Hillsborough. He spent four months out of the game before the position of manager became vacant at the JJB Stadium. 'I learnt how much I missed the game over those four months and I was desperate to get back in,' he said. Jewell sent off his CV, along with 31 other candidates for the job, which drummed up a great deal of interest.

Latics' Director of Football John Benson conducted Jewell's interview and by Dave Whelan's accounts he 'didn't interview very well'. But it was Jewell's past record with Bradford, coupled with his desire to succeed, which convinced Whelan he was the man for the job (ironically they didn't actually meet face-to-face until two days after his appointment) although he didn't get the dream start he had wanted.

'The day England beat Germany 5–1 in Munich [September 2001], we dropped to the bottom of the Second Division [League One],' recalls Jewell. 'We didn't have a game so I went to Cambridge to watch Dave Kitson. Other results went against us, so as I drove home we were bottom of the League. In October we went to Wrexham and lost 5–1 in the LDV Vans Trophy.' The players were ordered in for training the following day to watch a video of the game.

'In the November we were beaten 1–0 at home by Canvey Island in the first round of the FA Cup and the word on the street was that I was going to get the bullet. I was at my wits' end. At eight o'clock in the morning I went to see the chairman and said, "Look, this needs major surgery, have I got the time?" He said, "Do you want me to have a word?" I needed all the help I could get, so he came down to the dressing room and told the players, "He's staying. Anyone who doesn't want to play for him can f*** off!"

'After that, he came out and told me, "This year, make sure we stay up. Next season I want to be in the top six at Christmas, otherwise you'll be out". That Christmas we were four points clear at the top. That's when you realise if you can do the job and how strong you are. It's alright when it's all going well, it's when your

Jewell shares the cup with captain Jason De Vos as the team celebrate being champions of Division Two.

back is up against the wall and people have been calling for your head. I've always had the self-confidence you need as a manager. You're always up against it and you've got to make tough decisions. If the players see you're not confident they'll see through it. Half of it is a bluff, you've got to be able to do that in this job. It's easy to bluff when you're in a position of strength.'

Whelan's influence certainly kick-started Jewell's era into a fabulous, almost unbelievable run. But the JJB Sports supremo has never got involved with Jewell's daily running of team matters. 'The chairman doesn't interfere with the way I run the football side of the club's business. I send him to a match sometimes to watch a player for me. He knows the game to a certain extent, but what he doesn't know is that I send my own scout as well! To be fair, he's not a bad judge. I've never signed a player on his say-so, but I don't think it's unreasonable for someone who is putting up the cash to go and see what he thinks.

'We have a good relationship, but he's a ruthless guy who is not afraid to make changes and I'm not taking anything for granted. I don't think you should ever feel comfortable as a manager. The only certainty is one day you're going to get the sack, or walk out. We suffered a rocky spell when I first arrived but thankfully the chairman stood by me and I'd like to think I've repaid him.'

More success followed in the Championship. Here, Jewell lifts the October Manager of the Month Award.

Jewell admits, somewhat proudly, that his managerial style was honed by his formative years at Anfield. 'Something I learned from my Liverpool days is not to talk about our achievements,' he says. 'That's for other people to do. I'm just concentrating on doing the job to the best of my ability. You have to be humble in victory and magnanimous in defeat.'

By the end of the 2002–03 season, Wigan finished as champions of the old Second Division. The following year, Jewell saw his men miss out on the Division One play-offs on the last day of the season (remember Brian Deane?). But he knew

Jewell salutes the JJB faithful at Latics' promotion party after winning a place in the Premiership.

he had a squad good enough to make it to the top flight and subsequently guided Wigan to automatic promotion, again behind champions Sunderland – an air of déjà vu after his heroics at Bradford. But Jewell admits: 'If we hadn't gone up when we did, maybe it would have been time to move on and let someone else have a go.'

Armed with Whelan's bulging wallet, Jewell knew he would have to sign some reinforcements ahead of the Premiership campaign. A club record bid of £7.5 million was accepted by Chelsea for Scott Parker, but the talented midfielder

Taking centre stage, alongside Chelsea's Jose Mourinho on the opening day of the season.

wouldn't even get round the negotiating table and subsequently moved to Newcastle instead for £7 million. 'If I had the chance to sign for Newcastle or Wigan, I'd choose Newcastle every time,' Jewell said. 'It's so hard to try and sign players and convince them to come here because we're new to this League and aren't seen as an attractive club. I can't blame them.'

He has always backed his own judgement in the transfer market. But the £10 million he shelled out on former captain Arjan De Zeeuw, Rotherham's Mike Pollitt as well as Ryan Taylor, Josip Skoko, Damien Francis, David Connolly, Stephane Henchoz, Henri Camara and the unknown Pascal Chimbonda didn't have supporters, pundits or other clubs tipping them for a push for Europe. Jewell said: 'I never had a problem with anyone saying we'd go straight back down. If I'd been a reporter, looking at the history of the teams coming up and the size of Wigan as a club, I'd have thought the same. My only issue is with those people who said certain things about us without taking the trouble to find out what we're about. I like to think we've gained their respect.'

Jewell has earned the respect of his players, including Graham Kavanagh, for his honest approach and desire to succeed.

After defeats in their first two matches against Chelsea and Charlton, Jewell's men won eight and drew one of their next nine League games. It was form which made their sceptics sit up and take note. Amazingly, Jewell's men were second in the League in mid-November. Paul Scharner and David Thompson joined in the new year, while Neil Mellor and Reto Ziegler arrived on loan to make it 13 new faces since the previous summer.

It was the man from Guadeloupe, however, who really took the Premiership and the town of Wigan by storm. Chimbonda quickly earned himself cult status with a run of stunning performances. Stunning enough, in fact, to be named in the PFA Team of the Year.

Jewell almost pulled another rabbit out of the hat when Wigan came within a whisker of bringing Real Madrid and England striker Michael Owen to the JJB

Stadium before his £17 million move to Newcastle. 'We set our sights high and going for Michael Owen was no publicity stunt,' Jewell said. 'That one was the chairman's idea. We were struggling to get players and he said to me one day, "What about Owen?" I said, "Yeah, and see if you can get me Ronaldo while you're at it". But he said, "I'm serious, do you want to call his agent?" I blinked and told him, "No, this is a big one, you call the agent".

'It wasn't as daft as it sounded and we got pretty close. Michael wanted to come back to Liverpool, that was his dream. So the chairman put a deal to his agent whereby we'd buy him from Real Madrid for £11 million and if he wanted to go to Liverpool in the January window or at the end of the season, he could, as long as we got our money back. It definitely had its appeal for both sides. We were getting there when Freddy Shepherd (Newcastle chairman) came in and blew us out of the water. But the fact that we were serious showed the extent of our ambition.'

It was that ambition off the pitch which was reflected through onto the pitch and emulated by the players, who went on to take the Premier League by storm. 'We have built not just proper facilities, but a work ethic and a winning mentality,' Jewell says. 'I feel as if I underachieved as a player and my great desire is to leave my players feeling that I got the very best out of them. I will leave no stone unturned for that. I know we've pulled up trees this season, our first in the Premiership. There's no secret, just the desire and endeavour to work hard and be the best that you possibly can be.'

Jewell lives in Ilkley, in West Yorkshire, with his wife and two children, Sam and Alexandra. The Paul Jewell seen on a Saturday afternoon bursting blood vessels is not the same man behind the scenes, but in his five years at Wigan he has revealed little about his private life. Indeed, he stated one of the reasons he would not like the England manager's job was the amount of press interest – and intrusion – that is inevitably part of the baggage. He prefers his private life to remain private.

That's not to suggest he is rude and cold – on the contrary, Jewell is humorous and kind, but he realises the need to be strong, honest and decisive to be successful. 'You can't be afraid to make decisions in this game,' he said. 'You need to be strong and be able to tell your players the truth. There's only 11 players who think you've picked the right team on a Saturday afternoon. The rest and their wives and girlfriends, or boyfriends, think you've got it wrong.'

Jewell tries to unwind from the game with a round of golf with his talented son Sam, who is destined to make it onto the circuit. He also finds time to socialise in his local golf club with Wigan Warriors coach Brian Noble, and has a clutch of close friends from the game. But try as he might, his mind is never far from the job at Wigan Athletic. 'The minute you take your eye off the ball in this game you will get kicked in the teeth,' he concludes. 'There's no getting away from it.'

Football is always on Jewell's mind... no matter how he tries to relax.

PAUL JEWELL'S sharp scouse wit and impeccable comic timing would have served him well on the stand-up circuit. Here are a selection of his best, funniest and most memorable quotes from Wigan's historic debut season in the Premiership...

'Do I envy Jose Mourinho? No, not at all. Plus, I'm much better looking than him.' – as Latics prepared to face Chelsea on the opening day of the season.

'We were all over them for 12 seconds!' – after Jason Roberts's penalty was awarded straight from the kick-off against Sunderland.

'Jimmy Bullard is an alien, though' – when questioned about using the midfield in an unfamiliar 'alien' position against Sunderland.

'Play for Germany? Jimmy, you're not even good enough for Scotland!' – overhearing a *Sunday Times* journalist asking Bullard about playing for Germany.

'I passed English Literature. If you want to talk about Wilfred Owen or Siegfried Sassoon, I'm your man.' – showing his literary credentials.

'I don't know what the stats were but if it was a boxing match they'd have asked for it to be stopped

Always one to lighten the mood when need be, Jewell mocks trainer Joey Gallanagh as he has his picture taken in the Christopher Park gym.

I think.' – after a string of missed chances against Fulham.

'Stevie Wonder wouldn't have given that goal.' – after Phil Dowd's performance in a 1–1 draw at Blackburn when he allowed Shefki Kuqi's controversial goal to stand after Lucas Neill's foul on John Filan.

'I won't be at home all weekend, that's for sure – and I don't mean I'm going on holiday.' – preparing to look abroad for new signings before the January transfer deadline.

'I hate the transfer window – I wish I could throw a brick right through it!' – on his frustrations with signing new players before the 31 August transfer deadline.

'If it had gone to extra-time, some of the Bournemouth players would have had to go to bed they were that young!' – after struggling to overcome Bournemouth 1–0 in the Carling Cup first round.

"My worst nightmare is having to go to Highbury on the last game of the season needing one point to get into Europe.' – in October after Wigan's flying start.

'My heart bleeds for Graeme Souness. He has the England captain partnering the former England captain up front, a team full of internationals and 50,000 fans watching them every other week. Like I said, my heart bleeds.' – ahead of the Newcastle game in October.

'I think we need to get Henri a watch – I'd love to know what the French words are for "lazy bastard"!' – joking about Camara's time keeping.

'We're on TV more times than Coronation Street!' – in November, after Wigan's fourth successive televised game.

'I got the players in and told them, "Some of you have got wives, some of you have got girlfriends, some of you have got both. Go out and do it for them!"' – on his half-time team talk in the Carling Cup semi-final against Arsenal in January.

'I've got some ugly players but they aren't allowed to defend ugly.' – getting serious. Sort of.

'United had one shot on target and won 2–1 – go and work that one out.' – coming to terms with defeat, when Pascal Chimbonda scored a last-minute own-goal.

'People see Wigan as being about pies, rugby and Uncle Joe's Mintballs. We want to change that.' – at the start of their historic season in the Premiership.

8: November: The Wigan fan living in 10 Downing Street

THE TABLE at the start of November said Wigan were in second spot. In reality, they were on top of the world. Around the globe, newspapers carried stories about this small Lancashire club who had come from nowhere to take on some of the biggest clubs in sport. Their scheduled November fixtures, against Portsmouth, Arsenal and Tottenham, were punctuated by a free weekend with a tie against Newcastle in the Carling Cup squeezed on the end.

Bookmakers were monitoring their progress keenly, cutting their odds to qualify for the Champions League to 66–1 and to reach the UEFA Cup to 20–1. Their explosive start even impressed the Prime Minister. Tony Blair nominated Wigan captain Arjan De Zeeuw as the Premiership player he admired the most during a television interview (Fulham's Steed Malbranque and West Ham's Teddy Sheringham were the other two top-flight players Mr Blair praised).

Manager Paul Jewell, famous for his sharp wit, pounced on the announcement, grinning, 'It proves he doesn't get everything wrong,' though privately he must have been delighted by the news, and the club asked Labour party chairman Ian McCartney, the Makerfield MP, to present Mr Blair with a shirt signed by De Zeeuw.

The Dutchman and a clutch of teammates were watching *Football Focus* in a south-coast hotel on the morning of Wigan's game at Portsmouth (they had flown down the day before) and heard Mr Blair announce his favourite players on air. Cheers went up from some of his teammates, and De Zeeuw said modestly, 'It was a great honour for me.'

Tony Blair's praise was not the only reason De Zeeuw was in the spotlight. His first return to Fratton Park was given an intriguing twist following his disagreement with Pompey manager Alain Perrin in the summer, which prompted a £100,000 move back north to Wigan. 'Me and Perrin aren't the best of friends,' admitted De Zeeuw days before the match. 'When I left he said how he would love to show that Portsmouth are a better team than Wigan. He's said he wants to make sure that we finish below them, but that's not going to happen. I had a chat with him in the summer about my position in the team and he didn't give me an honest answer if I would be playing or not.'

De Zeeuw arrived in England 11 years ago with Barnsley, where he earned the nickname Patrick Swayze (presumably for his hair, setback eyes and chiseled

Arjan De Zeeuw made a winning return to former club Portsmouth.

features rather than his dancing ability). 'I was studying to be a doctor in Amsterdam when this opportunity came to play English football,' recalled the articulate Dutch defender, eagerly describing his journey through the heart of English football.

'I flew with my then girlfriend, now my wife, to Manchester and drove over the moors with the rain throwing down, pitch black, driving through these lanes, these dips. "Where the hell are we going?" I thought. The next morning I opened the curtain, and the sun was shining. Maybe not so bad! I was accepted by the Barnsley people, because I do my best. My dad used to be a carpenter but there wasn't much work so he worked in the steel-works for a long time. He gave me that belief that it doesn't matter how good you are, as long as you give it your best shot. He would cane me [verbally] if I didn't work hard enough in a match.'

De Zeeuw spent three years at Portsmouth after leaving Wigan in 2002, winning promotion to the top flight in his first season under Harry Redknapp. 'I had a good time there,' he said. 'Wigan were still in the Second Division at the time and I knew I needed to make the step up. I was just about to go on holiday at the end of the season and Harry rang me up when I was on my way to the airport. He asked me to go down to Portsmouth there and then for a chat. I told him my wife would divorce me if I did that so I went on holiday first! We had a good camaraderie at Portsmouth like there is here. When I retire, the first thing I will miss is the banter in the dressing room. Whatever you wear at Wigan, you'll get stick. Jason Roberts gets a lot of stick because he dresses a bit strange. Everyone takes the stick on the chin. The lads at Wigan are like family. A big strength of this team is everyone really gets on. There are no groups. We know this is a fairytale, but we've worked hard for this.'

De Zeeuw spoke to his teammates to warn them of the hostile environment they would face at Fratton Park, arguably the most archaic ground in the Premiership, and told of one fan who was particularly passionate about Portsmouth, Joel Smith. 'He rings a bell on the sidelines during the game to get the crowd going,' he laughed. 'If you see him away from Fratton Park he's so quiet. He's got a book shop and his family are antiques dealers and are really calm. But when he gets near the football ground he turns into a lunatic. I remember in 2003 when we got automatic promotion and we played Ipswich away with four games to go. We were getting beat 3–0 and he was still trying to spur us on. He climbed onto the roof of one of the stands and was provoking the police and stewards. They were all scared to go up there and bring him down in case they fell through the roof!'

The significance of De Zeeuw's return, with Portsmouth in 14th spot, did not go unnoticed by the national press, who requested him as the nominated player at Wigan's main press conference to preview the match. But after Perrin went public in the local *Portsmouth News* newspaper criticising De Zeeuw and claiming he did not want the former Barnsley player to leave, Paul Jewell moved to end the public grudge match.

In the conference, a formal question and answer session, De Zeeuw was asked: 'You must take great satisfaction to be where you are in the table and where they are given the circumstances of your departure?' De Zeeuw replied, 'Yeah, of course. It's something special for me. We've had a great start and they've had a bad start.' But before he could elaborate, Jewell interrupted. 'Can I just come in there?' he said. 'I don't think this is an Arjan De Zeeuw against Portsmouth thing. Okay, Arry is going back there, but it's where we are that matters. The only satisfaction he'll get is if we get three points.'

By 6.50pm on Saturday 5 November De Zeeuw was satisfied. Very satisfied. Emerging from such a hostile cauldron with a 2–0 win was a bigger achievement than some critics recognised and, unfortunately, those who did credited the victory not to Paul Jewell or his squad… but to a hypnotist named Marisa Peer.

Jason Roberts had been under her spell for several years and he invited Leighton Baines, Alan Mahon, Lee McCulloch and Ryan Taylor to see her. Roberts bagged the clincher against the club who stole him from Wigan's grasp when his first move to the JJB Stadium fell through, but he was embarrassed to talk about his meetings with Peer. 'I don't really want to go into that,' he shrugged coyly, seemingly embarrassed that their meetings had been trivialised in the tabloids. *The Sun* even ran a two-page spread on Peer's supposed influence as 'the hypnotist who has turned Wigan into the kings of football.'

Fulham-based Peer, 44, was described as 'the club hypnotist who has been their secret weapon' and told the national newspaper: 'I aim to have players who go out on to the pitch with unshakeable conviction in their ability.'

'I was a bit gob-smacked when I heard about it,' revealed De Zeeuw. 'I came down for breakfast before the game and someone asked me "Have you been hypnotised for the game Arry?" 'I said "What the hell are you on about?" and then they told me what had been going on. I certainly don't need a hypnotist. I'm too set in my ways to change now.'

Wigan, whose only victory in six previous League encounters against Pompey came in February 1979 with a 2–0 win at Springfield Park, completely deserved their three points. They controlled the second half and the game always looked safe after Pascal Chimbonda claimed his second goal in a week, when he nodded in Jimmy Bullard's 48th-minute corner. Roberts, a jovial and media-friendly person, was less restrained in praising fans' favourite Chimbonda. 'Pascal has come over here from France and has made himself an integral part in our dressing room,' enthused Roberts. 'He deserves all the credit in the world for coming over and conducting himself the way he has done.'

Pascal Chimbonda celebrates scoring Latics' opening goal with Jason Roberts and Lee McCulloch.

The Sun's two-page centre spread on the hypnotist, Marisa Peer, whom the tabloid credited with Wigan's blistering start to the season.

HYPNOTIST WHO HAS TURNED WIGAN INTO KINGS OF FOOTBALL

SALLY BROOK

LOOK INTO MY EYES

(INTO THE EYES, NOT AROUND THE EYES)

AND WIN THE PREMIERSHIP

Unlikely local heroes

Saturday 5 November 2005

Portsmouth 0 Wigan 2

PORTSMOUTH: Ashdown 6, Primus 6, Priske 6, Stefanovic 7, Griffin 6, O'Neil 7, Hughes 7, Taylor 6, Vignal 6, Vukic 6, Silva 6. Subs: Robert 6 (for Vignal 60), Lua Lua 6 (for Vukic 68), Diao (for Griffin 76)

WIGAN: Filan 7, Chimbonda 8, De Zeeuw 8, Henchoz 9, Baines 8, Bullard 6, Kavanagh 8, Francis 7, McCulloch 7, Roberts 7, Camara 6. Subs: Jackson (for Roberts 88), Taylor (for Camara 90). Wigan star man: Henchoz.

Goals: Chimbonda (48), Roberts (79)
Half-time: 0–0
Referee: Mark Clattenburg
Attendance: 19,102

	P	W	D	L	F	A	Pts
Chelsea	12	10	1	1	28	7	31
Wigan	11	8	1	2	13	5	25
Bolton	12	7	2	3	14	11	23
Man Utd	11	6	3	2	16	11	21
Arsenal	10	6	2	3	16	8	20
Tottenham	12	5	5	2	13	8	20
Man City	12	6	2	4	15	11	20
Charlton	11	6	1	4	16	14	19
West Ham	11	5	3	3	15	10	18
Newcastle	12	5	3	4	12	10	18
Blackburn	12	5	2	5	15	15	17
Liverpool	10	4	4	2	9	8	16
Middlesb'h	12	4	3	5	15	16	15
Fulham	12	3	3	6	12	16	12
Portsm'th	12	2	4	6	11	15	10
Everton	11	3	1	7	4	12	10
Aston Villa	12	2	3	7	10	21	9
West Brom	12	2	2	8	9	22	8
Birm'ham	12	1	3	8	7	17	6
Sunderl'd	12	1	2	9	11	24	5

Wigan nearly went behind after 13 minutes when John Filan flapped at Gregory Vignal's cross and Dario Silva put a free header over. Jewell continually rallied his troops, yet it was only as half-time approached that the message seeped through.

The returning Lee McCulloch saw a goal-bound shot blocked before Roberts dragged a shot horribly wide from the edge of the box. The panic subsided after Chimbonda's back-post header nestled in the corner. Stephane Henchoz was a colossus at the back while Graham Kavanagh was everywhere, though it was left to Chimbonda who helped wrap it up when he played a neat one-two with Camara and then teed up the unmarked Roberts for an easy tap-in.

The win helped silence the critics... as well as the bell of Joel Smith, the Portsmouth fan whom De Zeeuw had warned his teammates about. After the game, walking between interviews, De Zeeuw passed Perrin in the tunnel. The pair exchanged glances, before timidly shaking hands.

Eight wins dismissed Rodney Marsh's claim that Wigan wouldn't win more than seven all season. Asked for his reaction to the pundit's shocking tip, Jewell simply replied, 'Next question,' and looked away.

With a free weekend ahead of them, Jewell gave his players a few days off, although Henri Camara's rest and recuperation took place largely on an airplane seat. Camara was withdrawn at Fratton Park in the last minute after complaining of a hamstring strain. Wigan immediately informed his national team of the injury and told them he would not be fit to take part in their upcoming friendly. But Senegal insisted that their own doctors assessed his problem and, under FIFA rules, requested the £3 million star made a 20-hour round trip to prove his injury.

Wigan made *Sky Sports News* for a five-minute feature, but it was their reserves who took the spotlight for once, thanks to a freakish length-of-the-pitch goal by 'keeper Floyd Croll. Croll's powerful punt from his own box beat Manchester United's American international Tim Howard, who was back-pedalling towards his own goal. 'I hope it's not the last goal I score,' said Croll, whose side lost 2–1 at Ewen Field in Hyde.

Meanwhile, Chimbonda's cult status was growing among Wigan's expanding army of supporters. Website tshirts365.com launched a blue, unofficial T-shirt in

Damien Francis and Jason Roberts enjoyed some time off during November's free weekend.

What the opposition said...

'You have to take the example of Wigan, you must play well in defence and know when to counter. It is difficult for the confidence of the players because they badly want to give a win to the fans. But sometimes they attack too much and don't defend. Wigan scored two good goals and deserved to win the game. We just have to play better if we want to win. It was not a good day.' – Portsmouth manager Alain Perrin.

What the Wigan fan said...

'It was a long day – we only got back at 12.30am, but the game made it worthwhile. Wigan were by far the better side. We commanded midfield but our defence was the best area – all four players were superb. Leighton Baines had his best game in the Premiership.' – East Stand season-ticket holder Mark Fulton.

homage to the French star, with his name and iconic gloves on the front. His sparkling performances also prompted Jewell to renegotiate his contract to remove a clause that allowed him to leave for a relatively small fee. The Guadeloupe-born defender's agent, Willie McKay, told Sky Sports: 'A few clubs have contacted me about Pascal possibly doing a deal in January, but I could not do that to Paul Jewell after he took a chance on him.'

Teammates had been convinced by Chimbonda's value to the team. 'I have not seen everyone in the League play but Pascal must be up there as one of the best,' wrote Jason Roberts in his BBC online column. 'He is performing every week... he hardly speaks any English but he has fitted straight in, within two days he was part of the banter and everything. His English is about primary school level but he makes himself understood somehow!'

Jewell handled the early season success with honesty and modesty in equal proportion. But there was never any danger of him drowning in the gushing praise being poured on them ('It would be no disgrace not to get another point from our next five games'). He turned down an invitation to go to Dubai, alongside some of the bigger names in football – Sam Allardyce, Sir Bobby Robson, Graeme Souness – for an ill-disguised jolly. 'I got asked to go but the trip eats into next week,' Jewell told the *Mirror*'s Oliver Holt. 'I don't want to sound like a workaholic and I don't want to sound like I can't enjoy myself. But it's not really my scene at the moment. If I went I think people might say, "look at him, he thinks he's cracked it". I just didn't think it was right.'

The coverage given to the hypnotist, Peer, was blown out of all proportion and the evidence was overwhelming that critics regarded Wigan's marvellous start as a fluke. David Miller wrote in the *Daily Telegraph*: 'Cast your mind back some 10 years: think Wimbledon, early nineties. Wigan, likewise, may be about as pretty as the parson's nose, but how tenacious their moral challenge. Here is football's equivalent of Masefield's "dirty British coaster with a salt-caked smoke stack".'

Steve Brenner in *The Sun* wrote, 'Wigan are having a laugh – and they are loving every minute.' Rick Broadbent in *The Times* went a step further by questioning the abilities of the players who had taken the Premiership by storm. 'The revelation that Tony Blair is a fan of Arjan De Zeeuw is positively mind-boggling,' Broadbent wrote. 'We now await the summit meeting between Dubya and Graham Kavanagh

The Pacal Chimbonda T-shirt paying homage to the Latics star.

11. G. KAVANAGH
12. M. POLLITT
13. G. WALSH
14. A. MAHON
15. D. WRIGHT
17. D. FRANCIS
24. J. SKOKO
19. R. TAYLOR
20. G. TEALE
21. J. BULLARD
26. L. BAINES
32. L. JOYCE
22. D. CONNOLLY
BARCLAYS
MANAGER OF THE MONTH

(Previous page) In early November Paul Jewell received his Barclays Manager of the Month award for October, and then launched an attack at his 'disrespectful' critics.

with interest. Strange days indeed. De Zeeuw and Stephane Henchoz have carthorse pace, the midfield is flair-less and the strikers would struggle to get into most top-flight sides.'

'Some people are being a bit disrespectful,' said Jewell, in an understatement. 'At the end of the Sky coverage (of the United-Chelsea game), Richard Keys said that the champions' lead has now been cut to 10 points. And I thought to myself, "That's funny, I could have sworn we were only six points behind". I think there should be some respect along the line. There was a lot made of the hypnotism thing the other day, but as far as I know only Jason Roberts and Leighton Baines have done it and Leighton said it was a waste of time. We're certainly not the new Crazy Gang, we don't model ourselves on them. People can say what they want about us, I can't stop that, but I wish they'd give us a bit more credit. We are where we are because everyone here works hard and they are damn good at their jobs. I know we aren't going to finish second in the League, but even though we're there now people don't see us as a threat.'

Holt made an impassioned plea on Jewell's behalf, writing in his column: 'It's time to stop patronising [Jewell] and his team. Whether he likes it or not, he's earned his admission to the private club.'

Over the international break, Michael Owen's two late headers secured England a memorable 3–2 friendly win in Switzerland, and allowed Jimmy Bullard home to East London for the weekend to pursue his own international ambition. As well as taking up his second favourite pastime, fishing (his favourite is golf: he plays off a handicap of one and says he will turn pro once he retires from football) he went to visit his grandmother, Rose, who was born in Germany but moved to England during the war. Bullard's agent had made German manager Jürgen Klinsmann aware of Bullard's eligibility for their national side.

Paul Jewell milked the situation for humour, telling him, 'You're not even good enough to play for Scotland,' but the wisecrack did little to mask Jewell's admiration for the workaholic and tireless midfielder. In many ways, Bullard embodied Wigan's remarkable journey. As a youngster he was talented enough to earn an apprenticeship at West Ham but was considered too slight by a succession of coaches to make it in professional football. At 20, he was working as a decorator.

His path to the Premier League came via non-League Gravesend, Peterborough and Wigan and he was described by *The Sunday Times* as 'one of the most effective midfielders in the Premiership'. From painter and decorator to the World Cup Final? 'Ha, we'll see what comes of it,' he smiled. 'Probably nothing, but my agent wanted the certificate just in case.'

Brought up in Canning Town, Bullard admitted he had never been to Germany – 'The closest I've got is Denmark. But I'm up for it,' – although he also pointed out that, when Wigan approached him in January 2003, 'I had no idea where Wigan even was.'

The players returned from their free weekend to step up their training for their visit from a side five points behind them in the League: Arsenal. According to Bullard, Jewell focussed his training on building a winning mentality though he says the team morale was galvanised by their friendships off the pitch. 'Jewelly loves a competition in training,' he says. 'And a forfeit for the losers. Every day here's winning on your mind... and you never know the forfeit beforehand. The togetherness is the same as when I arrived. I've just moved next door to Steve

Jimmy Bullard checked his German qualification.

Arsene Wenger takes his seat at the JJB Stadium.

Saturday 19 November 2005

Wigan 2
Arsenal 3

WIGAN: Filan 6, Chimbonda 7, Henchoz 8, De Zeeuw 7, Baines 8, Bullard 9, Kavanagh 6, Francis 7, McCulloch 7, Roberts 7, Camara 7. Subs: Taylor (for Francis 78), Connolly (for McCulloch 87). Wigan star man: Jimmy Bullard.

ARSENAL: Lehmann 7, Lauren 7, Toure 7, Campbell 6, Cygan 6, Pires 7, Silva 7, Fabregas 8, Ljungberg 7, Van Persie 8, Henry 9. Subs: Flamani (for Pires 75), Bergkamp (for Van Persie 75), Senderos (for Ljungberg 90).

Goals: Van Persie (11), Henry (21, 41), Camara (28), Bullard (45)
Half-time: 2–3
Referee: Graham Poll
Attendance: 25,004

What the opposition said...

'You can understand why Wigan are second in the table and I would argue against many people saying they are in a false position. They are very intense as a unit and I think they are one of the favourites to finish in the top six. I was surprised by the intensity of their commitment. They showed tremendous resilience and the quality of their performance was outstanding. It needed to be a great Arsenal side to win.' – Arsenal manager Arsene Wenger.

McMillan and several of the lads live on the same estate. You end up being semi-brothers – it gives you that extra when you're fighting for each other on the park. We don't want to play in the Championship again now we've tasted the Premiership. I'd hate it. Three points in the Premiership feels 10 times better than three points in the Championship.'

Josip Skoko was missing from the squad after helping Australia book a place at the World Cup with a 4–2 penalties win over Uruguay in the second leg of the Oceania play-off in Sydney (Skoko came off the bench in extra-time). 'I haven't got Sky at home, so I couldn't watch the game, but a mate of mine was talking me through it and it certainly was edge of the seat stuff,' beamed Wigan 'keeper, and former Socceroo, John Filan.

In the days ahead of the Arsenal clash, there were memories of the opening day with the blanket media coverage. The most unusual was clue number 22 of *The Guardian*'s crossword puzzle, 'Law, cheating it (anag)'. The answer? Wigan Athletic.

This was not the first time Arsenal had visited Wigan. Leslie Knighton brought his North London side to Springfield Park on 4 May 1921, which saw Wigan Borough's first-ever game at the ground as a League club. The friendly encounter saw the home side run out 2–1 winners. The decades after that were largely kind to Arsenal, especially the years since Arsene Wenger took control in September 1996. Since that day, the Gunners have enjoyed nigh on a decade of unbridled success, having not finished outside English football's elite three teams, and the Professor, as Wenger is known (he completed a degree in economics before signing professional terms with Strasbourg) made the team one of the biggest draws in domestic football.

Arsenal forged an aura of invincibility as they marched onto a 49-game unbeaten run. That had abruptly ended the previous season, when Manchester United proved they were not bulletproof.

And while the men in red and white (or vintage claret as they were during their centenary season) attached themselves limpet-like to the top of the tree, an unfancied and unheralded Wigan side, whose success was unashamedly based on hard work, had slowly crept its way up from the lower branches to the lofty perch it occupied ahead of the game. This was Wigan's first major test of their courtship of a high League placing, and they aced it.

Wigan lost the match, ending their 11-game unbeaten run, but they gained so much more. Incredibly, ironically, Wigan's 2–3 defeat earned them something that their nine-game unbeaten run had not: respect. Not from the Wigan fans – that had been showered on Paul Jewell and his squad in abundance for more than three years. But respect from the rest of the nation and the Premiership followers throughout the world who had been too eager to dismiss their astonishing achievement, as if the side's only prized signing was Lady Luck.

Their heroic display in defeat against Chelsea, they argued, was fuelled by the euphoria of playing their opening game in the top flight, while their victories since were against lower placed sides, or big clubs at a time of turmoil. Now, after playing Arsenal, Wigan had proved they could not be ignored.

The fact that Arsenal were so brilliant and technically proficient only served to amplify the quality of the Wigan team. Their battling spirit, galvanised by flashes of genuine attacking class in Jason Roberts and Henri Camara, and midfield invention

in the slight, rangy shape of Jimmy Bullard, proved that they deserved their place among the football elite.

Under the spotlight, in front of a million TV fans, Latics played their part in a modern-day classic. The game was a reminder of why sport is so great. The tension and the excitement was at times unbearable, as the drama unfolded at break-neck speed in front of a new club record crowd of 25,004.

Five goals in the first half blew away widespread predictions of a bore draw or a landslide win, while the second half was about as entertaining and engrossing as any scoreless draw. That Wigan were on the wrong side of a 3–2 final scoreline did little to sour the occasion: even the most stoic supporter realised they had witnessed an epic. And to think people were debating whether the Premiership was getting boring just a few weeks earlier.

In a game which produced many heroes, it was as if John Filan had unselfishly nominated himself as a reluctant villain for his mistake, which had allowed Robin

Thierry Henry and Arjan De Zeeuw shake hands at the kick-off.

What the Wigan fan said...

'Although we lost, that was the best game I've seen so far this season. The first half was so exciting because every time Arsenal scored Wigan just went back at them. The atmosphere was incredible. Wigan lost but they still played really well.' – East Stand season-ticket holder Claire Chapman.

Leighton Baines shoots past Arsenal's Robert Pires.

	P	W	D	L	F	A	Pts
Chelsea	13	11	1	1	31	7	34
Wigan	12	8	1	3	15	8	25
Man Utd	12	7	3	2	19	12	24
Arsenal	12	7	2	3	19	10	23
Bolton	12	7	2	3	14	11	23
Tottenham	13	5	6	2	14	9	21
Man City	13	6	3	4	15	11	21
West Ham	12	5	4	3	16	11	19
Liverpool	11	5	4	2	12	8	19
Charlton	12	6	1	5	17	17	19
Middlesb'h	13	5	3	5	18	18	18
Blackburn	13	5	3	5	15	15	18
Newcastle	13	5	3	5	12	13	18
Fulham	13	3	3	7	14	19	12
Aston Villa	13	3	3	7	13	22	12
West Brom	13	3	2	8	13	22	11
Portsm'th	13	2	4	7	11	18	10
Everton	12	3	1	8	4	16	10
Birm'ham	12	1	3	8	7	17	6
Sunderl'd	13	1	2	10	12	27	5

van Persie's strike to squeeze under him – the first goal conceded by Latics in eight hours, three minutes.

Yet on reflection, the Australian – so many times a saviour for Wigan in the past – could take comfort from an otherwise solid performance in which he was helpless to prevent two stunning goals from Thierry Henry, a player who turned the JJB Stadium pitch into a playground.

After going 2–0 down against one of Europe's most potent sides, other teams would think about damage limitation. Not Wigan. They fought back with venom and precision, first through a Camara header and then with a well-crafted goal

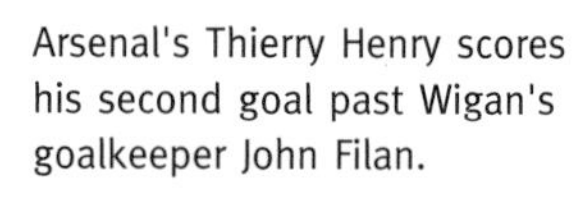

Arsenal's Thierry Henry scores his second goal past Wigan's goalkeeper John Filan.

from the tireless Bullard, or 'Marathon Man' as Arsene Wenger appropriately described him, after Henry's second on the stroke of half-time.

The Arsenal striker's goal, a stunning free-kick placed to the inch, eventually proved decisive after the visitors survived an onslaught of Wigan flair and fire in the final 20 minutes. Even Jewell, one of the most frank and straight-talking managers in football, fell back onto a trusty cliché to best summarise the match, conceding that 'Football was the real winner'.

The game marked the four-year anniversary of Wigan's 1–0 FA Cup defeat to non-League Canvey Island. Now, 197 games on, Jewell recalled: 'There were a lot of people who expected me to be fired after that. Now here we are, four years down the line, second in the Premiership and we're pushing Arsenal all the way in front of a sell-out crowd.'

Latics officials queued outside the visitors' dressing room afterwards, but not Bullard. 'I'm not into swapping shirts or asking for autographs,' he smiled. 'I can't understand why no one's asked for my autograph yet!'

Though the Arsenal players were not chasing Bullard's signature, they were full of praise for him and his teammates, with England defender Sol Campbell admitting, 'Wigan aren't where they are in the table by a fluke. They work so hard for each other and we had to match them. They'll be up there come the end of the season if they continue with that level of performance. The two lads up front have a lot of pace and Wigan will be upsetting a lot of other teams this year. Paul Jewell has done a great job and you have to take your hat off to what he has achieved. They kept going right up until the end and gave us a really tough time.'

In the after-match press conference, Arsene Wenger said Wigan could make a serious challenge for Europe and Jewell hinted he was beginning to raise his sights from survival to European qualification. 'Thierry Henry said to me after the game if we play like that all season we'll be right up there,' said Jewell. 'It was a genuine comment and it's true what he says. I did say before a ball was kicked at the start of the season that I hoped we didn't need to get a point on the last game of the season at Arsenal to get into Europe. I got sneered at. But we can't go through the season on compliments, we've got to go out there and do it. I just hope the supporters don't expect us to go and blitz everyone in front of us because that's what people are starting to think. It's given us heart that we pushed a team of Arsenal's stature all the way. I heard some people saying after the game that so-and-so didn't play well which annoyed me. Do these people know who we were up against? We were up against some of the best players in the world. We pushed them to the wire and that's something to be proud of.'

The following day, the *News of the World* ran a photo-montage of chairman Dave Whelan as Mr Potato Head with an accompanying article, with quotes from captain Arjan De Zeeuw claiming Whelan interfered with team matters and forced the squad to eat jacket potatoes and beans every day as a cost-cutting exercise.

The pair met at Christopher Park the following day and Whelan put the 'mischievous' story down to naivety on De Zeeuw's part, though he insisted their relationship remained as strong as ever. 'We knew certain stories would start appearing to try and portray us in a different light,' the JJB tycoon said. 'My relationship with Arjan and the rest of the players is first class and mischievous stories aren't going to interfere with that.'

Fredrik Ljungburg looks unrepentant as Pascal Chimbonda writhes in pain against Arsenal.

Jewell said the cheeky story highlighted the media scrutiny they were under in

the Premier League. 'They've set us up, it's a good story and they're looking to throw a spanner in the works,' he shrugged. 'We're in this big league and we've got to be careful what we say and how we say it because things can look different in print.'

Wigan's success meant there was little surprise when they declared an interest in departed Manchester United captain Roy Keane, who opted for Celtic instead, while the club also gave a trial to Chinese international Sun Xiang, though a permanent deal was not offered.

Above: Jimmy Bullard celebrates his stunning goal against Arsenal.

Right: Jason Roberts has words with the linesman against Spurs.

Wigan's match with Tottenham at the end of November marked the first time the two sides had faced each other. Martin Jol was celebrating a year in charge of the famous club, having guided Spurs to ninth the previous season. Jol took over at White Hart Lane in November 2004 and took the club to ninth in the table. The Dutch coach spent £7 million on former Newcastle midfielder Jermaine Jenas in the summer and also brought in Edgar Davids on a free transfer from Inter Milan.

Saturday 26 November 2005

Wigan 1 Tottenham 2

WIGAN: Pollitt 6, Chimbonda 6, De Zeeuw 6, Henchoz 6, Baines 6, Bullard 6, Kavanagh 7, Francis 6, McCulloch 6, Roberts 6, Camara 6. Wigan star man: Kavanagh. Subs: Connolly 5 (for Francis 67).

TOTTENHAM (4–4–2): Robinson 7, Stalteri 7, Dawson 8, King 7, Lee 7, Jenas 7, Carrick 7, Davids 8, Tainio 7, Mido 7, Keane 8. No subs used.

Goals: Keane (8), Davids (77), McCulloch (88)
Half-time: 0–1
Referee: Mike Riley
Attendance: 22,611

De Zeeuw, unfortunately, helped Tottenham take a 2–1 win. The Wigan captain failed to deal with Teemu Tainio's hopeful ball forward in the eighth minute and Robbie Keane capitalised. 'If anyone comes here and is given a goal on a plate it's a massive start for them,' offered Graham Kavanagh, Wigan's best player. 'But Arry has been outstanding all season. He won't be getting the blame from us. I'm sure we'll all make silly mistakes over the course of the season. It was his turn against Spurs, but what a player he's been for us this season – he's been immense.'

Jewell, who took charge of his 100th League game at the JJB, remained defiant after seeing his side slip down to fourth in the table. He said: 'We've lost against Arsenal and Tottenham – is this turning into a crisis now? There are 16 other teams in this division who would want to swap places with us right now.'

Latics' enthusiasm never waned, even when Edgar Davids delivered the killer second with 13 minutes to go, leaving Stephane Henchoz in his wake before firing past the re-called Pollitt. 'Davids showed what a great player he is with that goal,' said Lee McCulloch, whose last-minute strike, Wigan's one and only shot on target, set up a frantic finish. Tottenham's opener did come against the run of play, but they were the side with all the quality in possession.

McCulloch did have a great chance to hit back five minutes after Keane's goal, but sent a seven-yard header over. Henchoz was lucky not to concede a penalty after

Pascal Chimbonda and Teemu Tainio chase the ball.

assaulting the Spurs striker in the box, while Leighton Baines was unlucky to see his well-worked free-kick deflect over off McCulloch's head.

The second half was more of the same as the visitors controlled matters, with Pollitt doing well to push Tainio's drive round his post. The result was put beyond doubt when Davids's trickery broke through the defence, although McCulloch did bag his second of the season late on after Paul Robinson pushed Camara's cross into his path. 'It hurts against anyone to lose by the odd goal, be it Chelsea, Arsenal, Tottenham or Canvey Island,' Jewell added. 'We're still fourth in the table, so we can't be too down. If you'd offered us that before the start of the season we'd have been doing cartwheels down Wigan high street.'

Just days later, fans nearly were doing handstands down Standishgate (Wigan's high street) when Wigan beat Newcastle 1–0 to march into the quarter-finals of the Carling Cup (see the separate Cup chapter). It was a 1–0 win. But it was a 1–0 hammering.

What the opposition said...

'We had to work really hard for the points but we deserved to win in the end. Wigan are a team which puts in a lot of effort, maybe more than any other team in the League. I think they play the English style, but they do all the right things. They play with a 4–4–2 formation and build from the back. The midfield is always attacking the space and their two forwards work amazingly hard.' – Martin Jol, Tottenham manager.

What the Wigan fan said...

'On the balance of play it was a fair result. The finishing wasn't quite there and when you gift teams like Spurs you'll be punished. Wigan have lost two games, so what? They are still playing decent football. No team expects to win every game but the problem with some folk is that they can't wait for Wigan to fail.' – John Heeley, editor of fanzine *Cockney Latic*.

	P	W	D	L	F	A	Pts
Chelsea	14	12	1	1	33	7	37
Man Utd	13	8	3	2	21	13	27
Arsenal	13	8	2	3	22	10	26
Wigan	13	8	1	4	16	10	25
Tottenham	14	6	6	2	16	10	24
Bolton	13	7	2	4	15	13	23
Liverpool	12	6	4	2	13	8	22
Man City	14	6	3	5	15	12	21
West Ham	13	5	4	4	17	13	19
Middlesb'h	14	5	4	5	20	20	19
Charlton	13	6	1	6	17	18	19
Newcastle	14	5	3	6	12	14	18
Blackburn	14	5	3	6	15	18	18
Fulham	14	4	3	7	16	20	15
Aston Villa	14	4	3	7	14	22	15
Everton	13	4	1	8	5	16	13
West Brom	14	3	3	8	15	24	12
Portsm'th	14	2	4	8	11	20	10
Birm'ha'm	13	2	3	8	8	17	9
Sunderl'd	14	1	2	11	12	28	5

Paul Jewell reflects on defeat.

WHEN Wigan became a Premiership club, they made sure they retained some of the values of lower League outfits. They took a pro-active stance on their community projects and tried their best to answer all requests for player appearances. 'People were knocking our door down,' admitted club spokesman Matt McCann. 'And we have tried our best to help where we can.'

As well as backing a We Are Wigan community bus, Latics made visits to hospitals, schools, charities and social groups. McCann added, 'There are no big-time charlies at Wigan – the players really enjoy going out into the community and giving something back.'

Mike Pollitt and Pascal Chimbonda at the official launch of the Wigan Athletic Media Bus at St Peter's Catholic High School, Orrell.

Year Seven pupils at St Peter's Catholic High School, Orrell, take photographs on their mobile phones of Latics stars Mike Pollitt and Pascal Chimbonda at the official launch of the Wigan Athletic Media Bus.

Wigan Athletic's Reto Ziegler and Warriors winger Brett Dallas teamed up to launch a new football and rugby league complex at St Jude's, on Parsons Meadow. They are pictured with St James CP School pupils Amy Concannon and Matthew Burne.

Nathan Taylor, nine, meets his hero Pascal Chimbonda during Wigan Athletic's visit to Wigan Infirmary at Christmas.

Laura Sherratt controlled community projects at the JJB Stadium.

Latics club captain Matt Jackson with young reading champions at the JJB stadium for the launch of the Premiership reading scheme. Jason Roberts also helped with the Kick Racism Into Touch scheme. Jackson is pictured with Laura Enion, Cameron Pearce, Daniel Coffey, Matthew Dean and Liam Welsh.

The entire Wigan squad visited children at Wigan Infirmary at Christmas 2005 to give out gifts. They crowned the visit with a carol concert!

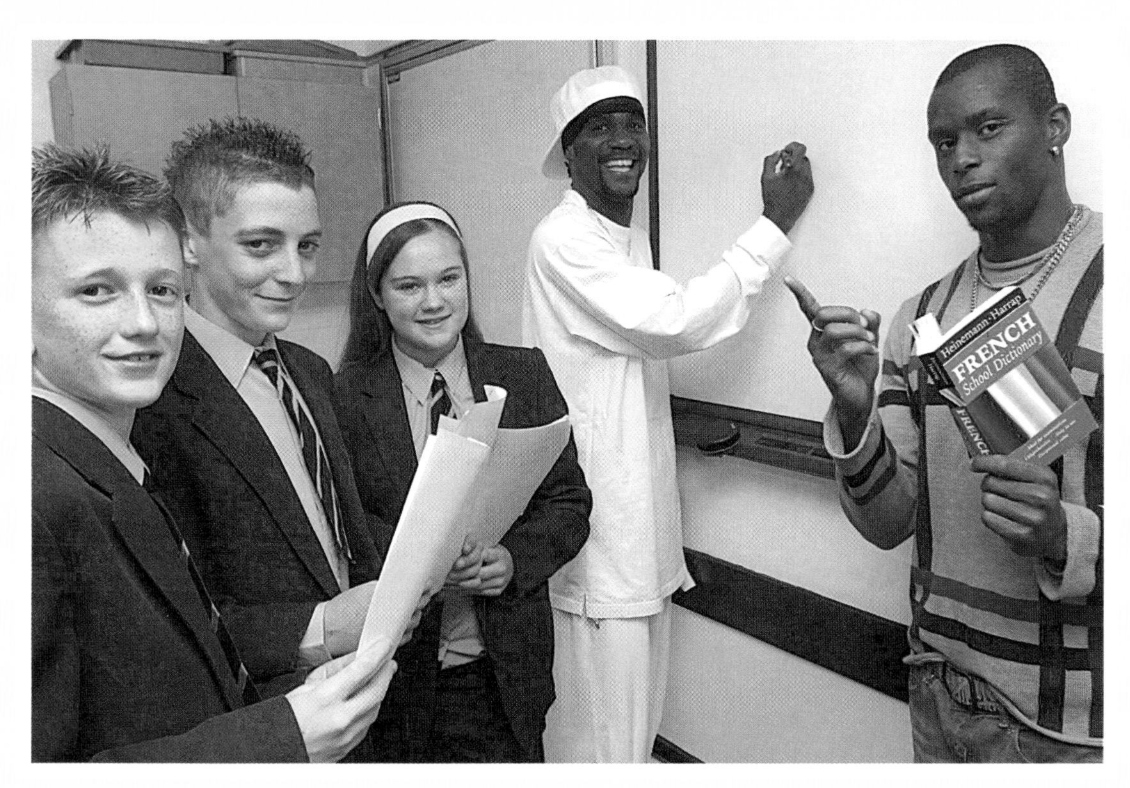

Latics stars Pascal Chimbonda and Henri Camara visited Hawkley Hall High School to take part in a Q&A session with the French class.

Damien Francis, Steve McMillan, Jason Roberts, Leighton Baines, Mike Pollitt and Gary Teale with Michael Wood, 12, during Wigan Athletic's visit to Wigan Infirmary.

9: Lights, cameras, action: Behind the scenes with Sky Sports

'IF YOU Think it's serious now, wait until the game starts... it's like the Death Star then.' Julian Sheldon is whispering, afraid of being overheard as the director shuffles through his notes inside one of Sky Sports' three production trucks parked in the shadows of the JJB Stadium. Director Duncan Walkinshaw is replaying a video package of Wigan defender Matt Jackson interviewing his teammates. He is scrutinising each detail meticulously, his sombre appearance only releasing a small laugh as Jackson, on all but 12 of the 116 television screens inside this one portable studio, asks teammate Jimmy Bullard: 'You've bought a new house and two new cars since you got promoted. How are you liking life in the Premiership?'

It is a little before 11.30am on Saturday 19 November. Sheldon, one of Sky Sports' eight-strong PR team, has travelled up from London to give a behind-the-scenes glimpse into the finely tuned machine that is a televised Premiership match. In truth, such a statement is incorrect: all Premier League games are televised to some degree, to some location. But this live broadcast – or OB, as they prefer to label them – had the added intrigue of pitting the rookies against the veterans, David against Goliath... or any one of a dozen similar analogies.

Wires protrude from the trucks to the stadium.

Wigan went into the game in second spot, and a staggering three places above Arsenal, making it an obvious selection for television. But Sky's coverage of the Premiership season actually started two months before the campaign began, when the fixtures were announced.

'Right from the kick-off in August, each person knows exactly what his or her role is in the build up to each game,' says Tony Mills, executive producer of football coverage. 'It means that we can be planning a match two weeks away and at the same time be involved in a run of five live games in seven days. Once the fixtures were announced, we requested the games we liked and the Premier League put those to the clubs, who discussed the proposed dates with the local authority and police.'

Outside the JJB Stadium, the most striking thing about the Sky production was

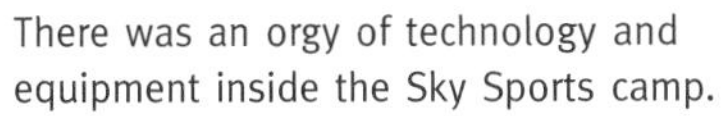

There was an orgy of technology and equipment inside the Sky Sports camp.

One of Sky Sports' production trucks outside the JJB Stadium.

the vast quantities of equipment. The technology was everywhere – hundreds of wires protruded from various ports from the three hi-tech Sky trucks on the carpark. Microphones and cameras lay on racks under shelter, like a Hollywood studio. A Hollywood studio that could shut up and relocate across the country within hours.

Sky's slick, polished broadcasts have raised the bar in sports coverage over the last few years. They were the first to utilise sweeping graphics and sound effects and were the pioneers of the super-slow-mo camera in 1993, which revolutionised football coverage. By shooting film at three times the normal speed, the action could be replayed with remarkable clarity. These days, hi-tech video dish machines act almost like video jukeboxes, providing immediate access to an extensive range of relevant replays. The staff take it as a huge compliment that their final product looks so natural and effortless, although covering a match is anything but.

For the Arsenal match, there were 96 staff on site. Sometimes Sky use a crew of up to 130 people. No wonder they need to operate with military precision. Outside the catering van, a portable table had been set up with two kettles, a tower of styrofoam cups and a large jar of Nescafé on it. Biscuits disappeared as swiftly as they arrived.

Martin Tyler, Sky's seasoned commentator, was sipping hot coffee and chatting

Behind the scenes with Sky Sports.

Security was paramount.

to three 'techies' when he spotted our photographer. He approached with a warm smile across his face and, after a brief greeting, enquired about our presence. 'Wigan deserve a book about them. You could write three books about them,' he said, with genuine enthusiasm. 'It's incredible what has happened here. Jagger has done a remarkable job.'

Jagger? The origin of Paul Jewell's nickname was a guarded secret – and one Tyler probably knew. He spoke of Jewell with such familiarity that it would seem impossible that nicknames would not occasionally creep into broadcasts. 'Ha, I've not said "Jagger" so far,' he smiled. 'I treat nicknames like swearing... they are outlawed.'

Tyler spent the previous evening at Wrightington Hotel and Country Club, reading through player profiles and statistics in the same way an actor would rehearse a script. But his knowledge of the game is so encyclopaedic he could no doubt cope admirably without his strict pre-game routine. An amiable man, he recalled his memories of Wigan and the strides the club has made until he was interupted by Kim Lawson, the production manager.

Lawson looked concerned. A rumour that the game might have to be called off because of a fault with the underground heating was filtering through the staff. Fortunately, as they chatted, Lawson's mobile phone rang. It was the stadium management telling her not to worry. The game would go ahead.

If Sky's matchday operation was like the Death Star, Lawson was Darth Vader, though she was far less frightening and she didn't carry a light sabre or wear a mask. Obviously. As production manager, she was responsible for every detail at the JJB – from the laying of cables to booking satellite links. She visited Wigan two weeks prior to the match to arrange hotels, draw up plans for camera positions and decide on power requirements and cable routes.

The day before the game, she oversaw the layout of nearly 10 miles of cables for cameras and microphones and when the power checks were made, she double checked them. She was already familiar with the layout of the JJB Stadium from Wigan Athletic and Wigan Warriors' televised matches – modern stadia do not throw up the same problems that the older ones do.

Director Duncan Walkinshaw in the Match Truck.

There was an obscene amount of technology.

Duncan Walkinshaw with other members of the production team in the Presentation Truck.

Inevitably, with so much equipment, things have gone wrong. Mistakes have been made. But the fear of having a howling error amplified around the country – and the world – has made the staff vigilant and ready for every contingency. 'If the power fails, we have a generator,' Sheldon explained. 'And if the generator fails, we have a back-up one. You're never going to get it flawless but you can minimalise the risk.'

At the heart of Sky's OB camp parked outside the JJB are three production trucks. Costing more than a million pounds each, they are the engine of a Sky Sports machine finely tuned over 300 live games a year. One looks after the visual footage, one houses the sound department and the third the graphics.

Each production truck is like a Tardis. From the outside, they look like glorified lorries. Inside, they are complete studios decked out with seemingly endless rows of monitors, microphones, PCs and control panels. The silence is eerie, and only punctuated by occasional whispered small-talk.

Producer Steve Tudgay in the Presentation Truck.

Sarah Cheadle, Associate Producer, in the VT Truck.

Richard Keys's image flicked onto the main screen inside the visual truck. He had been inside the main TV studio since 10am, though he hadn't yet changed into his sharp suit. Dressed casually in jeans and a sweater, he was in constant discussion with the programme director about the upcoming game. 'Is it nine or 10 games unbeaten for Wigan?' Keys asked. Walkinshaw relayed the question to one of the eight statisticians down at Sky's HQ in London, who replied instantly, 'Nine in the League, 10 including their Cup win over Bournemouth.'

Keys may have one of the most sought-after jobs in football but, according to Sheldon, it is more demanding than it appears. A live match will often include various video packages, highlights compilations, interviews and analyis before, during and after the game, and Keys often spends hours rehearsing the running order with the director. 'He works bloody hard,' offered Sheldon. 'He comes in early and makes sure he knows what's going on because if anything goes wrong, he's the one left with egg on his face.'

Redknapp, Quinn and Keys face the cameras before kick-off.

Keys, content with the script, left his seat to go to 'wardrobe' to change. We took his cue as a chance to explore the studio where Keys presents the match action, and left the trucks to head for the main reception. Walking around the front of the JJB Stadium, the number of fans had multiplied.

Hundreds thronged around the metal barriers near the main reception, waiting for the Arsenal team coach to arrive so they could get a close-up glimpse of superstars such as Thierry Henry and Sol Campbell. Incredibly, in all the madness and with all eyes trained on the approaching coach, Jewell managed to walk past them through the main doors relatively unnoticed. A polite nod to Kerry, who stood in the porch area handing out the executive tickets, and he was in. No trouble, no fanfare, no security. No problem.

Access to the television studio is via the second floor of the stadium, and across one of the banqueting suites. 'Can you do me a big favour?' asked hospitality manager Jill Gregory apologetically. 'While we're setting up, can you go the other way?'

'The other way' involved snaking through service corridors but eventually we found a door with a 'TV studio' sign on it, and a solitary security guard outside. A polite greeting, a glance at the accreditation cards and we were inside with Keys, Jamie Redknapp and Niall Quinn. And at least a dozen crew members.

The studio was compact and hot. Very hot. The commotion was feverish, with bodies constantly on the move obeying various instructions. Keys, Redknapp and Quinn faced a wall of cameras, screens, lights and an autocue from which Keys took his prompts. They were rehearsing their opening conversation and though Redknapp and Quinn did not script their answers, they outlined areas that each wanted to address. As they talked, a lady walked from one to another straightening their ties and applying foundation to reduce the reflection of the burning lights.

Sheldon, cautious not to discredit an impressive yet injury-plagued footballing career, says Redknapp was born to work in the media. A natural in front of the

Richard Keys may have a sought-after job but he works tirelessly before a match.

Jamie Redknapp, Niall Quinn and Richard Keys inside the studio.

camera, his insights appease the men and his looks please the women. Intelligent, yet a knockabout bloke. A celebrity, and one half of a celebrity couple, but not someone who craves celebrity.

Even the runners – the gofers hopeful of launching a career in television – report that he is polite and courteous. 'When he asks you for a drink, he asks "are you sure you don't mind?"' says one. 'Some of the others you get in here don't even say, "thanks".'

They watched an interview with Arsene Wenger on the monitor, and as they did, we were ushered out of the studio. They were ready to go live. So we climbed the steps to the gantry, from which the radio broadcasters and the TV commentators have the perfect vantage point to call the action.

A capacity 25,004 packed into the JJB Stadium, and the game did not disappoint. It was an epic. Thierry Henry's virtuoso talents thrilled the fans, as he made the JJB a stage for his wizardry. Wigan's resilience, though, was equally admirable as they battled their way back into the game through goals from Henri Camara and a brilliantly taken shot from Jimmy Bullard.

Unlike the popular stereotyped image, there were two directors – the programme director and the match director. The first was responsible for the show surrounding the game – video pieces and statistics compiled days in advance. Seconds before kick-off, he handed over to the match director – and prepared for his 15-minute slot at half-time – and the match director took control of selecting camera angles and co-ordinating action replays (a team of 11 VT operators studied the live footage for possible highlights).

Behind the scenes.

By half-time, five goals had been scored and though the Gunners hung onto the 3–2 lead until the final whistle, the supporters left buoyant and happy.

Jamie Redknapp, Niall Quinn and Richard Keys.

After the match, footage of Thierry Henry's stunning free-kick was analysed by Keys, Redknapp and Quinn. Sky use a special package, Replay 2000, to measure the speed and distance of the shot (the system was derived from Israeli missile research). As they were digesting the action, Paul Jewell and Arsene Wenger were marshalled in turn through the after-match media routine. Matt McCann, as the home team's media officer, dictated the order of the interviews, which today ran like this: live TV interview immediately after the game; a main press conference for the Sunday papers; a separate conference for the Monday and weekly papers; radio interviews; and then the BBC's *Match of the Day*.

The TV interview room featured backdrops for both Sky Sports and the BBC, and though they are corporate competitors, the two crews enjoy a healthy, friendly relationship.

Dealing with the demands of the media are recommendations – not requirements – of the Premier League. But Jewell has always looked at his media responsiblities as being a part of his job, and is generally well liked for his honesty and humour. Before the game, he had joked that he had found a chink in Henry's armour. 'He doesn't score many with his head,' he pointed out.

'He's more cooperative than most of 'em,' said John, one of the cameramen. 'I hope they stay up. We need more managers like 'im.'

Half an hour later, the coverage was over. The credits rolled. The equipment was packed up. Four hours later, the trucks were on the road.

The vantage point from which Martin Tyler and Andy Gray made their commentary of the Wigan v Arsenal game.

10: December: No time for Christmas

'WAKE ME UP, when September ends,' bellowed Green Day in their monster hit of 2005. But for Wigan, September was easy. December would be crunch time, and a ferocious test of their top of the table credentials. Seven games in one month including away fixtures at Liverpool, Chelsea and Manchester United – so much for Christmas shopping, office parties and relaxing.

For Paul Jewell, the month's opening fixture was one he had looked forward to ever since promotion was secured in May. It was more than just a game. More than 90 minutes. Much more than just 'another three points.' The trip to Anfield was an emotional pilgrimage for Jewell, a proud Kopite who has been a Red ever since his dad, Billy, first took him to see Liverpool. Football may be part of the social fabric throughout Britain, but in Liverpool it is religion, and for Jewell, Kenny Dalglish was his god. As a schoolboy he would follow his heroes around the country and then, like so many others, try and emulate them on the schoolyards and playing fields.

Paul Jewell before the game at Anfield, the ground where he worshipped his heroes as a youngster.

Jewell showed enough desire and talent to eventually earn an apprenticeship at Liverpool and though he never managed to fulfil his dream of playing for the Reds – the closest he went was as a travelling reserve – his experiences shaped his attitude. Immersed in a squad featuring the likes of Graeme Souness, Ian Rush and Kenny Dalglish, Jewell honed his impeccable training habits and strong work ethic, which he traces back to his teenage days at Anfield.

'You try and bring into management what you learn when you're growing up in the game and I was at the perfect place,' he says. 'I was at Liverpool when they were winning more or less everything. They didn't want players to run with the ball. They wanted it moving quickly and simply and that's what I try to instil in the players here at Wigan. Give the ball and go. Pass and move. I think we all try to complicate football too much these days, talking about systems and formations, but it means nothing. The game is all about players and getting the best out of them.'

Wigan's last appearance in Liverpool saw them beaten 5–2 in a second-round League Cup tie in September 1989. They lost the first leg 3–0 in a game which was switched from Springfield Park to Anfield to allow a bigger crowd to see the game.

On the eve of the game, Jewell admitted he still looks for Liverpool's results first, and still cracks a smile when they win. He doesn't like to see them lose, with the obvious exception of when he is in charge of their opponents: his Bradford side beat them on the last day of the season in 2000 to stay in the Premiership and deny their opponents a Champions' League place. 'The first result I look for after ours is always Liverpool's,' he says. 'One of the nicest things that has ever happened to me was when the Kop sang "Paul Jewell is a Kopite."'

Wigan sold out their 3,000 ticket allocation for the Anfield game and, with the game followed by away dates at Chelsea and Manchester United, fans basked in visiting three famous stadiums steeped in glory. Despite being perched above Liverpool in the table, the Wigan squad travelled to Anfield as underdogs. In front

Wigan Athletic captain Arjan De Zeeuw and Liverpool counterpart Steven Gerrard shake hands before kick-off.

of the Sky cameras, Wigan didn't manage to return with the three points, as they tumbled to a 3–0 defeat that, for Reds fans at least, was remembered as the match in which England's beanpole striker Peter Crouch finally managed to break his Liverpool goal-drought following his £7 million switch from relegated Southampton in the summer.

The tabloids seemed to take satisfaction in labelling Mike Pollitt as the villain for forcing the Crouch critics into submission. The Wigan 'keeper did, admittedly, drop a clanger to gift Liverpool an easy opening goal. But he redeemed his mistake with a string of breathtaking saves, and the final scoreline would have been nearer six or seven to the rampant home side had it not been for the intervention of the former Rotherham man.

Peter Crouch salutes the Kop after his first goal for Liverpool against Wigan after a 24-hour goal drought. 'It's sod's law,' said Dave Whelan.

After the game, chairman Dave Whelan rushed to the sombre visitors' dressing room to rally his players and to remind them of the strides they had made. He delivered a wake-up call – pointing out that they had lost to Liverpool and their next games were against Chelsea and Manchester United. 'We didn't play well – anyone could see that,' Whelan said. 'Liverpool did to us what we usually do to other teams. They came out and they were straight at us. They deserved to win, we've got no complaints. But I'll tell you something – we'd sooner be losing against Arsenal, Tottenham and Liverpool than Torquay, Grimsby or Gillingham. You're not going to come to these kind of places and expect to get good results. But you try and put in the effort and give a good account. We tried to put up a good show and for 20 minutes we looked alright.'

Unfortunately, that's when it all went wrong. Crouch's harmless looking shot took a massive deflection off Leighton Baines and, as the ball looped high up into the air, the 44,098 spectators expected Pollitt to make a routine save. Incredibly, impossibly, the ball ended up in the back of the net after Pollitt made a misjudged save. 'He jumped too soon,' said Whelan. 'It's sod's law. Crouch never scores for Liverpool for more than 24 hours and then ends up doing it against us.'

At half-time, Jamie Redknapp presented the case that the goal belonged to Crouch and was not a Pollitt own-goal, but Liverpool managed to score twice more – once each side of half-time – to become the first side to inflict more than a single-goal defeat on Wigan since Plymouth the previous November.

Steven Gerrard celebrates as Mike Pollitt is left in a heap after being beaten by Peter Crouch's shot.

Pollitt could have lost his head after his suicidal moment, but recovered superbly in a first half where the visitors were simply chasing shadows. De Zeeuw's header, which glanced the top of the bar, was their only highlight, and the skipper was forced to go off after injuring his knee following the effort.

The Wigan 'keeper made a brilliant stop to deny Gerrard when he burst through, but was helpless to keep out Crouch when he raced onto Steve Finnan's long ball and lobbed his effort into the far corner three minutes from the break.

Latics did start the brighter in the second half. Sami Hyypia timed his block to perfection to the frustration of Jason Roberts, while Graham Kavanagh saw a left-foot drive fly just over. Fernando Morientes's looping header came back off the bar before Jimmy Bullard registered Wigan's first shot on target on the hour – Jose Reina saving his timid effort.

The game was all done and dusted with 20 minutes to go when Gerrard's corner was headed goalwards by Morientes and Luis Garcia chested the ball home. Pollitt kept the score to a respectable level when he turned Gerrard's free-kick round the post and made an incredible double save from Morientes.

A 3–0 loss to the European Champions was no disgrace but Jewell was still disappointed with his own players' efforts. 'We were frightened in the first half. It was very unlike us because we usually start well,' he said. 'We sat off them and allowed them to win easy. Liverpool have got some world-class players, but we never caused them a problem. The only positive is that we didn't concede more. Mike held his hands up. He made a mistake, but he didn't let it affect him – he made four tcp class saves after that.'

Fed up Wigan fans after the defeat at Anfield.

Saturday 3 December 2005

Liverpool 3
Wigan 0

LIVERPOOL (4–4–2): Reina 6, Finnan 7, Hyypia 8, Carragher 7, Warner 7, Garcia 8, Gerrard 9, Alonso 7, Kewell 7, Morientes 7, Crouch 8. Subs: Risse 6 (for Kewell 62), Hamman 6 (for Alonso 68), Cisse (for Crouch 74).

WIGAN: Pollitt 7, Chimbonda 6, De Zeeuw 5, Henchoz 6, Baines 6, Bullard 6, Kavanagh 6, Francis 5, McCulloch 5, Roberts 6, Camara 5. Wigan star man: Pollitt

Goals: Crouch (19, 42), Garcia (70)
Half-time: 2–0
Referee: Uriah Rennie
Attendance: 44,098

What the opposition said...

'I want to see them working really hard and I think our players are doing those things. The statistics had to change at some time. We have a lot of clean sheets now, but we'll concede a goal at some point. We are winning games, but we will lose one. And Peter Crouch is a centre-forward, so he was always going to score.' – Liverpool manager Rafael Benitez.

Jewell preferred to run with smaller squads. Big squads means a big number of players, meaning more players left out of the team, and more disappointment. But with the Premiership abiding by UEFA's transfer window system that prevents clubs recruiting outside the summer months and January, such a choice brings its own challenges when players are injured, suspended or on international duty. Or tired.

With his Wigan side facing seven games in 20 days – and their next fixture at Chelsea followed by Manchester United four days later – Jewell was well aware of the need to rotate his squad to cope with the gruelling winter schedule. 'We've got to give some players a rest,' he said. 'The season is taking it's toll. I've spoken to other managers and they say by January some players are almost shot. The players who have got us to seventh in the table have played most of the games. I think some will benefit from a break.'

Wigan slipped out of the top six but Jewell, ever the realist, said fans who thought they could maintain their winning momentum against the big clubs were getting carried away. 'They thought we could play Arsenal, Tottenham and Liverpool and shoot them aside,' said Jewell. 'I knew that wouldn't be the case. When some of our fans were talking about getting a Champions' League spot this season I was trying to remind them that it would be a long, hard winter. I'm concerned at the fact that we're losing games. But I'd be more concerned if we only had nine points on the board rather than the 25 we've got. We're brand new to this League and we've got to make sure we don't let our heads go down. We desperately need the fans to be with us now it's not going our way. They should really go and appreciate these kind of games. It's what a lot of them had only dreamed of.'

Chelsea, 10 points clear at the top of the table, had only conceded seven goals all season and though having lost only one match, they had received an opening day bloody nose at the JJB Stadium. Wigan's glorious defeat was obviously mentioned in the pre-match build-up, but Jewell's instruction to his players was simple: concentrate on eradicating mistakes.

Wigan Athletic's Pascal Chimbonda, a friend of Michael Essien, in training ahead of the trip to Chelsea.

Jewell actually helped Wigan draw 2–2 at Chelsea in a third-round FA Cup tie in January 1985 (they lost the replay 5–0 at Springfield Park), and though he could reminisce fondly on the result – 'We went 2–0 up and I scored... we'd settle for the same outcome on Saturday' – he conceded that the football landscape had changed, particularly with the arrival of Roman Abramovich.

Again, Jewell devised a game-plan based on grit, a hard work ethic and self-belief. 'We'll try

What the Wigan fan said...

'We didn't deserve anything out of the game the way we played in the first half. It wasn't that Liverpool were too good but that we just didn't compete and seemed to wilt on the big stage. But it's hard to criticise a team that has done so well this season. It was brilliant to go to Anfield.' – East stand season-ticket holder Tom Humphreys.

	P	W	D	L	F	A	Pts
Chelsea	15	13	1	1	34	7	40
Man Utd	14	9	3	2	24	13	30
Liverpool	14	8	4	2	18	8	28
Tottenham	15	7	6	2	19	12	27
Arsenal	14	8	2	4	22	12	26
Bolton	14	8	2	4	17	13	26
Wigan	14	8	1	5	16	13	25
Man City	15	7	3	5	20	14	24
West Ham	14	6	4	4	19	14	22
Middlesb'h	15	5	4	6	20	21	19
Newcastle	15	5	4	6	13	15	19
Charlton	14	6	1	7	19	23	19
Blackburn	15	5	3	7	15	20	18
Fulham	15	4	4	7	16	20	16
Aston Villa	15	4	4	7	15	23	16
Everton	14	5	1	8	7	16	16
West Brom	15	3	4	8	15	24	13
Portsm'th	15	2	4	9	11	23	10
Birm'ham	14	2	3	9	9	19	9
Sunderl'd	16	1	2	13	14	33	5

and maximise what we've got,' he said. 'If they play well and we play well then we'll lose. But we pushed them all the way on the first day of the season and we've got to go there and believe we can win.'

One of the many heroes from that August Sunday afternoon was Pascal Chimbonda, who thrilled fans with an energetic and slick display at right-back. His performances in the weeks that followed alerted clubs across Europe, with Bayern Munich among those to watch him despite the former Bastia star signing an improved, three-year deal.

Chimbonda's personality contradicts his appearance. His colourful choice of clothing and brash style off the pitch suggest a flamboyant character, but he is modest and quiet, and though Latics travelled to Stamford Bridge just three points adrift of a Champions' League spot, he was not getting carried away. 'Survival is still our target,' he said. In truth, he didn't say that, but his translator, Edmund Jones, did. Chimbonda's grasp of English was showing marked signs of improvement, though he did not feel confident enough to use it in an interview. 'Psychologically that first game was a massive bonus for us. It gave us a sense of belief that we can match them.'

The 26-year-old, a strong fans' favourite, revealed a friendship between himself and Chelsea's superstar Michael Essien. 'He's a player I know from my time in France,' he added. 'We talk to each other on the phone and he's a great player. I've also played against Didier Drogba when I was with Bastia and he played for Marseille. He's a great player as well. It helps that I know what they can do and know what their strengths and weaknesses are.'

Chelsea's primary strength was winning. Sometimes they won beautifully, other times they just won, and their game against Wigan certainly fell firmly into the latter category. Chelsea did not play champion football. They did not look like a

Wigan's Leighton Baines holds off Chelsea's Arjen Robben.

Graham Kavanagh makes a pass in front of Frank Lampard. Teammate Lee McCulloch was accused by Jose Mourinho of cheating.

champion team. But history has shown that scraping out 1–0 wins is often the mark of a champion.

It was a game of few chances from either side, and though Wigan's attack did not have the same edge as their previous encounter on the opening day, they did not deserve to lose. Chelsea could not have argued with 0–0, but John Terry condemned them to their fourth straight loss for the first time in more than a decade. Interestingly, the last time they had lost four on the bounce, in April 1995, was under Graham Barrow's control when they were beaten by Preston, Walsall, Rochdale and Bury. None of those sides contained the likes of Thierry Henry, Robbie Keane, Steven Gerrard and John Terry. 'We're coming to the end, thankfully, of this run of tough games,' said Jewell, who took positives from their performances against Arsenal, Tottenham, Liverpool and Chelsea. 'There has only been the one game out of the four games where we didn't look like a decent side and that was at Liverpool.'

In their previous three games, basic individual mistakes had contributed to Wigan's downfall. And so when Chelsea won a 67th-minute corner, Jewell ran from his dug-out and instructed David Connolly to tell Lee McCulloch to keep a close eye on Terry, whom he had earlier felled with a first-half rugby tackle. Jewell's call proved in vain, as Frank Lampard swung in a perfect ball for the England defender to connect with. 'I'm disappointed we got beat by a set piece,' Jewell said. 'It's a harsh lesson we've learned because someone has lost concentration at a vital time. When they beat us on the first day of the season we can take that because it was a wonder goal. But when it's a gimme goal it's disappointing.'

It was tough on the visitors who had battled all afternoon to keep Jose Mourinho's superstars at bay. Matt Jackson made his first Premiership start in almost 10 years – his last being for Everton in February 1996 – and Josip Skoko, who celebrated his 30th birthday at Stamford Bridge, also marked his first League

Saturday 10 December 2005

Chelsea 1
Wigan 0

CHELSEA (4–3–3): Cudicini 6, Gallas 7, Carvalho 7, Terry 8, Del Horno 7, Cole 8, Essien 7, Lampard 7, Robben 6, Crespo 7, Duff 6. Subs: Drogba 7 (for Duff 45), Gudjohnsen 6 (for Robben 59), Geremi (for Crespo 69).

WIGAN (4–4–2): Pollitt 9, Chimbonda 7, Jackson 8, Henchoz 7, Baines 8, Taylor 7, Kavanagh 7, Skoko 8, McCulloch 7, Roberts 6, Connolly 6. Subs: Camara (for Roberts 73), Bullard (for Kavanagh 72). Wigan star man: Pollitt.

Goal: Terry (67)
Half-time: 0–0
Referee: Howard Webb
Attendance: 42,060

What the opposition said...

'We had six players out there with a great performance. It's easy to congratulate Wigan for their work this season – they are doing brilliantly. They will soon start winning again – there's no doubt about it because they are a very good team.' – Chelsea manager Jose Mourinho.

What the Wigan fan said...

'Chelsea did enough to win the game and showed why they are running away with the Premiership. Before John Terry's header there was always the chance Wigan could go up the other end and sneak something.' – *Cockney Latic* fanzine editor John Heeley.

start. 'It was a big birthday for me – it's just a pity the result didn't go our way,' reflected the Australian international, who was given a chance ahead of Jimmy Bullard, ending the midfielder's 123 consecutive League match run.

Latics were chasing shadows in the opening 20 minutes, Pollitt producing a great stop to keep out Joe Cole and Leighton Baines producing an unbelievable block on the line to deny Hernan Crespo. The efforts fuelled Wigan's confidence and as the game wore on, they attempted to pick it up a gear, and appeared good value for a 0–0 draw until Terry's intervention.

As a spectacle, it was forgettable, though Jose Mourinho guaranteed the game's exposure on the back pages by branding Lee McCulloch a cheat for feigning injury. The midfielder stayed down after a challenge and, after a Wigan player kicked the ball out so he could receive treatment, Mourinho defied the unwritten gentleman's rule and sent out the instruction not to throw the ball back to the visiting team. 'I am not stupid – he was cheating,' shrugged Mourinho.

Jewell didn't join Chris Hutchings in the Portuguese manager's office afterwards and, though he was critical of Mourinho's decision, he offered to defend him after the FA launched an investigation into his frank outburst. The word 'cheat' was pounced upon by the FA adjudicators. 'I thought [Mourinho's decision] was unsporting,' said Jewell. 'And I didn't like the comments because the word "cheating" is not something associated with Wigan. It's just one of those things said in the heat of the moment. I just don't think it's a big issue. I know the FA are looking into it, but if he wants me to write a letter or speak to them on his behalf then I will do because there are worse things that go on. I just took it as a flippant comment. I did think it was cheap but you won't be getting any more complaints from me because the issue is finished as far as I'm concerned.'

Jewell had other things to worry about than a 'flippant' remark: A Wednesday night trip to Old Trafford. The game marked his 200th League match as a manager and with United losing more and more pace on rampant, runaway leaders Chelsea, some were giving Wigan far more hope than they could have expected back in the summer.

The fixture was originally scheduled as Latics' third, but had to be postponed because of United's Champions' League commitments. 'That was a blessing in disguise for us,' said Jewell. 'We'd lost the first two matches and to go to United after that would have been a big ask for us. We played Sunderland instead and that's where our season started.'

United drew 1–1 at home to Everton three days before playing Wigan, and had won just three times in the League at home in seven attempts. Sir Alex Ferguson faced bruising criticism and repeated calls to quit but he found an ally in Jewell, who not only provided stoic defence of the Scot's glowing record but also insisted that United were still the biggest club in the country.

'Sir Alex Ferguson has been the best manager in this country for the last whatever number of years,' he offered. 'He's been there, seen it, done it. It would be both dangerous and naive to consider United vulnerable. We have the greatest respect for what they've done and what they stand for. United are the biggest club in the land at the moment. Chelsea have the mantle of being the champions, but Old Trafford is still Old Trafford.'

The praise did little to taper Ferguson's frustrations with sections of the national

Jimmy Bullard tries to stop Ryan Giggs at Old Trafford.

	P	W	D	L	F	A	Pts
Chelsea	16	14	1	1	35	7	43
Liverpool	15	9	4	2	20	8	31
Man Utd	15	9	4	2	25	14	31
Tottenham	15	7	6	2	19	12	27
Bolton	15	8	3	4	18	14	27
Arsenal	15	8	2	5	22	13	26
WIGAN	15	8	1	6	16	14	25
Man City	16	7	3	6	16	14	24
West Ham	15	6	4	5	21	17	22
Newcastle	16	6	4	6	14	15	22
Charlton	15	7	1	7	21	23	22
Blackburn	16	6	3	7	18	22	21
Middlesb'h	16	5	4	7	20	23	19
Aston Villa	16	4	5	7	16	24	17
Everton	15	5	2	8	8	17	17
Fulham	16	4	4	8	16	21	16
West Brom	16	4	4	8	17	24	16
Birm'ham	15	3	3	9	10	19	12
Portsm'th	15	2	4	9	11	23	10
Sunderl'd	17	1	2	14	14	35	5

press. In the official media conference ahead of the match, he refused to answer journalists' questions, swiftly leaving after just 74 seconds and providing even more ammunition for the tabloids to fire at him. In his statement, though, were some kind words about Wigan. His full statement was: 'I've got to be brief. Mikael Silvestre is a slight doubt, but should be okay. John O'Shea is fit again after missing Sunday's game with a toe injury. Wigan have been fantastic this season. I am pleased more for the chairman Dave Whelan than for anyone else at the club because he's the one that has driven the club to where they are. He's a straight-talker who cuts through the niceties very quickly. He's got a determination that has more or less forced Wigan to where they are now. He has had a few managers but he seems to have struck up a terrific bond with Paul Jewell, which is refreshing and I think it's the reason why they are there. So, that's all I've got. See you later boys. I'm busy.'

Skoko kept his place in the heart of midfield after some fine touches against Chelsea, and was bubbling in the build-up to the match after his native Australia were drawn against Brazil, Croatia and Japan in the World Cup. 'I'm really looking forward to it – we've drawn an easy group,' laughed the 41-cap veteran. 'It's going to be an eye opener for us over there in Germany.'

An injury to John Filan handed Mike Pollitt his first match at Old Trafford since an FA Youth Cup game against Mansfield at the tender age of 15, when he was on United's books. Fittingly, Pollitt impressed, though his performance was drowned out by the final scoreline: Manchester United 4, Wigan Athletic 0. Latics, though, could have been looking at double figures had Pollitt not been in goal, with Ferguson remarking afterwards: 'Pollitt made three or four great saves.'

Wigan certainly arrived at Old Trafford willing to take the fight to Ferguson's under-fire side. Jewell threw caution to the wind and went into the clash with three strikers – the first time he'd ever done so during his reign. Jason Roberts and David

Wednesday 14 December 2005

Manchester Utd 4 Wigan 0

WIGAN (4–3–3): Pollitt 9, Chimbonda 6, Henchoz 5, Jackson 6, Baines 6, Skoko 6, Bullard 6, Mahon 6, Camara 5, Roberts 5, Connolly 5. Subs: Kavanagh 6 (for Skoko 45), McCulloch (for Mahon 74). Wigan star man: Pollitt.

MANCHESTER UNITED (4–4–2): Van Der Sar 7, Neville 7, Ferdinand 7, Brown 7, O'Shea 7, Fletcher 7, Scholes 8, Smith 8, Giggs 8, Rooney 9, Van Nistelrooy 9. Subs: Bardsley 6 (for Ferdinand 65), Park (for Giggs 74).

Goals: Ferdinand (30), Rooney (34, 55), Van Nistelrooy (pen 69)
Half-time: 2–0
Referee: Alan Wiley
Attendance: 67,793

What the opposition said...

'I think it clicked for us after the second goal. I thought it was going to be tight the way Wigan started and they played some good football. Rio's goal has been a long time coming – almost three years – and Wayne put us in a comfortable position with his goals. We are still nine points behind Chelsea and the only thing we can do is remain consistent and hope they slip up.' – Manchester United manager Sir Alex Ferguson.

What the Wigan fan said...

'The trip to Old Trafford came amidst the much heralded five game "nightmare" run – we didn't expect anything and we didn't get anything. Wayne Rooney showed why he is held in such high regard and although we battled well, the highlight was taunting the United fans with chants of "USA, USA" and "Go Manchester Dolphins".' East Stand season-ticket holder Dave Webster.

	P	W	D	L	F	A	Pts
Chelsea	16	14	1	1	12	3	43
Man Utd	16	10	4	2	16	9	34
Liverpool	15	9	4	2	7	4	31
Tottenham	16	8	6	2	9	6	30
Bolton	15	8	3	4	9	12	27
Arsenal	15	8	2	5	6	11	26
West Ham	16	7	4	5	11	12	25
WIGAN	16	8	1	7	7	10	25
Man City	16	7	3	6	11	11	24
Newcastle	16	6	4	6	6	9	22
Charlton	15	7	1	7	12	8	22
Blackburn	16	6	3	7	5	13	21
Middlesb'h	16	5	4	7	8	11	19
Aston Villa	16	4	5	7	9	14	17
Everton	16	5	2	9	5	12	17
Fulham	16	4	4	8	6	14	16
West Brom	16	4	4	8	3	12	16
Birm'ham	15	3	3	9	5	7	12
Portsm'th	16	2	4	10	9	16	10
Sunderl'd	17	1	2	14	7	15	5

Connolly were joined by Henri Camara, who was given a breather in the defeat at Chelsea. The omens, strangely, were with Wigan: they had won on this ground before, during an FA Cup victory over Port Vale in November 1969.

United were like bulls to a red rag, and even many Old Trafford optimists admitted they had not seen such passion from their players in weeks. Darren Fletcher had an early goal ruled out for offside and the much-criticised midfielder's point-blank header was kept out by Pollitt.

The Wigan 'keeper made saves from Wayne Rooney and Ruud van Nistelrooy, but his admirable resistance was finally broken on the half-hour mark when Rio Ferdinand claimed his first goal in United colours and nodded in Giggs's corner. 'It was disappointing to concede from a set piece,' said Jewell, who had stressed the importance of not making elementary errors.

Pollitt again denied Rooney, but the striker netted in the 34th minute. A quick step inside Leighton Baines and a thrash of the left boot saw the ball fly in at the near post. Wigan's only effort on target came when Mahon saw his right-foot shot kept out.

Jewell tried to tighten the situation in the second half with Graham Kavanagh brought on to sit in front of the back four, but the United siege continued. Pollitt saved a shot from Van Nistelrooy, but the game was effectively ended in the 55th minute when the Dutch hitman released Rooney with a sensational put-through, and his jink over Pollitt was textbook stuff.

Van der Sar was called into action again by Mahon and did enough to push his goal-bound effort wide. But it got worse for the visitors in the 69th minute when Van Nistelrooy fell easily under a challenge by Pollitt in the area and rammed in the resulting penalty.

The defeat followed losses to big guns Arsenal, Tottenham, Liverpool and Chelsea, but Jewell was happy with his players' attitude. 'It's not a time to be critical

Henri Camara tangles with Rio Ferdinand, who scored his first goal for the club in three years.

because they gave their best, but it was not good enough tonight,' he said. 'Confidence takes a bit of a knock when you lose games but the last five games we've had would test any team, in any league, in any part of the world. It's important we don't use terms like "bounce back" because the bigger picture is after 16 games we've 25 points – Bolton lost six in a row last season and got into Europe.'

Wigan's five big matches were great experiences. Fans, some of whom had supported Wigan from their days in non-League football, marvelled at seeing their club battling it out against names known across the globe, bolstering the legend of Paul Jewell and Wigan Athletic. Now, though, with a game at home against Charlton, it was time to earn some points. Latics were beaten by Darren Bent's goal at the Valley in their second game of the season, but it was the manner of the loss against Alan Curbishley's men which upset Jewell the most. 'The players let themselves down at Charlton earlier in the season,' he said. 'But we've come on leaps and bounds since then and have made great strides.'

The Addicks arrived at the JJB Stadium having already ended their own five-game losing streak by beating rock-bottom Sunderland 2–0 at home the previous weekend. But they were no match for Wigan. And they were no match for Henri Camara.

After four games without a goal, against some of the meanest defences around, Camara showed why Jewell was willing to take a £3 million summer gamble on him. The speedy frontman developed a reputation as an *enfant terrible* for refusing

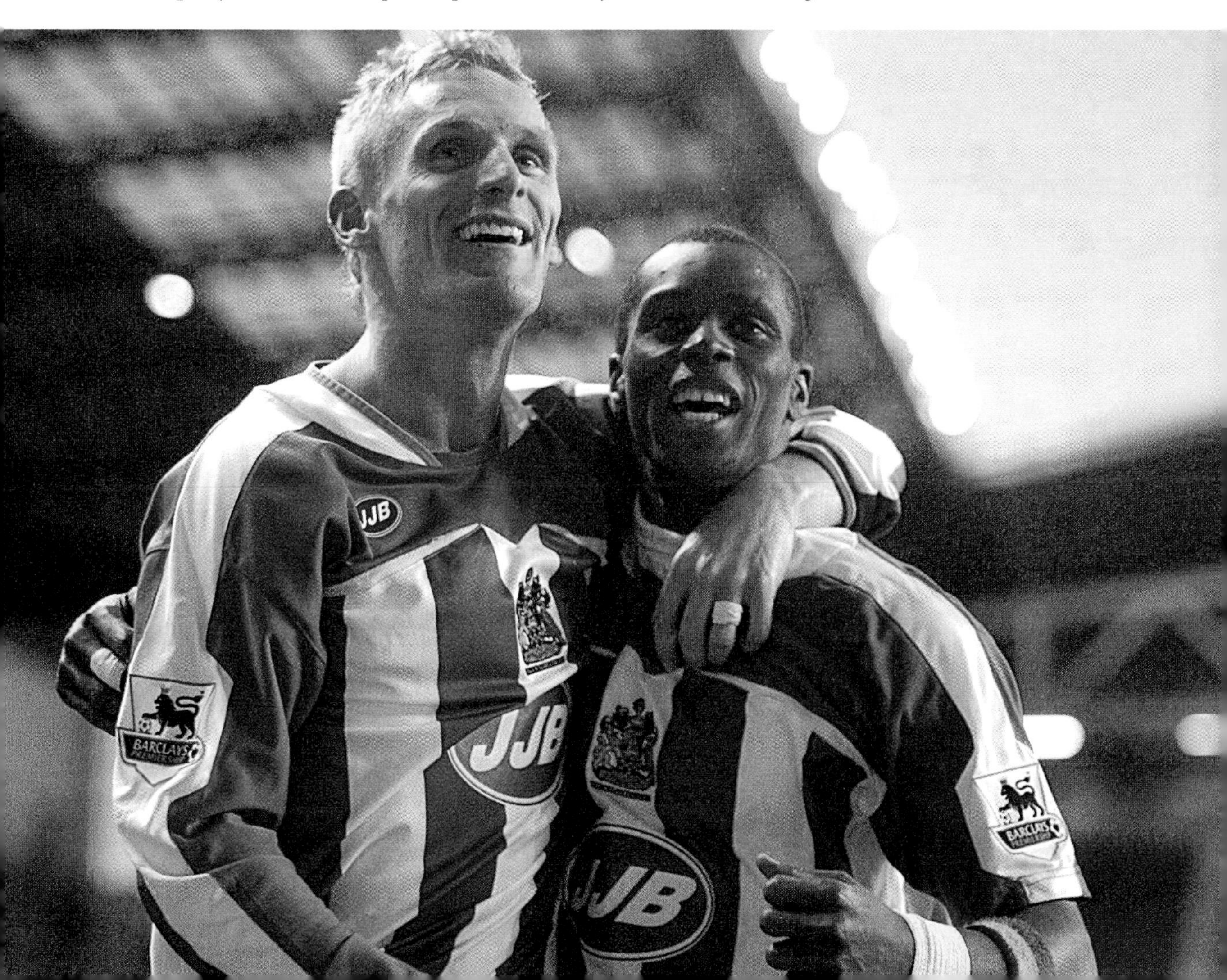

Camara celebrates the second goal of his hat-trick against Charlton with teammate Gary Teale.

to play for Wolves when they were relegated from the Premiership. But on 17 December, he made different headlines by writing another paragraph of Wigan's history/fairytale/Hollywood blockbuster with the club's first hat-trick in the top flight. 'I was speaking to Sir Alex after the game last Wednesday and he was saying what a threat Henri is because he's got unbelievable pace,' revealed Jewell after his striker's sparkling hat-trick. 'Henri's so quick – he can catch pigeons.'

Nathan Ellington's trio of goals to sink West Brom in the Worthington Cup in October 2002 was the last time a Latics player had walked off the field clutching the match ball. Andy Liddell was the last man to do it in the League, against Cambridge in March of that year. No Latics star has ever bagged four in one game. But Camara's crackers, which propelled his goal tally to six in 15 games, ensured Latics were sitting comfortably in sixth spot in the Premiership on 25 December. Merry Christmas.

Matt Jackson wins the ball against Charlton.

Camara, who had not struck a treble in four years (for Sedan against Troyes), said the goals were his way of dealing with the frustrations of an otherwise difficult month. 'We were really angry after the five defeats before this game – it really wound us up,' he said. 'It was important to come back with a confidence-boosting performance.' That it was. This was Wigan's best performance of the season and proved the demons of the previous five games had been well and truly exorcised.

The Addicks were played off the park from the first whistle and the scoreline flattered them. Whelan's decision to re-lay the pitch proved a masterstroke, as the surface acted as a catalyst for a free-flowing Wigan performance from which Camara took full advantage. 'Henri was a different class,' Jewell enthused. 'The lads want the pitch to get re-laid every week after that! We trained on it the day before the game and the players got a boost when they saw how nice it was.'

Saturday 17 December 2005

Wigan 3 Charlton 0

WIGAN (4–4–2): Pollitt 7, Chimbonda 7, Jackson 8, De Zeeuw 8, Baines 8, Teale 6, Bullard 8, Kavanagh 7, McCulloch 7, Roberts 7, Camara 9. Subs: Taylor (for Teale 83), Johansson (for Camara 87). Wigan star man: Camara.

CHARLTON (4–5–1): Kiely 6, Young 5, Perry 5, Hreidarsson 5, Powell 5, Ambrose 6, Smertin 6, Kishishev 6, Murphy 5, Thomas 5, Bent 5. Subs: Bartlett 5 (for Thomas 45), Spector 5 (for Ambrose 69), Hughes (for Kishishev 84).

Goals: Camara (9, 51, 63)
Half-time: 1–0
Referee: Martin Atkinson
Attendance: 17,074

The opener, with nine minutes gone, had all the hallmarks of a typical Liddell goal. Lee McCulloch allowed Leighton Baines's throw-in to drop over his shoulder before rifling in a shot which crashed back off the bar, Camara smashing home the rebound. Jimmy Bullard, back in central midfield in place of the injured Josip Skoko, ran the show in the first half. McCulloch and Bullard were left cursing when they couldn't convert Camara's cross before the redundant Mike Pollitt kept Bent out with a fine stop when he burst clear.

It was game over six minutes after the re-start when Arjan De Zeeuw's ball was flicked on by Roberts and Camara toe-poked the ball over the line as Kiely and Hermann Hreidarsson collided. Wigan's number seven, though, wasn't finished yet and saved the best until last. Baines's ball into the box was cleared by Perry straight to Camara's feet. He nipped past Danny Murphy like he wasn't there and set off towards goal like an Olympic sprinter. Perry and Kiely got in a calamitous tangle, which allowed Camara to stroke the ball home and lap up the congratulations. His day was complete with three minutes to go when Jewell substituted him to a standing ovation.

The victory brought to an end a run of five straight League defeats for Paul Jewell's men. But Arjan De Zeeuw insisted the spirit and belief inside the camp never dipped during the toughest run of fixtures in Premier League history. 'The atmosphere in the dressing room before the game was good,' he said. 'We were all up for it. We may have lost the five previous games, but they were all decent sides we played. It was a great team performance on Saturday. We dominated the game. We were in their faces and we didn't let them settle.'

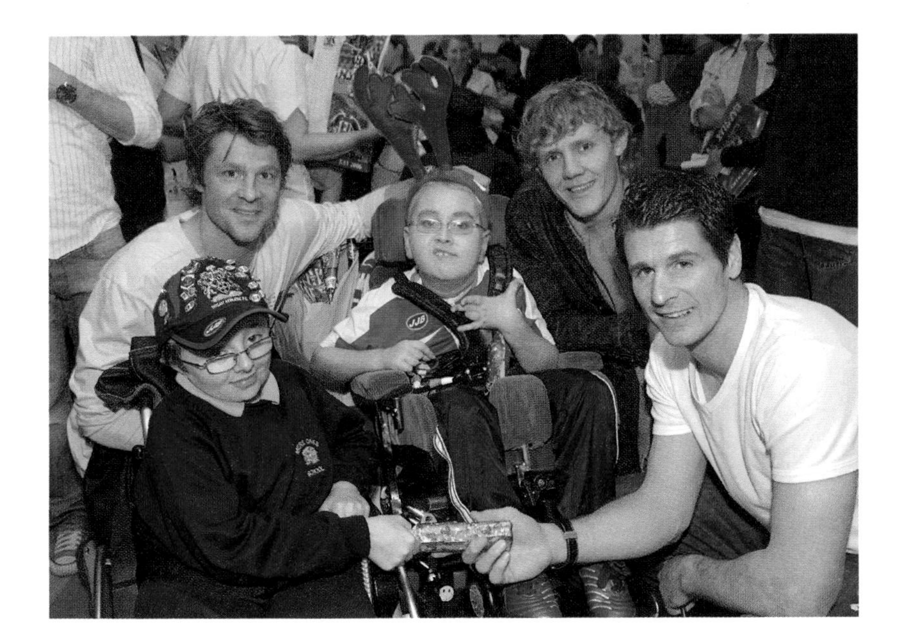

Arjan De Zeeuw, Jimmy Bullard and Mike Pollitt with Mere Oaks School pupils Daniel Dawoud, left, and Tom Barrow during Wigan Athletic's Christmas visit to Wigan Infirmary.

With 28 points on the board, Jewell acknowledged his sixth-placed side could reach the fabled 40-point safety mark with the four games over a gruelling, eight-day Christmas schedule against Manchester City, West Ham, Blackburn and Birmingham. 'We'd have to be Devon Loch not to stay up now,' he joked, before adding, 'But the year I stayed up with Bradford there was 10 games to go, Wimbledon were seventh or eighth and had their cigars out. They got one point out of their last 30 and got relegated. There will be no complacency from us. It's going to be a hectic time for us and it's important to keep rotating the players.'

Jewell's confidence was supported by recent history, after a pattern emeged from previous seasons that teams in sixth spot by Christmas finished the campaign in the top half of the table (Norwich were the highest-placed team at Christmas to be relegated. They were seventh in 1994 and finished 20th the following May). 'We needed to get some more points on the board before Christmas,' chairman Dave Whelan said. 'It's a good indication of where you will finish in the table when you've played half of your games.'

With Wigan hosting Manchester City on Boxing Day, Jewell maintained their regular pre-match preparations which meant his players had to train on Christmas morning. 'As players, we don't really have a proper Christmas, to be honest,' McCulloch said. 'You've got to watch what you are eating – you can't really have a proper Christmas dinner. But I'll still get to see my family, which is the main thing.'

The players lightened the mood with a Secret Santa on Christmas Day, swapping presents after training had finished late morning. David Connolly's gift for Graham Kavanagh proved fitting – an Action Man with a JJB logo emblazoned across his chest – in a box labelled Major Kav. The moniker was adopted as the midfielder's nickname. 'It has a big head and shoulders and shouts a lot of nonsense,' says Kavanagh. 'I can't think why I got it!'

The following day, the Wigan fans continued the town's tradition of turning out in fancy dress. No one is quite certain of the origins of the Wigan tradition but, as the years have rolled on, it has become part of the cultural fabric of the town and fancy dress hire stores report that many of their costumes are booked weeks in advance.

What the opposition said...

'Wigan played well but we don't have a prayer if we don't want to go that extra yard. The basic art of defending has gone out of our team. My players are incapable of defending at the moment and it's got to change. We've been too easy to knock over in recent weeks. Wigan will say they made their own luck, but I'm completely and utterly shocked at the manner of the defeat.' – Charlton manager Alan Curbishley.

What the Wigan fan said...

'It was a really great performance. The scoreline flattered Charlton. We played them off the park and we could have easily scored four or five more. Henri Camara was just too much for them. It was great to see him score a hat-trick.' – East Stand season-ticket holder Claire Chapman.

	P	W	D	L	F	A	Pts
Chelsea	17	15	1	1	37	7	46
Man Utd	17	11	4	2	31	14	37
Liverpool	15	9	4	2	20	8	31
Tottenham	17	8	7	2	25	16	31
Bolton	16	9	3	4	22	14	30
Wigan	17	9	1	7	19	18	28
Man City	17	8	3	6	24	17	27
Arsenal	16	8	2	6	22	15	26
West Ham	17	7	4	6	25	22	25
Newcastle	17	7	4	6	18	17	25
Charlton	16	7	1	8	21	26	22
Blackburn	17	6	3	8	19	24	21
Middlesb'h	17	5	5	7	23	26	20
Fulham	17	5	4	8	18	22	19
Aston Villa	17	4	5	8	16	26	17
Everton	17	5	2	10	9	23	17
West Brom	17	4	4	9	17	25	16
Portsm'th	17	3	4	10	13	26	13
Birm'ham	16	3	3	10	11	23	12
Sunderl'd	17	1	2	14	14	35	5

Latics fans in the Christmas spirit for their Boxing Day derby with Manchester City. Latics offered a prize for the best fancy dress, won by a Pascal Chimbonda 'double'.

Stuart Pearce's side arrived at the JJB Stadium trailing Wigan by one point in the table. The only previous occasion that the two clubs had faced each other in the League on Wigan soil was in October 1998 when Shaun Goater claimed the only goal of the game.

For Latics striker Jason Roberts, the game offered a chance to test his skills against his hero, Andy Cole. 'It will be a pleasure to be on the same pitch as him,' Roberts admitted. 'He's my idol.' Both strikers scored to leave the 25,017 sell-out JJB Stadium record crowd breathless – it was a game that bristled with great goals, great saves and a great atmosphere.

Monday 26 December 2005

Wigan 4 Manchester City 3

WIGAN (4–4–2): Pollitt 8, Chimbonda 8, Jackson 7, De Zeeuw 7, Baines 8, Teale 7, Bullard 8, Kavanagh 8, McCulloch 8, Roberts 9, Camara 9. Subs: Francis (for Kavanagh 72), Taylor (for Teale 83), Connolly (for Camara 86). Wigan star man: Roberts.

MANCHESTER CITY (4–4–2): James 6, Sommeil 6, Distin 5, Onuoha 5, Thatcher 5, Sinclair 7, Barton 7, Reyna 6, Jihai 5, Vassell 5, Sibierski 7. Subs: Dunn 5 (for Sommeil 66), Cole 6 (for Reyna 66).

Goals: Sibierski (3), Roberts (11, 45), McCulloch (23), Camara (71), Barton (77), Cole (88)
Half-time: 3–1
Referee: Dermott Gallagher
Attendance: 25,017

Jason Roberts and strike partner Henri Camara stole the show with their terrific power, pace and movement – the stuff of nightmares for Man City's bruised, battered and bowed back-line, epitomised by a confused-looking David James, sitting on the deck after Latics' fourth wondering just what kind of hurricane he'd been hit by.

Grenadan Roberts bagged a glorious first-half brace, while the Senegalese hit-man made it four goals in two games with a sweetly struck effort after the break to make it 4–1. In between, Lee McCulloch got in on the act when he bagged his third of the campaign, while Mike Pollitt pulled off a string of great saves to deny the visitors.

But Wigan fans had to nervously endure a valiant comeback by City, which nearly earned them a point at the death. 'When I came off and it was 4–1 I thought to myself "lovely, that's the job done",' Kavanagh smiled afterwards outside a pumping home dressing room. 'But it really was heart in your mouth stuff at the end.'

City opened the scoring with 1 minute 55 seconds on the clock as David Sommeil's cross to the back post was nodded in by the unmarked Antoine Sibierski. But, fuelled by a vocal support, Wigan rallied to storm into a 3–1 lead by the break. Camara had two sights of goal before that man Roberts rammed in his seventh goal of the season after 11 minutes.

Mike Pollitt's quick throw was gathered by Gary Teale and his through ball sent the front man away. His first touch was sublime to take him away from Sylvain

Distin and his second was even better as it pinged off the post and nestled in the corner of David James's net. McCulloch then sent Latics on their way to their 10th League victory when he headed in Teale's inch-perfect cross from 13 yards out.

'We showed great character in the first half,' said Paul Jewell, who stuck with the same side who beat Charlton in the previous League game. 'We bounced back well after a kick in the teeth in the first few minutes. We looked really dangerous on the break and could have scored two or three more goals.' But Latics rode their luck and less than a minute after McCulloch's goal City could have been level. Joey Barton's chipped shot over Pollitt came back off the inside of the post, rolled across the line and Matt Jackson booted it to safety.

Just as City began to get on top Camara's hopeful ball forward hit Ben Thatcher on the back of the head, and fell kindly for Roberts, who outmuscled Distin on a charge towards goal and coolly slotted home past the onrushing James. But according to Jewell, they came close to paying the price for over-confidence in the closing stages. After the break City huffed and puffed and Barton had a shot

Jason Roberts celebrates a goal against Manchester City on Boxing Day.

What the opposition said...

'Jason Roberts and Henri Camara looked like world-beaters out there and caused us havoc. But we had a great deal to do with that because of the way we defended. They've both got pace and power and can finish when they get in. Paul Jewell will be lauding them up and so he should because they were great for him.' – Manchester City manager Stuart Pearce.

What the Wigan fan said...

'It was unbelievable – it had everything. It's the best match I've seen all season by a long way. It was so exciting and end to end all the way through. We had plenty of chances, but so did City and Mike Pollitt had to make some good saves. Wigan deserved to win.' – West Stand season-ticket holder Len Marsden.

	P	W	D	L	F	A	Pts
Chelsea	18	16	1	1	40	9	49
Man Utd	18	12	4	2	34	14	40
Liverpool	16	10	4	2	22	8	34
Tottenham	18	9	7	2	27	16	34
Bolton	17	9	4	4	22	14	31
Wigan	18	10	1	7	23	21	31
Arsenal	17	9	2	6	23	15	29
Man City	18	8	3	7	27	21	27
West Ham	18	7	5	6	26	23	26
Newcastle	18	7	4	7	18	19	25
Blackburn	18	7	3	8	21	24	24
Charlton	17	7	1	9	21	27	22
Middlesb'h	18	5	5	8	23	28	20
Aston Villa	18	5	5	8	20	26	20
Fulham	18	5	4	9	20	25	19
Everton	18	5	2	11	9	27	17
West Brom	18	4	4	10	17	28	16
Portsm'th	18	3	5	10	14	27	14
Birm'ham	17	3	3	11	11	25	12
Sunderl'd	18	1	3	14	14	35	6

superbly saved by Pollitt and saw his rebound cleared off the line by Pascal Chimbonda.

Pollitt kept Barton at bay again, the rebound this time falling to Vassell, and his shot deflected off Chimbonda and the Wigan stopper somehow turned it around the post. Pollitt was forced to save from Trevor Sinclair and Andy Cole before Latics went up the other end and robbed a fourth. Kavanagh's ball sent Camara on his way and he nutmegged the mesmerised Richard Dunne and sidefooted into the net past James.

Barton's volley, flying in with 13 minutes still to play, made it 4–2. Then, with two minutes to go, Cole fired in a loose ball from Pollitt's save. In injury-time Sibierski put a free header just wide and then James made his way forward when City won a corner in the dying seconds. But when the England 'keeper committed a foul on David Connolly and the ref blew up there was a shake of the fist in celebration by Jewell, as his men got over the line to take all three points and stay sixth in the table.

And then the party really started.

During such a hectic schedule, Paul Jewell managed to find time to negotiate the signing of Austrian Paul Scharner from Norwegian side Brann Bergan for £2.5 million. Jewell had first spotted him playing against England at Old Trafford in October. The all-action defender, who says his hobbies include bridge jumping, was unveiled to the press with a blue stripe in his hair, wearing a heavy sheepskin jacket.

While his style was questionable, his stock certainly was not, with Birmingham among the clubs who were keen to sign the 12-cap international. 'It is two steps up from Norway and is the goal for each footballer to play in England,' said Scharner, who agreed terms but could not officially be called a Wigan player until January.

The day after Boxing Day, Wigan's players travelled down to London and played West Ham United on 28 December. If they were feeling lethargic, they did not show it as they stormed to a thoroughly well-deserved 2–0 win. Jason Roberts and Henri Camara took their tally to 17 goals between them as they hammered, battered and bruised the Hammers with their own one-two double punch. Their first-half strikes silenced the home support, while the Latics fans lucky enough to make the game were sent into raptures.

Paul Scharner with blue and white stripes in his hair after arriving at the JJB Stadium.

Charlton were on the receiving end of a Camara hat-trick earlier in the month, and this was followed up by Roberts, who claimed braces against Bolton and Manchester City. The pair certainly arrived in East London full of confidence and they didn't disappoint. Both goals were gifts. But both were class finishes.

Anton Ferdinand's back header in the 42nd minute was never going to find former Wigan favourite Roy Carroll and Roberts nipped in before slotting his shot into the corner. And it got even better on the stroke of half-time when Camara's cheeky flick and turn inside the box totally out-foxed Paul Konchesky, who should

Gary Teale runs at the West Ham defence during their 2–0 win.

Wednesday 28 December 2005

West Ham 0 Wigan 2

WEST HAM (4–4–2): Carroll 6, Dailly 6, Ferdinand 5, Collins 6, Konchesky 5, Fletcher 5, Reo-Coker 6, Mullins 6, Etherington 5, Bellion 5, Harewood 6. Subs: Zamora 6 (for Fletcher 25), Newton 6 (for Bellion 45), Aliadiere (for Harewood 81).

WIGAN (4–4–2): Pollitt 7, Chimbonda 7, De Zeeuw 7, Jackson 7, Baines 8, Teale 6, Bullard 7, Kavanagh 7, McCulloch 7, Roberts 8, Camara 8. Subs: Connolly (for Camara 81), Francis (for Teale 83). Wigan star man: Jason Roberts.

Goals: Roberts (42), Camara (45)
Half-time: 0–2
Referee: Steve Bennett
Attendance: 34,131

have cleared the ball. But the Senegal striker wasn't waiting for him and took a touch before hammering his shot past the helpless Carroll. And the scoreline could have been even greater. Former West Ham reserve and self-confessed Hammers fan Jimmy Bullard had never scored at Upton Park, though he almost did on the half-hour mark, with Carroll having to be at his best to turn away his fierce 25-yard drive.

What the opposition said...

'I can have no complaints – we were second best on the night. We got punished at the back by two quality strikers. We charged kids just £1 to get into the ground to watch the match and I think they were ripped off.' – Alan Pardew

What the Wigan fan said...

'This win was all about the pace, skill and power of Henri Camara. Upton Park was stunned by Camara's trickery to set up Jason Roberts for the first goal before making one of his own. The striker demonstrated why he's been so instrumental to our success this season.' – East Stand season-ticket holder Tom Humphreys.

Jason Roberts scored a goal against West Ham.

	P	W	D	L	F	A	Pts
Chelsea	19	17	1	1	41	9	52
Man Utd	19	12	5	2	36	16	41
Liverpool	17	11	4	2	25	9	37
Tottenham	19	9	7	3	27	18	34
WIGAN	19	11	1	7	25	21	34
Arsenal	18	10	2	6	27	15	32
Bolton	17	9	4	4	22	14	31
Man City	19	8	3	8	27	22	27
West Ham	19	7	5	7	26	25	26
Newcastle	18	7	4	7	18	19	25
Blackburn	18	7	3	8	21	24	24
Charlton	17	7	1	9	21	27	22
Aston Villa	19	5	6	8	23	29	21
Fulham	19	5	5	9	23	28	20
Middlesb'h	18	5	5	8	23	28	20
West Brom	19	5	4	10	19	28	19
Everton	19	5	2	12	10	30	17
Portsm'th	19	3	5	11	14	31	14
Birm'ham	18	3	4	11	13	27	13
Sunderl'd	18	1	3	14	14	35	6

West Ham had to go for it in the second half and the space they left at the back just created more pressure from Latics' quick breaks through Gary Teale, Bullard, Roberts and Camara. None of their efforts brought goals, but a 2–0 win left everyone delighted. Everyone, that is, except the Wigan fans on the three supporters' coaches, who missed the game when the drivers were forced to turn around at Birmingham on the M6 because of traffic chaos.

As newspapers and television channels continued their end of year reviews, tributes poured in for Paul Jewell and Wigan Athletic. Arguably the best, though, belonged to Niall Quinn, who wrote in his column in the *Guardian* newspaper his roll of honour for 2005. 'I hold up my hands, I doubted Wigan,' he wrote. 'At first they got

Saturday 31 December 2005

Wigan 0
Blackburn 3

WIGAN (4–4–2): Pollitt 6, Chimbonda 6, De Zeeuw 7, Jackson 6, Baines 6, Teale 5, Bullard 6, Kavanagh 6, McCulloch 6, Roberts 6, Camara 6. Subs: Francis 5 (for Kavanagh 56), Connolly 5 (for Teale 56), Wright 5 (for Baines 66). Wigan star man: Arjan De Zeeuw.

BLACKBURN (4–4–2): Friedel 7, Neill 7, Khizanishvili 7, Nelson 7, Gray 8, Bentley 8, Savage 7, Reid 9, Pedersen 9, Kuqi 7, Dickov 7. Subs: Bellamy 7 (for Dickov 57), Emerton (for Pedersen 84), Thompson (for Bentley 87).

Goals: Pedersen (15), Reid (53), Bellamy (85)
Half-time: 0–1
Referee: Mark Clattenburg
Attendance: 20,639

Arjan De Zeeuw curses a missed header at goal against Blackburn. 'It was a shame we finished the year like that,' said the captain.

by on adrenaline but gradually they have also shown steel. Not only are they proving me and everyone else wrong… they are doing it with a smile.'

Unfortunately, the year ended on a sour note with a 3–0 home thrashing by Blackburn – but nothing could take the shine off a memorable year. This was the first time the two clubs had met in the League – Rovers had won the previous four meetings in the FA and League cups.

Mark Hughes's side had enjoyed the luxury of a day off after their clash with Sunderland was called off due to a frozen pitch four days earlier. By contrast, Paul Jewell's men were 220 miles away chalking up an impressive victory at Upton Park, and three games in six days took its toll.

Rovers looked as fresh as daisies, and never looked back after Morten Gamst Pedersen opened the scoring with a cracking strike after 15 minutes. Two Lee McCulloch half-chances and an effort from Arjan De Zeeuw were the highlights of a brief first-half rally, but Blackburn effectively sealed the win with Steven Reid's 25-yard rasper, eight minutes after the restart. 'Polly said he dived for it but it was a token gesture,' De Zeeuw shrugged.

Substitute David Connolly did get a rare sight of goal, but Friedel smothered his close-range shot superbly. It was left to Craig Bellamy to wrap it up when Damien Francis inadvertently sent him in and he placed it beyond Pollitt.

'It was a shame we had to finish the year off like that,' captain De Zeeuw added. 'We looked tired and we didn't play our usual game. We left too many gaps and spaces for them. It's been a tough schedule and a lot of the lads looked leggy. We always put a lot into our games and it takes a lot of effort. We would have liked to have played a team who had a game two days before as well.'

Being New Year's Eve, fans reflected not just on the game but on the year… and they did so with wide grins. They knew that, thanks to Wigan Athletic, they would never forget 2005.

What the opposition said...

'I thought we were in control for the whole game. In the first half we expected Wigan to test us and we stood up to them. Once we got our noses in front I was confident we would see the game out. We created a lot of chances, but we needed more care in front of goal. We feel we're a top 10 side and now we're up there I think we'll stay there.' – Blackburn manager Mark Hughes.

What the Wigan fan said...

'Mark Hughes's men came to the JJB Stadium to do a job and they executed it perfectly. By hassling, hurrying and closing us down they succeeded in nullifying our pace and attacking football while producing three goals – including two class strikes – to take the three points.' – East Stand season-ticket holder Chris O'Brien.

	P	W	D	L	F	A	Pts
Chelsea	20	18	1	1	15	3	55
Man Utd	20	13	5	2	20	11	44
Liverpool	18	12	4	2	10	5	40
Tottenham	20	10	7	3	12	11	37
WIGAN	20	11	1	8	9	10	34
Arsenal	19	10	3	6	7	11	33
Bolton	18	9	4	5	16	5	31
Man City	20	8	4	8	14	15	28
Blackburn	19	8	3	8	11	15	27
West Ham	20	7	5	8	12	15	26
Newcastle	19	7	4	8	10	15	25
Charlton	18	8	1	9	12	11	25
Aston Villa	20	5	7	8	12	17	22
Middlesb'h	19	5	6	8	8	11	21
Fulham	20	5	5	10	8	18	20
Everton	20	6	2	12	6	16	20
West Brom	20	5	4	11	3	17	19
Portsm'th	20	4	5	11	9	20	17
Birm'ham	19	3	4	12	6	15	13
Sunderl'd	19	1	3	15	7	15	6

Latics boss Paul Jewell, assistant Chris Hutchings and his Rovers counterpart Mark Hughes.

JJB

11: From the outhouse to the penthouse

An ecstatic Paul Jewell celebrates promotion to the Premiership.

WIGAN ATHLETIC'S 73-year rise from the Cheshire League to the Premier League may never be matched by any team in English football. The club's arrival in the top tier of this country's beautiful game is certainly a rags to riches story.

Wigan Athletic were formed in 1932 after taking the place of their predecessors Wigan Borough, who ran into extreme financial difficulty. Players were unable to collect a weekly wage from the debt-ridden club and on 26 October 1931 Borough played their last League game at Wrexham's Racecourse Ground where they were beaten 5–0. They officially resigned from the Football League on Monday 26 October. Borough's club secretary of the time, Frank Platt, said: 'From the information I have gleaned from the books of the club, I have no hesitation in saying that the Association Football public of Wigan have shown once again that they have no desire to maintain League football in Wigan.'

Just when it looked like the town might have had no football team to cheer about, Wigan Athletic were born on 9 May 1932. By 8 May 2005 that same club joined the elite of the English game as they smashed their way into the Premier League – just 27 years after gaining entry into the Football League. Wigan's Mayor, Cllr Hipwood, chaired a public meeting at Queens Hall which resulted in the founding of the newly established club.

They bought Springfield Park for £2,850 from the owners of Woodhouse Lane Dog Track and were accepted at the second attempt into the Cheshire League – they also unsuccessfully applied for the Football League. Latics were the fifth club to play at the ground, following the building of the premises in 1897.

Charlie Spencer – who played for Manchester United and England – took the reins at the club for the first five years of their life in the Cheshire League. He was on £6 per week and their first fixture on 27 August 1932 saw them beaten 2–0 by Port Vale Reserves at Springfield Park. But they followed it up by beating Tranmere Rovers Reserves four days later 5–1.

In the 1934–35 season Wigan won the Cheshire League Championship. They also beat Carlisle United 6–1 in the first round of the FA Cup at Brunton Park, a record victory that still stands for a non-League side over Football League opposition.

Manager Les Rigby leads out Wigan Athletic at Wembley for the Challenge Trophy Final against Scarborough in 1973.

After World War Two, Latics were elected out of the Cheshire League by the League's committee, after spending nine successive seasons at that level, prompting them to join the Lancashire Combination Division One. In 1950 they were almost rewarded with Football League status, but lost out on a third poll vote to Scunthorpe United.

The 1953–54 campaign was remembered as one of the most remarkable in the club's history. They retained the Championship, their third title in four years, won the Lancashire Junior Cup and completed a unique treble by lifting the Lancashire Combinations Cup. They also went on to claim national fame in the FA Cup. They beat Hereford in the second round in front of 27,526 fans, a non-League record which still stands, excluding Wembley finals.

In the next round they met Newcastle, who were at the height of their footballing prowess. A crowd of 52,222 at St James' Park saw Latics return with a 3–3 draw. The replay four days later on 13 January 1954 got off to an unsporting start as Newcastle's chairman, Stan Seymour, refused to let his team change in Latics' makeshift changing rooms, and insisted they used the Corporation Baths instead. He described the facilities at Springfield Park as 'crude'. The Main Stand had been destroyed by fire a year earlier, and the supporters and directors had worked hard to gain the money to rebuild – work that was still going on. Wigan narrowly lost the replay 3–2.

In 1961–62 Wigan sought election back into the Cheshire League. It had proved a struggle for the club and took 13 managers after Spencer's appointment to get them back up. Their application was accepted and during the 1964–65 season, legendary Wigan striker Harry Lyon bagged 66 goals, which included six in one match to claim a new club record.

Wigan remained in that league until becoming a founder member of the Northern Premier League seven seasons later for the start of the 1968–69 campaign. Throughout their time in the Cheshire League, Lancashire Combination and Northern Premier, Latics continued to seek election into the Football League.

In 1971, they won the Northern Premier and reached the third round of the FA Cup, losing to Manchester City at Maine Road. Election to the Football League looked a certainty, but Latics only polled 14 votes. The blame was laid at the door of chairman Ken Cowap, who had distributed £2 Parker pens to each club's voting representatives. It was a goodwill gesture, but rebounded dramatically, some seeing it as an attempt to influence the voting.

Latics centre-forward John Rogers celebrates his goal against Scarborough during the Challenge Trophy Final at Wembley in 1973.

Wigan enjoyed further Cup success two years later when Les Rigby led them to their first Wembley appearance in 1973. They met Scarborough in the FA Trophy, but were beaten 2–1, with striker John Rogers claiming the goal for Wigan.

But it was the Football League that Wigan really wanted to crack, and their passage into the League was finally unblocked in 1978 after 34 rejections. Ironically, it came at the end of the season when Latics had finished runners-up to Boston United in the Northern Premier. It had take Wigan 23 managers to break into the Football League, and Ian McNeill was the man with the honour of leading them to glory. Boston's ground wasn't up to scratch, which allowed Latics the chance to seek election.

They tied with Southport in the first vote, knocking Bath City, of the Southern League, out of the running. And on the second vote they edged out Southport, who dropped out of the League as Wigan celebrated. McNeill said: 'It was a privilege to be manager of Wigan when they got into the Football League. A lot of hard work was put in by us because we needed to visit every club to put forward our case for

The Wigan Athletic team which in 1985 won the Freight Rover Trophy at Wembley.

election. First and Second Division clubs had a vote each, while the Third and Fourth Division sides got 12 votes between them.'

It was a tense evening as votes were cast, with McNeill, chairman Arthur Horrocks and secretary Jack Farrimond travelling to London's Cafe Royal to hear the outcome. 'In the first vote we tied 26–26 with Southport,' McNeill said. 'In the re-vote, we then got the backing of a lot of clubs who voted for Bath City the first time around. We won 29–20. I was outside at the time because we only had two tickets and Arthur and Jack were in there. The first I knew of us winning was when the door swung open and a guy stomped out saying Wigan had won. We felt a million dollars and Arthur suggested we stay in London for the night to celebrate. But I insisted we went back to Wigan and although it was late when we got home, the party was still in full swing.'

Harry McNally at Springfield Park.

Their first game was a goalless draw at Hereford on 19 August 1978. Joe Hinnigan had the honour of being the first player to score, four games in against Newport. Peter Houghton netted the first League hat-trick in a 5–3 thriller over Port Vale – he'd scored the Latics' last goal as a non-League club at Matlock.

In their first season in the League, Latics finished in a credible sixth place. Two seasons later promotion was secured as they claimed second spot under player-manager Larry Lloyd. The late Harry McNally followed Lloyd through the Springfield Park door in March 1983. A stonemason by trade, he would often turn up to the ground in his builder's lorry, famously once blocking the path of the Chelsea team bus ferrying the players to training and back. By the end of his first season McNally's side had finished 18th in the old Division Three. They finished 15th the season after.

McNally oversaw the signing of a young, scouse striker named Paul Jewell and remained as manager for two years before departing in March 1985. He was replaced by Bryan Hamilton and on 1 June that year the club made their first appearance at Wembley when they beat Brentford 3–1 in the Freight Rover Trophy with goals from Mike Newell, Tony Kelly and David Lowe.

On 14 March 1987, Latics reached the sixth round of the FA Cup under Ray Mathias – their best ever run in the competition – before being knocked out at home by Leeds, who won 2–0. Mathias left the club in March 1989 when the club finished 17th in the Third Division and four years later Wigan were relegated.

Paul Jewell signed from Liverpool.

David Lowe and his Latics teammates reaction after hearing that they had drawn the mighty Leeds at Springfield Park in the quarter-final of the FA Cup in 1987. They lost 2–0.

Kenny Swain was in charge for 42 matches and managed just 11 wins – he was promptly shown the door.

The future of the club was far from bright. Wigan finished the next season fourth from bottom and were almost relegated to the Vauxhall Conference. They finished just three points ahead of Hereford after a win against Gillingham and a last day draw away at Shrewsbury. Graham Barrow took over the reins in September 1994 to try and turn their fortunes around. Barrow, a former Latics player, had signed for the club in 1981 from non-League Altrincham, with Larry Lloyd snapping him up. He said: 'We didn't have a proper training ground back then. After the game all the players would go into Springfield Park social club and chat with the fans. It was a very friendly and intimate club.' He was named the man of the match in the Freight Rover Trophy Final. But the club was stuck in the doldrums when he came back as manager.

Wigan Athletic played Liverpool in the League Cup second round at Anfield in 1989. Ian Rush has a shot at goal flanked by Darren Patterson and Peter Atherton. Latics lost 5–2 in the first leg and 3–0 in the second leg, both played at Anfield.

Barrow said: 'Wigan had no points from their first five games and I was horrified at the state of the club. That fifth straight defeat at home to Barnet saw just 1,438 fans pay through the turnstiles and the club was in a total mess. There were three players good enough to build a new team with – Simon Farnworth, Ian Kilner and Neil Rimmer – and I just had to start from scratch. We had to beg, steal and borrow and it was a desperate struggle. But I managed a 2–1 win at Hereford in the sixth League game, which was my first game in charge and I'll never forget that day. I can remember the scorers, a David Rennie penalty and a Neil Rimmer volley.'

But it wasn't until February 1995 that Wigan Athletic's fortunes began to change for the better when local millionaire businessman Dave Whelan took control of the club. The former Blackburn defender was seen as the saviour after Latics had run into more financial difficulties. Whelan said: 'I'd never really thought about it until the old Wigan president Stan Jackson came to me and said "Our wage bill is £586 and we can't pay it". I had enjoyed so many great times in football and my business was in sport so I said I would meet the bill. That was it. The bug hit me. The first match wasn't so special. Apart from Ian Kilford, who had signed from Nottingham Forest, I couldn't find a single member of our team I thought could actually play. I just thought that if we couldn't do better than that there was something really wrong with us.'

Dave Calderbank, who covered Wigan for Barnes News Agency from their non-League days, was one of the first journalists to report Whelan's ambitions for the club. 'When Dave Whelan came in and said he wanted to take the club into the Premiership within 10 years I think it was a bit tongue in cheek,' Calderbank said. 'I don't really think he believed it. He probably dreamt it but I don't think he would have expected it to happen.'

A snowbound Springfield Park during a match in 1987.

Whelan's early assessment of the team he had taken over proved to be spot on. The former Blackburn Rovers player immediately signalled his intent by signing the so-called 'Three Amigos' – Isidro Diaz, Jesus Seba and Roberto Martinez. By the end of the season Latics had finished the campaign in 14th position under the leadership of Barrow. He said: 'It was a great achievement when I thought we'd do well to stay in the League.'

Just three months into the next season, though, Barrow was shown the door after a 6–2 home defeat to Mansfield Town. Whelan replaced him with John Deehan after he resigned from his post at Norwich City. It proved to be a good appointment as the new boss steered the club to 10th in Division Three in his first season. Things were to get even better for Deehan in the 1996–97 season as he led his side to the Championship with 87 points.

Latics rough tough centre-forward Bobby Campbell gets involved after a clash with the goalkeeper in a match at Springfield Park in the late 1980s.

Wigan made a steady start to life in Division Two as they finished the campaign in 11th place – just eight points off a play-off spot. In the summer of 1998 Deehan decided to leave Springfield Park and signed a three-year contract with Division One side Sheffield United. Whelan decided that Mathias should be given another crack at managing Wigan and brought him back on board before the start of the 1998–99 season.

This proved a popular and welcome appointment as the Liverpudlian led the side to sixth place and a play-off shot at the First Division. But it was all to end in tears for all parties. Latics drew the first semi-final leg 1–1 against Manchester City and then Shaun Goater's hand-ball goal sent the Blues to Wembley to face Gillingham, whom they beat on penalties.

Chairman Dave Whelan kisses the trophy, flanked by Martinez, as Latics won promotion to Division Two in 1997.

The demolition of Springfield Park in June 1999.

Whelan's decision to axe Mathias after coming so close shocked everyone. The JJB Sports tycoon saw John Benson as the natural replacement for the departed Mathias. Benson had joined Latics as assistant manager to Deehan, a position he continued to hold under Mathias. In June 1999 he made his way into the hot-seat and became the first manager to lead the club out at the £28 million JJB Stadium as Springfield Park closed its doors.

The new stadium came as a welcome relief for reporters and broadcasters who had to put up with less than adequate facilities at the old ground. Calderbank said: 'They had no press box so Derek Fuller, the general manager at the time, stuck one in the corner and so Wigan became famous in press circles for being the only stadium in the Football League where you could only see one goalmouth from the press box. One of us would take turns acting as a runner who would stand outside and then come in and inform the press what had happened. There's no comparison between now and then. If anything needed doing the staff would all get stuck in.'

Benson led Latics to fourth place and another place in the play-offs at the end of the year. But if the season before was bad, this was even worse. This time Wigan got through to the Final where they faced Gillingham – the Gulls having been denied the year before by City.

Pat McGibbon scored an own goal, but Simon Howarth's strike on the hour saw the game move into extra-time. Stuart Barlow slotted home a penalty and Wigan thought they were on their way to the First Division. They were six minutes from achieving their goal when Steve Butler claimed a late equaliser. The goal knocked the stuffing out of Latics as Andy Thomson rattled in the winner four minutes later and just two minutes from time – heartbreaking stuff.

Dave Whelan with the JJB stadium model.

Whelan welcomes Sir Alex Ferguson to the JJB Stadium for the opening game.

Benson had seen enough after such a rollercoaster year and, after consultation with Whelan, decided to step down as manager and 'move upstairs'. Whelan was determined to bring the 'revolving door' syndrome of managers to an end. There had been four managers in charge during his first five years as chairman.

Bruce Rioch was the next chosen candidate to take over and he came with the credentials that Whelan believed could finally get the club out of the Second

Golden boy Stuart Barlow celebrated a hat-trick in a 4–1 win against Preston but the following year it ended in tears when Wigan lost to Gillingham at Wembley in 2000.

Division at the third time of asking. The Scot had taken Middlesbrough from a dire financial position and lifted them from the third to the First Division within two seasons. He had also taken Millwall to the Second Division play-offs before taking over at Bolton Wanderers. He achieved promotion in his first season at Burnden Park and also took them to the sixth round of the FA Cup. In 1995 he had taken the Trotters to the League Cup Final and promotion to the Premiership via the play-offs.

In 1995 Rioch was given the opportunity to manage Premier League giants Arsenal. He was the manager responsible for signing Dennis Bergkamp for £7.5 million from Inter Milan. But his stay at Highbury was to last only 15 months, after which he was sacked and joined Queen's Park Rangers as assistant manager. He had a spell at Norwich before Whelan persuaded him to take over at Latics in the summer of 2000.

It looked yet another wise move from Whelan as Rioch's side lost only one of their first 22 League games and seemed certain to make the play-offs in fourth spot. But after rumours of Whelan interfering in training ground tactics, Rioch stood down from his position, although Whelan later said he wasn't convinced he was the right man for the job. 'I just didn't get the impression that Bruce was hungry enough for the job. He was coming to the end of his career as a manager and I felt we needed to get someone in who was young, ambitious and hungry. I was proved right in the long run because when Bruce left here he never took a manager's role with any other club in the country.'

Stephen Roger Bruce isn't remembered fondly by Whelan. The former Manchester United favourite was plucked out of the wilderness when he was named as the new Wigan Athletic manager on 4 April 2001. Bruce had been out of work for six months after his sacking from Huddersfield Town before he got the call from the JJB Stadium.

Latics were banging on the door of the play-offs when Bruce took over. They duly finished the season in sixth place and came up against Reading in a two-legged semi-final affair. The Royals had finished the campaign in third place behind Millwall and Rotherham, who went up automatically.

The first game at the JJB Stadium on 13 May finished 0–0 – but it was a whole different story three days later at the Madejski Stadium. Latics took the lead in the 26th minute with a Kevin Nicholls strike and, as the clock dwindled down, it looked like Latics might be heading back on their way to Wembley for a second successive play-off final. But in the 86th minute Martin Butler claimed an equaliser and in injury-time Nicky Forster's winner sunk Latics in yet more heartbreaking circumstances.

The game was to bring to an end Bruce's eight-match run in charge. He went on holiday after the clash and Whelan was convinced he would sign a two-year deal to stay at the club upon his return. But Bruce snubbed his advances and chose to move to Crystal Palace instead – a move which infuriated Whelan. He said: 'We took Steve Bruce out of nowhere and gave him a chance to get himself back in the game and this is how he goes and repays us. He told me we'd need to shake up the squad and told nine players they wouldn't be getting new contracts at the club and then decides to leave himself. I'm astounded.'

But Whelan only had to wait 14 days before he found his new man. The vacant Latics job certainly attracted a lot of attention, with no fewer than 32 applications

Ray Mathias had two spells as manager of Wigan Athletic. He was sacked in 1999 and succeeded by John Benson, Bruce Rioch and Steve Bruce before Paul Jewell took the job.

arriving on Whelan's desk. Bryan Robson, John Aldridge, Ronnie Moore and Joe Royle were all interested in the position. But it was a man who had plied his trade as a young centre-forward at Springfield Park 13 years previously who was seen as the man to finally take the club out of the old Second Division.

Paul Jewell had the rare distinction of becoming the first manager under Whelan to sign a contract when a two-year deal was pushed under his nose on 12 June 2001. Whelan said: 'I've no doubt in my mind that we've got the right man on board. Paul was our first choice and I believe he can bring success to Wigan Athletic. Paul made his name at Bradford when he took them up to the Premier League and kept them there – if he can do it with them he can do it with us.'

Jewell had been out of work for four months following his sacking from Sheffield Wednesday. He was granted an interview at Tranmere before his arrival at Wigan, but said the vacant position at Prenton Park wasn't for him. He didn't think twice, though, when Whelan offered him the position of manager at the JJB Stadium. But if Jewell, who became the club's 35th manager, expected a happy ship when he took his place in the hot-seat he was sadly mistaken. Three successive near misses in the play-offs had seen Latics dubbed the bridesmaids of the old Second Division. It was a mystery to other fans around the country because of the millions poured into the club by Whelan. The players Bruce had left behind after his departure to Palace weren't the happiest bunch of motivated players, and were certainly not putting in the kind of performances their hefty wage packets warranted.

The first few months of Jewell's reign were by far the hardest. Trying to work out how his side could thrash Stoke 6–1 at home and then lose 1–0 to lowly Canvey Island in the FA Cup four days later was hard to explain. 'That was my lowest point as manager here,' Jewell said. The pressure was certainly on Jewell just a few months into his new job. Wigan were languishing in the relegation zone and they were then thrashed 5–1 in an LDV Vans tie at Wrexham. 'I was at the end of my tether at that point,' Jewell reflects. 'There were players here who certainly thought they'd be here far longer than the manager would.'

Paul Jewell at his first press conference to announce him as the new Wigan Athletic manager.

Neil Roberts and fans' favourite Andy Liddell celebrate the Division Two Championship, which they claimed with 100 points.

1932: Wigan Athletic founded as the latest football club in the Lancashire town, following Wigan County, Wigan United, Wigan Town and Wigan Borough, all of which folded.
1978: After 34 previously unsuccessful attempts, Wigan are eventually elected to the Football League, ousting Southport by 29 votes to 20.
1978: Wigan's first match as a League club ends in a 0–0 draw against Hereford at Edgar Street.
1982: Wigan promoted to old Third Division on the back of a 21-match unbeaten run, finishing third behind Sheffield United and Bradford City.
1985: Beat Brentford 3–1 at Wembley to win the Freight Rover Trophy.
1987: Reach the FA Cup sixth round for the only time in their history, eventually losing 2–0 to Leeds.

Whelan vowed to stick by his man and called the *Wigan Observer*'s sports desk one Monday afternoon from his Majorca holiday home to declare his support for the Liverpudlian. 'Paul Jewell is going nowhere,' Whelan said. 'He is what his name says he is "a jewel". If he can't do this job then no one can. If he resigns then I will resign.' True to his word, Whelan stuck firmly behind his man and opened the door for any players who weren't prepared to do it Jewell's way.

The manager was armed with a cheque book to rival any club outside of the top division. Peter Kennedy became his first signing from Watford for £300,000 and was soon joined by Jason De Vos. Tony Dinning smashed the club's record transfer fee when he joined from Wolves for £750,000. Matt Jackson, John Filan and Gary Teale all came in before the turn of the year.

Jewell managed to steady the sinking ship and they worked their way up from second bottom in the division. A huge breakthrough for the club came on transfer deadline day on 28 March 2002. Nathan Ellington was brought in from Bristol Rovers for £1.2 million. Jason Jarrett also signed from Bury and Latics finished their first season under Jewell in 10th place.

If Jewell's first season was difficult, his second season at the helm was anything but, as Latics stormed to the Division Two Championship, claiming 100 points and smashing 16 club records. They finished in pole position with three games still to play. 'It's a fantastic achievement by everyone at the club,' Jewell said. 'We proved this season that we were head and shoulders above everyone else in the division and it's testament to the players for all the hard work they have put in.'

Wigan beat Crewe into first place by a whopping 14 points – to say it was a one-horse race for the top spot was the understatement of the season. They had chalked up 29 wins from their 46 games, losing just four games all season. The streets of

Wigan turned blue as the players paraded the Division Two trophy around the streets of Wigan. Thousands of supporters paid homage to their heroes, who had finally taken the club to the next level after years of heartache.

Wigan Athletic chairperson Caroline Molyneux, a season-ticket holder for 20 years, wept at their remarkable achievement. 'For the first time in the club's history, the atmosphere on the terraces was electric,' she said. It was a far cry from her early days of watching the club at Springfield Park. She said: 'When I went to watch them play as child I would bring my lucky rabbit along'. But the charm, like the side, was hopeless. 'At school I was the team's only supporter, wearing their shirt underneath my blouse. The ribbing was merciless. Then there was the time when I watched fans walk out of a game against Portsmouth dressed as funeral directors and carrying a coffin to mourn their team's relegation into the Fourth Division.'

Jason De Vos, who lifted the championship trophy aloft with Jewell, said: 'It's an amazing feeling – the best of my career. All the lads have been absolutely fantastic and it's a great honour to be the captain of such a great group of players.'

Jewell, never a man to rest on his laurels, wasn't content with making up the numbers in the newly named Championship (the old Division One). He was always striving for more and to eager to push his troops to the limit. He said: 'We move on to the next level and now we've got to do even better. We can't afford to be sitting round here thinking how well we've done, now we want to make our mark at the next level.'

Jewell knew he would need more fire power going into the Championship. Nathan Ellington, who had finished the promotion-winning season with 22 goals, underwent a shoulder operation before the end of the campaign. He wasn't ready in time for the new season, meaning Andy Liddell and Neil Roberts were handed the responsibility of leading the line.

On 5 September 2003, Jewell thought he'd made a breakthrough when he snapped up Geoff Horsfield for £1 million from Birmingham.Weeks before his arrival, Jason Roberts had infamously turned round at Stafford services on the M6 on his way to the JJB Stadium for a medical to go and sign for Portsmouth instead. Horsfield quickly settled into his new home, banging in seven goals in his opening 16 matches. But he was travelling to Christopher Park from Birmingham every day for training. After some work by his agent behind the scenes, Horsfield was soon off as he engineered a quick move to West Brom.

Following Roberts's initial Wigan snub, Whelan told the *Observer* he 'would never work with his agent ever again.' But after some sweet talking and a grovelling apology, uncle Cyrille Regis, Roberts's agent, was back on the phone to Jewell to try and set up another deal.

Roberts eventually arrived on 13 January 2004 for a club record fee of £1.4 million. His 34-second debut strike at Preston North End four days later to grab another club record may never be beaten. It was the third-fastest debut goal of all time.

Latics adjusted well to life in the Championship. From the start of September until the beginning of April they only slipped out of the top six three times. They looked firmly on course for a shot at the Premier League through the play-offs, but began to falter as the season reached boiling point.

At the start of April Latics were sitting comfortably in fourth spot and looked good for a top-six finish. They forced Gillingham to swallow a bitter pill with a 3–0

1993: Wigan relegated back to new Third Division.

1994: Finish 19th, their lowest ever League position.

1995: JJB Sports supremo and former Blackburn player Dave Whelan acquires club in February and immediately signals his intentions by signing the 'Three Amigos': Isidro Diaz, Jesus Seba and Roberto Martinez.

1996: Under John Deehan, Latics approach the final three games needing just a point to clinch a play-off place. They lost the lot and missed out.

1997: Record a 7–1 win over Scarborough, the biggest League triumph in the club's history.

1997: Wigan win promotion to Second Division, clinching the title on goals scored from Fulham after a 2–0 home win over Mansfield.

1999: Win the Auto Windscreens Shield, triumphing 1–0 over Millwall.

Jason Roberts celebrates with strike partner Nathan Ellington and the Latics fans after scoring 54 seconds into the game, the third-fastest debut goal ever.

1999: Play the final game at Springfield Park, a 1–1 draw with Manchester City in the Second Division play-off semi-final.
1999: Move into the fantastic JJB Stadium, built at a cost of £32 million, with Manchester United's treble-winners taking part in the opening game.
2000: Reach the play-off final and are just seven minutes away from promotion when Gillingham score twice to snatch a dramatic 3–2 win.
2001: Sell Roy Carroll to Manchester United for a club record £2 million. After just six weeks in charge, Steve Bruce quits as manager to join Crystal Palace. Former player Paul Jewell confirmed as replacement.
2002: Splash out a club record £1.2 million to sign Nathan Ellington from Bristol Rovers.
2003: With Jewell at the helm, Wigan storm to the Second Division title by an

win at the Priestfield Stadium – victory coming three days after the game was called off due to a frozen pitch, less than an hour before kick-off. A 2–0 defeat at Norwich did little to rock the boat as Jewell's side responded with a superb 3–0 home win against Cardiff to maintain their strong position.

As the pressure increased Latics buckled in their last four matches as they failed to claim another three points. Jason Roberts and Jason Jarrett both saw red at play-off hopefuls Crystal Palace in a 1–1 draw. Sunderland showed all their resistance at the JJB as they left happy with a 0–0 draw. The lack of fire power also told at the City Ground against mid-table Nottingham Forest. Without Roberts to partner Ellington Wigan didn't pose the same threat as the hosts scrambled to victory, courtesy of David Johnson's strike. The 11th defeat of the season left Latics in a precarious position – they would need to beat West Ham on the last day of the season to secure a top-six finish.

Wigan had the luxury of trying to accomplish the feat in front of their own fans and 9 May 2004 looked like it would be another party when Neil Roberts put Wigan

Latics celebrate their promotion to the Championship with an open-top bus ride around Wigan.

ahead in the 34th minute. But the 20,669 fans inside the stadium – a record to watch Latics at the JJB at the time – will never forget what happened in the last minute of the clash.

Michael Carrick's free-kick at the death was headed in by Brian Deane. The striker had gone the previous 15 games without finding the back of the net, but his seventh of the campaign saw Latics finish the season two points outside the play-off spots in seventh place. The Hammers were to be denied promotion to the Premiership as Neil Shipperley's strike saw Crystal Palace beat them in the play-off final to join Norwich and West Brom in the top flight. 'To lose it so late when we played so well is a kick in the teeth,' Jewell said. 'I felt people knocked us at the beginning of the season, saying we were relegation favourites, but we battered West Ham for 40 minutes. We just couldn't get a second with it happening so late – it just gets worse and worse. We know what the division's all about, where we need to improve. It doesn't necessarily follow that we will do well next season, just look at Nottingham Forest, they got in the play-offs last year.'

But the manager was confident that with the quality he had within his squad they would be capable of having another go at promotion. He didn't feel the need to make wholesale changes. Brazilian defender Emerson Thome was drafted in on a free transfer from Bolton and was followed by Gareth Whalley a month later from Cardiff. Peter Kennedy, Neil Roberts and Tony Dinning all left the club after playing successful roles in Wigan's emergence as a new force.

Any fear that Wigan might have suffered a huge hangover from their disappointments was well and truly wiped out when the 2004–05 season kicked off. Latics were in a determined mood. Desperate to make up for the previous year's agony, they literally took the division by storm. They won 11 of their opening 17 games – it took until November for them to come unstuck, when they were beaten 2–0 at home to Portsmouth. That was quickly forgotten as Jewell's men hit fierce rivals Preston for five at the JJB. They ended 2004 by losing their last three League games. But Wigan were still in a fabulous position and weren't thinking about the play-offs – they were targetting automatic promotion. The goals were flying in from the boots of Messers Ellington and Roberts. They were to finish the campaign with

incredible 14 points, amassing 100 points.

2004: **Despite being in the top six until the last minute of the last game, Wigan miss out on the play-offs as Brian Deane's late header earns West Ham a draw at the JJB Stadium.**

2005: **Club confirm a new JJB Stadium record crowd for a football match as 20,745 see Sunderland win 1–0 in the battle of the top two. Promoted to Premiership on 8 May after beating Reading 3–1.**

2006: **With Wigan sixth in the Premiership, they reach the Carling Cup Final by beating Arsenal on away goals. A 1–0 home win is followed by a dramatic 2–1 defeat at Highbury, where Jason Roberts scores in the dying stages to take Wigan through on away goals, to meet either Blackburn or Manchester United.**

Paul Jewell is soaked in champagne as he lifts the Division Two championship trophy.

45 goals between them. The Duke bagged 24 to his best mate's 21. Their fabulous run was to continue at the start of 2005 with a 2–0 win at Sheffield United which was followed by wins against Wolves and Rotherham.

But anything Latics were doing, Sunderland and Ipswich were able to match and it transpired that the race for the top two would be a three-horse affair. Latics met the Tractor Boys at home on 5 March. Ellington's 43rd-minute penalty gave Wigan some breathing space as the season entered its climax. But then their form took a turn for the worse, as first West Ham and then Sunderland won at the JJB and thoughts started to turn to the play-offs rather than first or second place. Jewell remained optimistic, saying: 'This is going to go down to the last game of the season. It's going to come down to who can hold their bottle.'

Latics responded with wins at Cardiff and Leicester. With three games to go they were hanging on to second place as the Black Cats claimed pole position. Any chance Wigan had of winning the Championship ended when they drew at home to Queen's Park Rangers. Preston's Brian O'Neil cancelled out McCulloch's opener in the penultimate game of the season to set up another tense finale on the last day of the season.

Second-placed Wigan were at home to Reading while Ipswich, who were third, travelled to Brighton. Both sides were locked on 84 points, but Latics had a far superior goal difference. 'This is the biggest game of the players' lives,' Jewell said. 'They may never get this close to getting to the Premier League ever again.'

Wigan were well on their way when McCulloch netted in the 18th minute and Roberts put the supporters in dreamland three minutes later when he doubled the lead. With five minutes to go, the Duke planted in a storming header. Steve Sidwell's 90th-minute goal was no more than a consolation – no one could stop the Latics bandwagon. Off into the top tier of English football – after 73 remarkable years.

Did you know?

Graeme Jones holds the record for the most Latics League goals scored in one season: he bagged 31 goals during the 1996–97 campaign.

Wigan's crowd of 27,526 against Hereford in the second round of the FA Cup in 1953 remains the highest attendance between two non-League sides, excluding Wembley finals.

Wigan Athletic had a mascot when they were elected to the Football League. Sammy Springfield was the name of the seal invented by Derek Fuller that featured on all their letterheads. The seal, though, never existed.

Andy Liddell is Wigan's record League goalscorer with 70. He bagged the strikes between 1998 and 2004.

Manchester United legend Bobby Charlton was manager at Latics for eight games. The former Springfield Park director took charge for the games in 1983. Apparently, he got his 1994 knighthood for something else.

Former Wigan boss Sir Bobby Charlton.

Mikhail Gorbachev was never a Wigan fan. The story started after Wigan played Metalist Kharkov, who had Gorbachev as one of their officials, and he was apparently so impressed he followed Latics' progress even when he became President of the Soviet Union. Nice story. But not true.

Wigan fan? Former Soviet Union president Mikhail Gorbachev.

Gary Walsh and Roy Carroll aren't the only 'keepers to have starred for both Wigan Athletic and Manchester United. John Connoughton, from Abram, and Orrell-raised David Gaskell also played for both clubs.

Between 1959 and 1961, Wigan Athletic were not the highest-placed football club in Wigan. Wigan Rovers, now members of the Wigan Amateur League, played in the Cheshire County League while Latics were then members of the Lancashire Combination.

Wigan chairman Dave Whelan had the chance to buy Manchester United in 1989. Former Red Devils chairman Martin Edwards offered him control of the club for just £10 million after Michael Knighton pulled out of negotiations. But Whelan decided it would have a negative effect on his JJB Sports empire and rejected the offer. In 2005 the Glazers' takeover was valued at more than £800 million.

Former Wigan striker Nathan Ellington's middle name is Levi-Fontaine.

Wigan were awarded the fastest penalty in the history of the Premier League against Sunderland on Saturday 27 August 2005. Jason Roberts was upended by Black Cats skipper Gary Breen and tucked away the resulting 12-second penalty. It was Wigan's first goal in the top flight and marked Roberts's 100th career League goal.

Jason Roberts recorded the third fastest-ever debut goal when he scored for Latics at Preston after just 34 seconds on Saturday 17 January 2004. That can only be bettered by Barry Jones of Notts County, who scored after six seconds in 1962. Bernard Evans netted after 25 seconds for Wrexham in 1954.

In the family... John Regis.

Former Olympic sprinter John Regis is Jason Roberts's cousin, while three of the Latics star's uncles – Cyrille Regis, Dave Regis and Otis Roberts – all played football to a high level.

Jimmy Bullard made his 100th consecutive League appearance for Latics against Millwall on 12 March 2005. He joined centurions Colin Methven (117), Jeff Wright (110), John Filan (109), Colin Greenall (103) and Tommy Gore (102). Bullard's run came to an end at Chelsea on Saturday 10 December 2005 when he bowed out on 123 consecutive League games.

Paul Jewell set a new Premier League record when he kept Bradford in the division with the lowest number of points – they stayed up with 36 on the board. West Brom beat that record, staying up in 2004–05 with 34 points.

Paul Jewell took Bradford up to the top flight in second place behind Sunderland and Ipswich were third – a mirror image of the top three when he was in charge at Latics at the end of the 2004–05 campaign. Bradford went up with 87 points and Latics amassed exactly the same number of points.

Jimmy Bullard took 42 attempts to complete Soccer AM's 10-yard golf bucket challenge – but the midfielder plays off an enviable handicap of just two and wants to become a professional golfer when he retires from football.

Latics joined six other north-west clubs in the top division in 2005, with neighbouring Manchester United, Manchester City, Liverpool, Everton, Bolton and Blackburn all within a 30-mile radius of the JJB Stadium. The last time there were seven north-west clubs in the top flight was in the 1963–64 season.

Wigan Athletic started off life playing in a cherry and white jersey. They switched to playing in blue, hoping for a change in luck, when they were knocked out of the Cheshire League.

Latics became the 39th different club to make it to the Premiership since it began in 1992. Of the teams who have been promoted, 47 percent have been relegated after one year and 53 percent have survived at least one season.

The four teams Wigan had never played in a competitive match as they began their Premier League campaign were: Manchester United, Arsenal, Tottenham and Charlton.

Latics made the best start to a Premiership season since 1994 after getting 13 points after seven games. Nottingham Forest managed 17 points at the same stage 11 years previously and finished third.

Wigan's run of six wins and a draw in October 2005 was only bettered by Juventus across the whole of Europe.

Lee McCulloch and Arjan De Zeeuw were the only two members of the team playing in the Premiership who were also in the side when Latics were beaten by lowly non-League outfit Canvey Island in the FA Cup on 17 November 2001 at the JJB Stadium. Steve McMillan was at the club, but missed the game.

George Best's last game in the Football League was against Wigan. He played for Bournemouth aged 38 on 7 May 1983 in a Division Three game at Dean Court. The sides drew 2–2 and David Lowe and Alex Cribley played for Latics.

Wigan link – George Best.

Winger Keith Gillespie, famous for his stints at Manchester United, Newcastle and Blackburn, played 17 times for Wigan during two loan spells, in 1993 and 2000.

The only player to turn out for Latics in the League with a surname beginning with the letter 'Y' was David Young. The Mossley-born midfielder played three times for the club in the 1982–83 season.

Kevin Langley holds the record for the most League appearances for Latics. The midfielder had two spells at the club from 1981 to 1986 and from 1990 to 1994. He made 317 League appearances and 394 in total.

Latics smashed 15 club records on their way to the Second Division title in 2003. They were: highest-ever attendance at the JJB Stadium (16,922), highest average home League attendance (11,500), most points in a season (100), most wins in a season (29), most consecutive League wins (12), most consecutive away wins (five), best start to a season (four consecutive wins), most games without conceding a goal (four), most clean sheets in a season (29), least goals conceded in a season (25), least defeats in a season (four), least away goals conceded in a season (nine), least away defeats in a season (two), most players in PFA team of the season (five) and reaching the quarter-finals of the Worthington Cup.

No Wigan player has won an England cap but David Thompson went close when he was called up by Sven-Goran Eriksson in 2003 while at Blackburn. However, he failed to make it onto the pitch.

Roy Carroll has won the most caps while starring for Wigan. He got nine caps for Northern Ireland during his four-and-a-half years at Latics.

Jason De Vos and Archie Gemmill are the most capped players to have pulled on the Latics shirt. They won 43 caps for Canada and Scotland respectively.

12: January: Gone Shopping

Wigan boss Paul Jewell meets his predecessor and current Birmingham manager Steve Bruce ahead of kick-off at St Andrew's.

THERE was little New Year cheer for Latics as they began 2006 with a disappointing defeat at Birmingham.

Despite the convincing 3–0 loss at home to Blackburn two days earlier, Wigan's weary squad made the trip to the Midlands with the prospect of completing a productive festive period. Three points would have meant they'd taken nine from a possible 12 and Jewell handed four players the chance to cement their place in the starting 11 as he rang the changes. Josip Skoko, David Wright and Damien Francis were all given rare starts, while Stephane Henchoz was drafted back in at centre-back following an exhausting Christmas schedule.

Latics sat comfortably in fifth place but it was second-bottom Birmingham who looked more like the side who were pushing for Europe. Soft goals by Jermaine Pennant and Mario Melchiot saw Steve Bruce's side record a 2–0 win – and Jewell subsequently saw red over his side's inept display. 'I can't tell you what I really want to say because I'm really, really angry and I'm best keeping a lid on it,' he fumed. 'We didn't have enough fight and that's the most important thing, I can take getting beaten if my team goes down fighting.

'We did some silly things. I would rather players stick their head in the box and be brave rather than give silly fouls away and get yellow cards. It's childish – it was immature football at times. We had people in good areas, but then we'd kick and push players when their backs were turned – it's crazy.

'We didn't stop crosses or defend set pieces – all the things we were doing to get us into the top half of the division. Suddenly we started to think those things weren't important. I told them to have a right go at them in the second half, but we didn't even have a shot on target.'

Skoko registered Wigan's only shot in the 25th minute, though his 20-yard effort caused little trouble.

Though Wigan had suffered heavier defeats this season, this was their poorest performance, and confirmed Jewell's suspicions that he would need to use the transfer window to bolster his squad. Rotating his side from the existing talent pool did not pay the dividends he expected. 'I wanted to freshen it up because we've had a lot of players who have played a lot of games,' Jewell explained. 'So I decided to change it to give us a bit of spark, but it just didn't work. The players didn't look up for it and that's amazing. We haven't created any chances in the last two games and the hardest thing to do in the Premier League is to score goals. That isn't having a go at the forward-thinking players but at the whole team.'

Henri Camara is pulled back for offside during a frustrating match against Birmingham.

The performance was out of character for Latics, who had set the Premiership alight during the first half of the season with their unreserved attacking play. If the referee had pointed to the penalty spot after five minutes, when Kenny Cunningham looked to have pulled over Jason Roberts, then it could have been a different story, but ultimately they got what they deserved.

The nature of both Birmingham goals also upset Jewell. Pennant was presented with a free header at the far post on 20 minutes while Melchiot grabbed the second 13 minutes later after the Wigan defence failed to clear an innocuous corner.

Despite their heady position in the top flight a furious Jewell threatened to wield the axe after the Birmingham defeat. As the January transfer window was flung open, the Latics boss warned his players that he wouldn't hesitate to make 'drastic' changes.

'If you don't act and address the reasons why it's happening you can soon find yourself on the slide,' said Jewell, who put the complacency down to too many of

Monday 2 January 2006

Birmingham 2 Wigan Athletic 0

BIRMINGHAM: Taylor 6, Melchiot 7, Upson 8, Cunningham 8, Lazaridis 7, Pennant 9, Izzet 8, Johnson 7, Gray 7, Heskey 7, Jarosik 7. Subs: Taylor 7 (for Melchiot 45), Pandiani (for Jarosik 74), Kilkenny (for Izzet 84).

WIGAN: Pollitt 6, Chimbonda 6, Henchoz 6, De Zeeuw 7, Wright 5, Bullard 6, Francis 5, Skoko 5, McCulloch 6, Roberts 6, Camara 6. Subs: Teale 6 (for Skoko 45), Connolly (for McCulloch 71), Kavanagh (for Bullard 73). Wigan star man: De Zeeuw.

Goals: Pennant (20), Melchiot (33)
Half-time: 2–0
Referee: Peter Walton
Attendance: 29,189

What the opposition said...

'It was a vital result for us against a team who have been playing ever so well this season. These are games you have to try and take points from. The players were fabulous under difficult conditions and this was a massive result for us. There's no reason why we can't get out of the situation we're in and a result like this will give everyone a lift.' – Birmingham's assistant manager Eric Black.

What the Wigan fan said...

'We couldn't complain with the outcome. We never looked liked scoring and our defending was a bit dodgy, which allowed Birmingham to score two easy goals. We have to work hard to win games and it's difficult to maintain such a high standard at such an intense period of the season.' – Wigan Athletic chairperson Caroline Molyneux.

Former Wigan favourite Nathan Ellington returned to the JJB Stadium in West Brom's colours.

Paul Scharner trains with his new teammates.

Reto Ziegler arriving for training at Christopher Park.

	P	W	D	L	F	A	Pts
Chelsea	21	19	1	1	46	10	58
Man Utd	20	13	5	2	40	17	44
Liverpool	19	12	5	2	28	11	41
Tottenham	20	10	7	3	29	18	37
Wigan	21	11	1	9	25	26	34
Arsenal	19	10	3	6	27	15	33
Bolton	19	9	5	5	25	20	32
Blackburn	20	9	3	8	26	25	30
Man City	20	8	4	8	27	22	28
West Ham	21	7	5	9	27	30	26
Newcastle	20	7	5	8	20	23	26
Aston Villa	21	6	7	8	25	30	25
Charlton	19	8	1	10	24	30	25
Fulham	21	6	5	10	25	30	23
Everton	21	7	2	12	14	31	23
Middlesb'h	20	5	7	8	25	30	22
West Brom	21	5	4	12	20	31	19
Portsm'th	21	4	5	12	16	33	17
Birm'ham	20	4	4	12	15	29	16
Sunderl'd	20	1	3	16	15	38	6

his players believing the media hype. 'No one playing for Wigan is guaranteed of his place. It doesn't matter if they're the fans' favourites, I don't care who they are, if they continue to play like that they won't get in the team. I'm not going to accept it. Everyone has a bad day at the office, but I don't like too many of them.'

Top of Jewell's wish list was a striker and his chase for one was stepped up after he lost Henri Camara to the African Nations Cup. As Latics prepared to face Leeds United in the FA Cup, Camara was basking in the Egyptian sun having met up with his Senegalese teammates.

Wigan appeared to have put the Birmingham defeat behind them with an improved display in the Cup but needed a replay to beat Leeds after being pegged back by a late goal.

During a two-week break from League action – in which Wigan also beat Arsenal 1–0 in the first leg of the Carling Cup semi-final – all attention turned to transfer dealings. The club was linked with Norwich's Dean Ashton and Auxerre frontman Mwaruwari Benjani, while new recruit Paul Scharner arrived in Wigan following his £2.5 million switch from Brann Bergen. The amiable Austrian had bleached a blue and white stripe into his hair to celebrate the move.

The 25-year-old, who left David Wright on crutches after a bone-crunching

The Baggies' Darren Moore and Ronnie Wallwork combine to deny Jason Roberts.

tackle in his first training session, said: 'It has always been a dream for me to play in the Premier League. I am confident I can play in this division. Wigan are a good team and I want to help them hold their position in the table. I want to help them into Europe – that's a big goal.'

Another Latics defender enjoyed signing a contract at the JJB after an extension clause was activated by Arjan De Zeeuw's 19th League appearance of the season at Birmingham. 'I signed a contract for a year in the summer with the option of a further year,' revealed the happy Dutchman. 'I've always said if I feel fit and I'm not starting to annoy myself I will carry on as long as possible. I've been happy with how things have gone so far – this has been a great move for me.'

While Jewell was scouring the transfer market, his chairman Dave Whelan was making more headlines by calling for England coach Sven-Goran Eriksson to be sacked after the *News of the World*'s 'fake Sheikh' scandal. He suggested that his own manager or Manchester City boss Stuart Pearce should take over the national side, saying: 'The FA have grounds in my view for sacking Eriksson. You simply do not expect the England manager to openly discuss his future plans and to air his views about what he thinks about players in his squad. If it was up to me, I'd say goodbye to him and bring in City's Stuart Pearce and Paul Jewell. What a team they would be.' But Jewell would not be drawn on the mounting speculation while Pearce dismissed the suggestion as embarrassing.

The pre-match build-up to the clash with strugglers West Brom centred on the return of former fans' favourite and top goalscorer for three consecutive seasons, Nathan Ellington.

The Duke made a surprise £3 million move to the Hawthorns on the eve of the

Sunday 15 January 2006

Wigan Athletic 0 West Brom 1

WIGAN: Pollitt 7, Chimbonda 6, De Zeeuw 8, Henchoz 8, Baines 8, Teale 8, Kavanagh 8, Scharner 7, Bullard 6, McCulloch 6, Roberts 7. Sub: Johannson (for Baines 80). Wigan star man: Teale.

WEST BROM: Kuszczak 9, Watson 7, Davies 7, Moore 5, Robinson 5, Greening 6, Wallwork 7, Inamoto 7, Carter 7, Ellington 6, Campbell 7. Subs: Albrechtsen 8 (for Ellington 44), Earnshaw (for Campbell 79).

Goal: Albrechtsen (56)
Half-time: 0–0
Referee: Martin Atkinson
Attendance: 17,421

	P	W	D	L	F	A	Pts
Chelsea	22	20	1	1	48	11	61
Man Utd	22	13	6	3	41	20	45
Liverpool	20	13	5	2	29	11	44
Tottenham	22	11	7	4	31	19	40
Arsenal	21	11	4	6	34	15	37
Wigan	22	11	1	10	25	27	34
Bolton	20	9	6	5	25	20	33
Man City	22	9	4	9	30	25	31
Blackburn	21	9	4	8	26	25	31
West Ham	22	8	5	9	29	31	29
Charlton	20	9	1	10	26	30	28
Fulham	22	7	5	10	26	30	26
Newcastle	21	7	5	9	20	24	26
Everton	22	8	2	12	15	31	26
Aston Villa	22	6	7	9	26	32	25
West Brom	22	6	4	12	21	31	22
Middlesb'h	21	5	7	9	25	37	22
Portsm'th	22	4	5	13	16	34	17
Birm'ham	21	4	4	13	15	31	16
Sunderl'd	21	1	3	17	16	40	6

Premiership season and faced chants of 'Judas' when Wigan beat the Baggies 2–1 away earlier in the season. 'It will be weird going back,' he said philosophically. 'And I'm sure the supporters will give me a hard time, but I expect that and I've got to deal with it. I suppose it is part of football.'

But Ellington didn't steal the spotlight, it was the name of West Brom's Polish keeper Tomasz Kuszczak that was on the lips of every Latics fan as they trudged home following a surprise 1–0 home defeat. He pulled off an outstanding save at full stretch to deny Jason Roberts at the back-post in the 90th minute when it looked like the Grenadan international was certain to rescue a point. 'It was an amazing save – it looked like it was in,' said a frustrated Jewell. 'But we've got to do better than going all the way until the end before the 'keeper has got to make a save. Chances like that were few and far between. We had plenty of opportunities. Gary Teale did ever so well in the second half with a constant supply.'

Pascal Chimbonda searches for inspiration during Wigan's defeat by West Brom.

Latics laid siege to the visitors' goal after falling behind to a well-taken strike from right-back Martin Albrechtsen. After dominating the first half Jewell's men looked certain to go and claim all three points, but the sending off of West Brom's Darren Moore changed the game. The burly centre-back received two justified yellows for malicious fouls on McCulloch and Roberts, but instead of spurring Wigan on to victory it inspired the Baggies.

To the delight of the home crowd, Ellington was sacrificed to make way for Albrechtsen, who 12 minutes later latched on to a ball from Ronnie Wallwork in his own half. He cut into the box and fired past Mike Pollitt at the near post. That signalled a West Brom retreat and despite firing in 24 attempts at goal Latics couldn't bag the equaliser they deserved – they'd gone five hours and 15 minutes without a goal in the Premiership.

Despite the defeat, Wigan were still in sixth place and just six points off a Champions' League spot but Jewell was worried that his side was starting to wane. 'I said to the players at half-time: "If we aren't going to win the game we've got to make sure we don't lose it". I told them not to play in the wrong areas – sometimes they think they are better than they are,' he says. 'We've got to learn to start drawing games if we're not going to win them. After coming up to this division and having some success, if you start to think this game is easy it will hurt you – especially at this level. We've got to get back to what we're good at, which is a team of honest endeavour, full of energy and that looks a threat.'

Wigan Athletic's resilience and fighting spirit were put to the test again as they faced three games in a week. Following three straight League defeats, the quality of Jewell's team was being questioned... and they were to answer the detractors in fine style.

The boss held a training ground meeting in an attempt to rekindle the spark which had made Wigan into one of the teams of the season. He challenged his players to address the faults and unearth the root of their problems. 'They've said that there's so much more right here than wrong,' revealed Jewell. 'And that's a great point. It wasn't a crisis meeting – we just sat down and had a chat. I wanted the players to tell me why they've been flat of late.'

What the opposition said...

'You need everyone to contribute in games like this and Tomasz pulled off a marvellous save at the end. It's a situation you don't want to go through too often, but the players come out of it with a lot of credit. The circumstances asked questions of our character and belief and they can take a lot of positives from the game.' – West Brom assistant manager Nigel Pearson.

What the Wigan fan said...

'It would be unfair to say we shouldn't have got something out of the game. But I can't take anything away from how West Brom defended in the second half, the goalkeeper was outstanding and the 10-man defence scrapped heroically to stop us from scoring.' – fan Jason Taylor.

David Thompson and Neil Mellor both made goalscoring debuts against Middlesbrough.

Stephane Henchoz gets above Ugo Ehiogu at The Riverside.

Saturday 21 January 2006

Middlesbrough 2
Wigan Athletic 3

MIDDLESBROUGH: Jones 6, Bates 5, Riggott 5, Southgate 6, Pogatetz 6, Parnaby 6, Parlour 6, Cattermole 6, Downing 7, Viduka 5, Yakubu 6. Subs: Ehiogu 7 (for Riggott 27), Johnson 6 (for Bates 32), Hasselbaink 7 (for Viduka 45).

WIGAN: Pollitt 7, Chimbonda 7, Scharner 7, Henchoz 7, Baines 8, Teale 8, Kavanagh 8, Bullard 7, Thompson 8, Roberts 8, Mellor 8. Subs: Johansson (for Thompson 90). Wigan star man: Thompson.

Goals: Roberts (2), Thompson (29), Hasselbaink (56), Yakubu (66), Mellor (90)
Half-time: 0–2
Referee: Andre Marriner
Attendance: 27,208

What the opposition said...

'These are testing times for everyone at the football club. We have simply got to stick together and we must not panic. There are still a lot of games to play this season and we are determined to put things right. We're in a battle and we have to fight our way out of it.' – 'Boro boss Steve McClaren.

With only 24 players at his disposal, Jewell brought in three new players. David Thompson arrived from Blackburn while Reto Ziegler and Neil Mellor both signed on loan deals from Tottenham and Liverpool respectively. A deal to bring Southampton's Neil McCann fell through.

Jewell was still without Camara – who scored in Senegal's opening African Nations Cup game – while McCulloch was ruled out for a month after undergoing a double hernia operation. The bare-boned squad beat Leeds United on penalties in the FA Cup third-round replay before travelling north to the Riverside to face Middlesbrough.

Steve McClaren's side were languishing in 17th spot after a 7–0 drubbing at the hands of Arsenal the previous week and hadn't won in eight League games. But having beaten both Arsenal and Manchester United at home earlier in the season, 'Boro were to be no easy ride for the new-look Latics.

Both Thompson and Mellor made their debuts on a clear, crisp day in the North East, and what debuts they were! Linking up superbly with Jason Roberts, the duo ran the hosts ragged in the first half and Wigan were ahead within two minutes.

The Grenadan, whose game was transformed after taking on the responsibility of the captain's armband, smashed the ball past a hapless Brad Jones to break the temporary goal drought. Wigan began to dominate and grabbed a deserved second when the devastating Gary Teale broke down the right to latch on to a Mellor pass to cross for Thompson. The energetic scouser nodded the ball home neatly for a 2–0 lead.

Latics dropped off in the second half and looked to have thrown away three vital points when Jimmy Floyd Hasselbaink pulled one back before Yakubu levelled. However, the ecstatic home fans hadn't counted on Mellor. With one last throw of the dice, Roberts flicked on a Jimmy Bullard cross which fell invitingly for the 23-year-old to pounce and earn maximum points... and a pile-on from his teammates.

'It was special to get the last-minute winner,' smiled Mellor, whose career at Anfield momentarily peaked with a breathtaking goal against Arsenal in 2004, but had never climbed to such dizzy heights since. 'Paul Jewell asked me before the game to score the winner, so I did. When I got the goal everyone jumped on top of me, which shows you what a good team spirit Wigan have. I've been out for a long time through injury and I'm just pleased that the gaffer here has gambled and taken a chance with me. Hopefully I can repay him with some more goals and some more wins. There were a couple of offers for me. But once I knew the gaffer here, who is a young English manager, was in for me, I was keen to come here. A lot of people speak highly of him and I want to learn some things from him. It's the perfect start for me.'

His former Liverpool teammate Thompson was also enjoying himself at the JJB, having taken a pay-cut to earn first-team football. 'This is a great opportunity for me to try and kick-start my career. It was promising at one stage, but then it seemed to hit the rocks due to injury,' admitted the 28-year-old. 'But now I've been fit for a long time, I just wasn't getting a game at Blackburn. I hadn't played for a long time before the game at Middlesbrough and that's all I want to do now. The manager hasn't asked me to go out and impress him. He knows what kind of player I am – he's just asked me to go out there and play. The team spirit here is absolutely amazing. Team spirit can sometimes out-perform ability. I'm not saying that these

The players celebrate a stunning win at Middlesbrough.

lads haven't got ability because they definitely have. But the team spirit at the club is worth an extra 10 or 15 points this season.'

Wigan's two new boys followed in a long line of 26 other players including Paul Scharner, Jason Roberts, Nathan Ellington and Geoff Horsfield, who all managed to score on their Latics debuts.

Latics took a break from the Premiership and enjoyed contrasting fortunes in the domestic cup competitions. The highs of Highbury – when Roberts's last-gasp extra-time goal saw them through to the Carling Cup Final – were followed by the misery of Manchester City, who dumped Wigan out of the FA Cup with a 1–0 win. But there was no time to reflect as the end of January approached and Wiganers awaited the arrival of Everton at the JJB Stadium. They'd enjoyed a glorious day out at Goodison Park early on in the season when Damien Francis secured a memorable 1–0 win, but David Moyes's side were a different proposition come 2006.

More than 20,000, including a sold-out Everton contingent which saw dozens of away fans scattered through the home end, filed through the turnstiles on a cold winter's night.

David Thompson's dream start to his Wigan career at Middlesbrough was a distant memory when on nine minutes he inadvertently put the ball past a stranded Mike Pollitt while attempting to tackle Up Holland-raised Leon Osman. The goal stunned the home crowd and Latics almost went two down when Pollitt saved from James McFadden before they took a hold of the game.

Stephane Henchoz's punt forward was met by the familiar sight of Pascal Chimbonda charging in round the back of the defence to keep the ball alive. He headed across the box for Scharner and from close-range he sent a well-taken volley flying past Richard Wright.

Wigan edged the second half with substitute Reto Ziegler impressing and the returning Arjan De Zeeuw settling back into the side after three games out. The game looked set to peter out until the arrival of big Duncan Ferguson late on. After just seven minutes on the pitch, the notorious Scot bizarrely punched Scharner in the stomach and earned a straight red from referee Mike Dean.

What the Wigan fan said...

'Thompson and Mellor are two good additions to the squad; they both offer pace and power going forward. The Riverside is a nice ground and there was a really good atmosphere with us in full voice throughout. All in all it's looking very good.' – East Stand season-ticket holder Stuart Waterworth.

	P	W	D	L	F	A	Pts
Chelsea	23	20	2	1	49	12	62
Man Utd	23	14	6	3	42	20	48
Liverpool	21	13	5	3	29	12	44
Tottenham	23	11	8	4	31	19	41
Arsenal	22	11	4	7	34	16	37
Wigan	23	12	1	10	28	29	37
Bolton	21	10	6	5	27	20	36
Blackburn	22	10	4	8	27	25	34
West Ham	23	9	5	9	31	32	32
Man City	23	9	4	10	30	27	31
Charlton	21	9	2	10	27	31	29
Everton	23	9	2	12	16	31	29
Fulham	23	7	5	11	27	32	26
Newcastle	22	7	5	10	20	25	26
Aston Villa	23	6	8	9	26	32	26
West Brom	23	6	4	13	21	32	22
Middlesb'h	22	5	7	10	27	40	22
Birm'ham	22	5	4	13	20	31	19
Portsm'th	23	4	5	14	16	39	17
Sunderl'd	22	2	3	17	17	40	9

Reto Ziegler tussles with Alan Stubbs of Everton.

Everton's infamous striker Duncan Ferguson leaves the field after being sent off for punching Paul Scharner.

Tuesday 31 January 2006

Wigan Athletic 1 Everton 1

WIGAN: Pollitt 6, Chimbonda 7, De Zeeuw 7, Henchoz 6, Baines 7, Teale 7, Scharner 7, Bullard 6, Thompson 6, Mellor 6, Roberts 7. Subs: Ziegler 6 (for Thompson 45). Wigan star man: Paul Scharner.

EVERTON: Wright 6, Hibbert 7, Weir 7, Stubbs 7, Valente 6, Osman 7, Arteta 7, Neville 6, Kilbane 6, Cahill 7, McFadden 7. Subs: Ferguson (for Arteta 73).

Goals: Thompson (og, 9), Scharner (45)
Half-time: 1–1
Referee: Mike Dean
Attendance: 21,731

What the opposition said...

'I thought, in the first half, we played well enough at times. We never gave Wigan any opportunities until late on, and then their goal came from a stupid free-kick. Instead of us being 1–0 up at the break, we went in one each, and that only adds to the frustration.' – Everton manager David Moyes.

With some 10 minutes remaining Wigan pushed for a winner against the 10 men, but any hopes of three points were dashed by Dean. He sent Roberts off for an elbow against David Weir and ensured that he was the centre of every post-match pub debate. His dismissal meant Wigan were left facing a striker crisis. But Jewell was in philosophical mood. 'It was irresponsible of Jason, his elbow was up there and he's got to learn not to do that,' he said. 'But I know he's not a malicious type of player. If someone as big and as strong as Jason is wants to elbow you, you wouldn't get up – their trainer didn't need to come on.'

But Weir refused to exonerate Roberts following the explosive finale to the stalemate which put his appearance in the Carling Cup Final in doubt. Luckily the Spurs game had been rearranged, ensuring the striker would be available for Cardiff, but that didn't stop the double red card debate raging. 'I got caught on the jaw. That's all I know,' said Weir. 'It doesn't matter to me whether it was accidental, he has caught me and that's the end of the story as far as I'm concerned.'

Meanwhile, David Moyes was fuming with Ferguson and Weir revealed that the Scot hadn't apologised to his teammates. 'He hasn't mentioned it,' he said. 'Maybe we deserved to come away with a little bit more, but we can't be too disappointed.'

The point was enough to send Wigan above Arsenal into fifth and just two points off a Champions League spot with little more than three months to go.

Mike's incredible journey

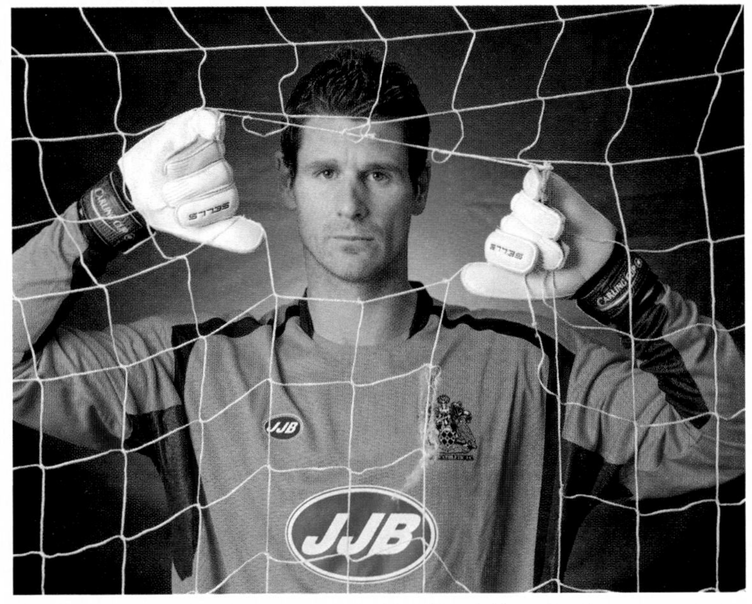

Mike Pollitt was thrust into the spotlight after his Highbury heroics.

BOLTON funnyman Peter Kay had a sketch in which he held his arms out like a plane and pronounces 'this time next week' with a nod and a wink in expectation of his holidays. But when Latics' Bolton-bred keeper Mike Pollitt looked back on his equivalent of 'this time last year', it was more of an arms-folded, eye-rolling nightmare in expectation of impending doom.

Stuck between Rotherham's posts, rooted to the bottom of the League, and heading for Football League One faster than Lee Bowyer travelled to Newcastle's training ground, Pollitt's future looked bleak. 'At Christmas 2004, we had only won one game,' he reflects. 'It was difficult week in, week out. We knew it was going to be very difficult to stay in the League. Obviously I knew that if I was going to get the opportunity to get away, I had to keep playing well – I was getting plenty to do. You put a brave face on things at the time and keep saying "we're not down yet" then the manager got the sack as well. In the back of the mind, you knew it was always going to be difficult. We won on Boxing Day and that took us to six points.'

One year on, and life in the Pollitt household couldn't be more different. His days as a goalkeeping journeyman firmly behind him – 12 clubs in 15 years since he started out as a trainee at Manchester United, more of which later – meant life was settled. 'Signing for Wigan wasn't a hard decision,' he smiled. 'Moving around here, there and everywhere a few years ago, it was hard times for me and my wife, Emma, but it's nice to come through them. Now we are settled back at home in Bolton and it's great to be in the Premiership.'

Several months into the season and not only had he established

Arjan De Zeeuw has words with Jason Roberts after he was red carded against Everton.

What the Wigan fan said...

'Overall a point was probably a fair result but if one team wanted to win it then it was Wigan. Ferguson's red was totally justified but Roberts could have some argument because Weir looked like he walked on to the elbow more than Roberts flung it back.' – East Stand season-ticket holder Chris O'Neill.

	P	W	D	L	F	A	Pts
Chelsea	23	20	2	1	49	12	62
Man Utd	23	14	6	3	42	20	48
Liverpool	21	13	5	3	29	12	44
Tottenham	24	11	8	5	31	20	41
Wigan	24	12	2	10	29	30	38
Arsenal	22	11	4	7	34	16	37
Bolton	21	10	6	5	27	20	36
Blackburn	22	10	4	8	27	25	34
West Ham	23	9	5	9	31	32	32
Man City	23	9	4	10	30	27	31
Charlton	22	9	3	10	27	31	30
Everton	24	9	3	12	17	32	30
Fulham	24	8	5	11	28	32	29
Newcastle	22	7	5	10	20	25	26
Aston Villa	23	6	8	9	26	32	26
Middlesb'h	23	6	7	10	30	40	25
West Brom	24	6	5	13	21	32	23
Birm'ham	22	5	4	13	20	31	19
Portsm'th	23	4	5	14	16	39	17
Sunderl'd	23	2	3	18	17	43	9

Mike Pollitt applauds the Latics fans.

himself as the number one, but the Wigan fans began to wryly chant: 'Pollitt for England', then 'England's number one.' He smiled: 'Playing in the Premiership and doing well, it's nice that the fans give you some encouragement. I've been quite pleased with my form. I thought my chance of playing in the Premiership had passed by. But I got this opportunity and we reached the final of a major trophy as well. I'm quite pleased with what's happened to me this year, it's been a good year. Hopefully I can stay in the side and go on to better things. I've always believed in my own ability, I've got the chance now to prove a few of my doubters wrong.'

Although his chances of a national call-up may have been more of the terraces poking a collective tongue into a cheek than a serious plea to Sven-Goran Eriksson, it underlined how Pollitt had rapidly become a massive fans' favourite at the JJB. A series of top-class saves in matches against Charlton Athletic, Manchester United and Bolton Wanderers while John Filan was injured cemented his place in the side and made him another of Latics' heroes in a season full of gallantry.

It sounded daft to say at the time, but the tip-top quality of his performances could probably be traced to a howler against Liverpool on 3 December. Pollitt was caught off-guard when an ambitious punt from that previously luckless lug Peter Crouch took a cruel deflection off Leighton Baines, and the looping ball was palmed into, rather than over, the net by the Wigan 'keeper. Pollitt's blushes were magnified as the goal ended Crouch's lengthy barren spell and led to endless TV replays.

Those video highlights, and the subsequent newspaper reports, failed to mention that Latics' stopper had redeemed himself by full-time with a string of world-class saves. 'I got a bit of stick over that as you'd expect, mostly from the press, it was just one of those freak things that happened,' admitted Pollitt. 'I could do that a thousand times in training and it probably wouldn't happen again, but it happened in front of 40-odd thousand people. I put it behind me and I thought I did okay after that. It does affect you, you do dwell on it over the weekend, but I think the more games you play, you can put it behind you.'

Pollitt's ongoing battle with Australian John Filan for the starting spot has not dampened the spirit between them. 'You can never rest on your laurels,' he says, shifting from one relaxed position to another in his press room seat. John's a fantastic goalkeeper, he's done well for the club in the three or four seasons he's been here. There's been competition all over the park and the goalkeepers are no different. I've never taken playing every week for granted.'

While many clubs failed to be satisfied with their first choice goalkeeper (Sunderland's Kelvin Davies anyone?), Wigan could count themselves fortunate to have two tip-top stoppers. 'There are no "big time Charlies" here – we all work for each other,' says Polly. 'The manager keeps our feet on the ground and seems to have a magic wand. Everything he's done this year has come up trumps and everybody's in it together, so hopefully we can continue that.'

Just how far he had come was reflected in a little tale he recounted about his time at Manchester United.

'Polly, get yersel' over here.' Alex Ferguson was trundling over the pitches at Manchester United's Cliff training ground towards the youth team. The United manager was short of a goalkeeper as he prepared an 11 against 11 match with his first-team squad to finish the day's gruelling session. Gary Walsh and Mark Bosnich were away with the reserves and Fergie needed someone to go between the sticks for the game to go ahead.

It was the autumn of 1989.

Young Mike Pollitt was minding his own business, but when the fiery Scot's voice piped up over in his direction, the 'keeper's heart began to race. It wasn't as much an invitation, as an instruction. Pollitt duly obliged, and took his place minutes before top-flight strikers Mark Hughes and Brian McClair fired rockets at him. Just a couple of years earlier, the Farnworth-born teenager had been playing for Bolton Schools, where he was spotted by United scout George Knight.

'I remember those days when I used to get over and train with the first team as a 16 and 17-year-old like yesterday,' Pollitt reflected. 'I was one of those cheeky little apprentices and Fergie quite liked that. I got on really well with him. It was a great experience and a good grounding for me. I would never have got that anywhere else. Jim Leighton was the first-team 'keeper there at the time, Les Sealey came later on and Bosnich and Gary Walsh were there. But sometimes they were away with the reserves and the first team only had one 'keeper training and he used to shout me over. It was a fantastic experience playing in training with the likes of Mark Hughes, Bryan Robson and Steve Bruce.'

Pollitt played for three years at United, between 1988 and 1991. Two years as an apprentice and one year as a professional. He never played for the reserves, but was a regular in their 'A' and 'B' sides on Saturday mornings in the Lancashire League.

His debut at the Theatre of Dreams came as a 15-year-old in the Youth Cup Final against Mansfield after the regular 'keeper was struck down by injury. 'We lost the game 2–1,' he said. 'But I'll always remember walking out to play at Old Trafford as a teenager.'

Time was called on his career with the Red Devils when Bury came calling. Pollitt said: 'It was just before they started to win everything that I left in 1991 when Peter Schmeichel came. I went to Bury, then had two years at Lincoln, played for Darlington, Notts County, Sunderland and Rotherham and various clubs on loan in between.'

But the wheel turned full circle for Pollitt when he faced his first club in the Carling Cup Final. And that appearance was in no small part due to his inspired performance at Highbury in the semi-final. A Jose Reyes penalty save was one of a catalogue of stunning stops to help book Wigan's place in the last phase of the competition. 'When you make an early penalty save like I did it gives you a lot of confidence,' Pollitt said. 'If they had scored that they may have kicked on and got a few more, so it was quite an important save. Psychologically, keeping the penalty out gave the lads a lift as well.'

'Mike gave a world-class performance,' enthused chairman Dave Whelan in the triumphant aftermath. 'He was absolutely wonderful. He had a nightmare at Middlesbrough (the previous game) and I was a bit surprised when I saw Mike was in the side, but that's Paul Jewell. He has faith in his players, he stands by them and he's very loyal to them. He was very loyal to Mike at Highbury and my word, did he repay his loyalty.'

And Pollitt's performance prompted a thoughtful Sir Alex Ferguson to wonder whether he might have made a mistake releasing him from United's books. 'I watched the other semi-final with some friends and I had told them I had let Pollitt go,' Ferguson recalled. 'After he made several saves, one of them looked at me and said, "Are you sure you did the right thing?"'

But this was one Wigan fairytale not to have a happy ending. It would be final heartbreak for Pollitt. After just three minutes of the Cardiff showpiece – an event he had waited his whole career for – he bent down to collect a regulation through ball on the edge of the six-yard area and – twang. His hamstring had gone.

As Pollitt was applauded off the field, teary eyes shielded by a massive glove, the sympathy of

Wigan's goalkeeper Mike Pollitt saves a penalty from Arsenal's Jose Antonio Reyes during the Carling Cup semi-final second leg match at Highbury.

69,000 people, red or blue went with him. His manager Paul Jewell summed it up: 'I felt sorry for Polly. He has played most of his career in the lower leagues and then when he has a big day like this he does his hamstring after two minutes, which is so unlucky.'

Despite the disappointment and following weeks spent on the sidelines, watching John Filan recapture some fine form before his chance came again, the big Boltonian remained stoical about his year. 'It's been a funny career but I'm having a bit of an Indian summer now – playing in the Premiership and getting to the Cup Final,' he said. 'Considering we were told we were down before we started and weren't given a chance – we were going to be down by Christmas – I think we've proved a lot of people wrong.'

Pollitt was including himself in that sentence – a jibe not only at those pundits who wrote Wigan off before a ball had been kicked, but also at those who had supposed he wasn't good enough at the highest level. His comments also reveal everything you need to know about what was driving Paul Jewell's side. Their survival push and League form was not dulled by a major Cup Final, nor did their season end raggedly after the defeat. Wigan and Mike Pollitt would continue to confound the critics. Time and time again.

13: On the Road

FROM the highs of Highbury to the perils of Arab TV, Latics fan and Wigan journalist Phil O'Brien takes an irreverent look at life on the road with Wigan Athletic as he follows his hometown club during their first season in the Premiership...

'THE RUGBY aren't playing today lads,' shouted a Mancunian voice from the back of the bus. We were on our way to watch Latics at the City of Manchester Stadium, and had just encountered our first City fan. 'Wrong shaped ball lads, you wanna stick to that other game,' he continued. I smiled back politely while the contingent of Wigan fans at the front of the double-decker burst into a rendition of *You Are My Sunshine.*

Over the years, especially the past few, I'd grown ambivalent to this sort of attitude. 'Who do you support?'

'Wigan Athletic.'

'Who do you support in the Premiership then?' they'd reply, looking confused. 'No one, I support Wigan.' It had become a familiar exchange, but one that I didn't think I'd have to go through again after our promotion to the English top flight last year. Those pre-conceived ideas and clichés didn't just fall away when the final whistle went against Reading on 8 May though. Over the 10 months of our first season in the Premiership they have been altered step by step; firstly by the way the team has played and also by how our fans have responded, travelling for hours up and down the motorways of England to see 90 minutes of football.

One of my highlights of the season used to be the FA Cup draw, when I'd sit nervously in front of the TV, palms sweating, unable to eat my tea until 'number 37, Wigan Athletic will play number...'. I longed for a trip to Burnden Park more than anything but Bramall Lane or even Boundary Park would have done. Our big draw never came out though, a 1–0 defeat at Grimsby was about as good as it got. But still, it was different to standing on the crumbling, open terraces of Springfield Park or later, sitting in the plastic blue or red seats of the JJB Stadium and as the years passed the away day wins became more familiar. Victories at places such as Tranmere, Bury and Rotherham were met with such fervent joy that it was impossible, only a few years ago, to see how Latics' fans hearts would stand up to claiming three points against Premiership clubs.

However, the club's rise under Paul Jewell had made us realise that anything is possible and by the time the trip to West Brom came on 10 September 2005 we almost knew what to expect. Wigan had tasted defeat away at Charlton a couple of

Journalist and lifelong Wigan fan Phil O'Brien travelled the country savouring the club's first season in the Premiership.

On the way home from Latics... fans make their way home over the footbridge over the Leeds and Liverpool Canal.

weeks earlier but, following our first win at home to Sunderland, the sold-out Latics allocation travelled south with optimism.

After taking a detour to avoid a pile-up on the M6, we made it to the Midlands with 20 minutes to spare, dumped the car on a grass verge in the middle of a dual carriageway and ran through the rain to the Hawthorns. Jonathan Greening had struck midway through the first-half to give the home side a 1–0 lead and I was comforting myself with a cheese and onion pie when rumblings that we were on the attack filtered down to the concourse.

Just as I turned to look at the TV David Connolly smashed in the equaliser. Everyone ran to get back in the ground but the stewards blocked our path. Instinctively we ran back to the TV with bottles and pies flying in the air.

A point would have been a fine result – our first away from home in the Premiership – but, when Jason Roberts squared for Jimmy Bullard, three were up for grabs. He side-footed, effectively passed the ball, into the bottom left corner and I emerged from the celebrating hordes some five rows from my seat. We rolled out of the Midlands that blustery, wet night feeling like we'd arrived in the top flight. For all Latics fans knew then, it could have been our only win away. Instead, it turned out to be the first of many.

Two weeks later a bleary-eyed gang of us boarded an early train to Merseyside. Among our contingent were four of our Everton mates, whose normally quiet journey was hijacked by dozens of Wiganers shoe-horned into two carriages. By the time we reached Pemberton, the train was full and as we flew through Orrell a smattering of confused Evertonians and Wiganers gazed in.

Despite both sets of fans mingling happily enough, on arrival Merseyside Police thought fit to detain the hundred or so visiting supporters for 10 minutes before setting us loose on the Liverpool suburbs. We cut through the red-bricked back streets for the sun-baked beer garden of the Black Horse on County Road. Young Evertonians played football with a squashed Coke can while inside their dads watched Liverpool on the big screen, praying for a Reds defeat.

Our trip to Goodison was particularly significant because I went to school with mainly Blues and their rival fans from across Stanley Park. While they would regale the playground with tales of Gary Lineker or John Barnes I'd be singing the praises of Donny Page. Finally we were on level terms with them and now, when I warned of Jason Roberts's power and pace, they actually had to listen.

We filed through the terraced streets around Goodison and into the rackety old ground, squinting up at the Merseyside sun as a cool breeze rolled in from the Irish Sea. A tight game was won by a Damien Francis goal. Jewell had signed the former Norwich midfielder for the type of performance he put in against the disappointing Toffees. Even with two minutes left he was overlapping our strikers and pushing for a second although, sadly, this performance was to be his best offering in a Latics shirt.

I caught a taxi back into the city centre to meet up with both my Wigan and Everton mates, who all seemed gently shocked by the result. It was a well-deserved win but this season was starting to get absurdly enjoyable.

Unbeaten in six, we made the familiar journey down the M6 to the Midlands again, this time to face Aston Villa on 22 October. Three of us, including my cousin and dad, had been to Villa Park before in 1994 but in very different circumstances. If we won today we could go fourth in the Premiership; in 1994 we were thankful of the distraction from our perilous position at the bottom of the Football League's basement.

We had enjoyed a surprise first-round win in the Coca-Cola Cup against Crewe to set up our trip to the former European champions, but in the first leg of the second round we got soundly beaten 5–0 by Ron Atkinson's side – a disallowed Pat Gavin goal was the highlight. As we walked around Villa Park on this pleasant autumnal day in 2005, it was surreal to think that we were now in the same division and above them after our surprise start to the season.

Villa Park is regarded as one of the best grounds in the country and, although it didn't stand up to that billing, it does have a warm traditional feel to it that other grounds lack. Uniquely, a food kiosk in the away end has been turned into a programme memorabilia shop – one of the gems on sale was the complete collection from our first season in the League. The expansive stadium is anything but intimidating and as we took our seats behind the goal, a wave of confidence flooded through the large Latics contingent.

Villa looked a reasonable side but lacked any real threat up front and when Aaron Hughes smashed the ball into his own goal it became apparent that another three points were up for grabs. The home fans were distinctly quiet throughout and they left in their droves when the under-used Alan Mahon pinged a sublime left-foot shot into the bottom right-hand corner to seal the win.

At last, revenge after more than a decade and we headed back to the North West with smiles as bright as Ron Atkinson's tan. The 2–0 victory had sent us to fourth in the Premiership, I'll repeat that, the 2–0 victory had sent us to fourth in the Premiership and to celebrate we headed to Manchester for a night out and sung our way around the city streets with four fingers thrust in the air.

Very unwisely I decided against travelling to Fratton Park, where Wigan beat Pompey 2–0 to go second in the Premiership. Fourth was incredible, but second!? Instead I saved my shrinking bank balance for the three visits to Liverpool, Manchester United and Chelsea.

Anfield was another ground I'd been to before, to see us lose 5–2 in the first leg of the League Cup second round in 1989. Goals from Bryan Griffiths and Dave

Wigan fans in the Anfield Road End of Liverpool's famous ground. The last time the club had played at Anfield was in 1989.

Two Wigan fans are left wondering how Peter Crouch's shot went in after it hit the back row of the Kop, bounced off the corner flag, ricocheted off the crossbar, rolled along Rafa Benitez's nose...

Thompson had put us 2–1 up that night, and if Jewell's side could match that team for spirit and endeavour against the odds then we wouldn't be far off causing an upset.

Again I boarded the Liverpool-bound train at Wigan Wallgate for the 12.45pm kick-off and this time I stayed on one extra stop for Anfield. It was a more precarious trip than our earlier visit to Goodison Park and the icy stares which greeted our group as we piled into a Wetherspoons pub near to the ground created an unease that grew as the day went on. Anfield isn't a particularly pleasant area. The rows and rows of impressive yet empty and desolate Victorian terraced houses point to a more prosperous era that is long gone.

You'll Never Walk Alone filtered down the steps and into the concourse as we made our way to our seats, but as that song turned into the awful 'We won it five times', the mood in the stadium changed. Instead of being proud of their heritage, on this day Liverpool appeared smug, in a way that I thought only Manchester United were capable of perfecting. Arguably the majority of Latics fans would have been pleased to see Steven Gerrard lift the European Cup the previous May, but by the end of the game I for one was cursing the patronizing scousers, Scandinavians and Brummies. What do we care if they've won the damn thing five times? My mood darkened as Peter Crouch struck a shot that hit the back row of the Kop, bounced off Pepe Reina's cross-bar, struck Jimmy Bullard's blonde ringlets, rolled along Rafa Benitez's nose and danced through the legs of Pascal Chimbonda before Mike Pollitt caught it and juggled it for a wee while before scissor-kicking it into his own goal. By sheer magnetism they were 1–0 up and Crouch – who was desperate to break his Liverpool duck – had the audacity to claim it as his goal.

The striker – I'm not going to make any reference to his ridiculous height – then claimed a well-taken goal that was undoubtedly his before Luis Garcia bagged their third. Throughout this comfortable win for their team, what did the Liverpool fans sing about? Winning that damn European Cup five times in a version of a Beach Boys song that Harry Seacombe would be proud of. The night that followed was slightly better thanks mainly to an unrelenting supply of Guinness and the fact that Liverpool has some of the finest pubs in the north-west – particularly the Doctor

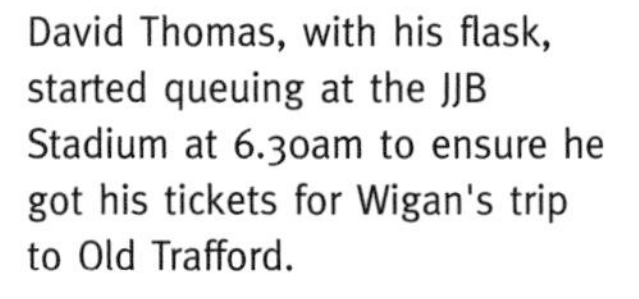

David Thomas, with his flask, started queuing at the JJB Stadium at 6.30am to ensure he got his tickets for Wigan's trip to Old Trafford.

Duncan – but I was reminded of the banality of Liverpool fans on the way home. We had to get a coach from St Helens station to Wigan and during the journey were treated to another rendition of 'We won it five times' by two die-hard Liverpool fans who had the broadest Wigan accents this side of Darlington Street. They were finally drowned out by 'You've never won the Freight Rover'.

The following week, 10 December, we faced an even sterner test at Stamford Bridge against the genuine champions. Leaving the JJB Stadium at 8am on a Supporters' Club coach, we arrived in the sunny London suburb some two hours before kick-off. Only myself and my brother had decided to make this trip from those we regularly go with but that gave us more chance of being allowed into a pub to grab a quick pint with the locals.

Venturing west of the ground we stumbled across a quintessential London boozer decorated with hanging baskets and classic maroon and beige tiling. Pre-match chatter escaped outside as I wormed my way through the bodies of blue to the bar to order a drink in the least northern accent I could muster. A game was being shown live on TV and there was a 'proper' big match atmosphere, which grew as we finished our pints and made our way back to the ground with the Chelsea fans.

At £48 a ticket it is understandable that some of our fans were reticent about visiting the Bridge but the away end was still sold out. Wigan fans covered two tiers, tucked neatly into the corner of the compact stadium.

With each game the players were looking more and more like they belonged in the Premiership and as a fan, instead of being petrified at the prospect of facing Chelsea, I took my seat with genuine pride and confidence. Latics' detractors said that there was no point in the club getting promoted to the top flight because we'd get battered every week, but by this stage of the season we'd proved that the performance against Chelsea on the opening day was no fluke. The return fixture was similar in the way that Mourinho's side threatened very little but seemed happy to cruise along, confident that the goal would come. Of course it did and we lost 1–0, but the trip and money it cost were worth it, for the superb veggie balti pie if nothing else. I lingered in the stadium for a few moments after the final whistle before heading out to join the Chelsea hordes and overhear more praise for Paul Jewell's side, which had become the most talked about in the League.

Four days later Latics headed to Old Trafford to play the last of their much-dubbed 'nightmare five-game run'. I had been working in Liverpool so I jumped on a train from Lime Street to Manchester Victoria, where I caught a Metrolink to the stadium. As we got into the city centre the tram filled with United fans who largely bemoaned the demise of their once all-conquering side and insisted to a group of not-so-sure Wiganers that Latics could get something on what was a cold, clear December night.

The doors were finally flung open as we reached the station next to Old Trafford cricket ground and we all piled through the underground tunnel out on to the long, straight street that leads to the imposing football ground. Red, white and black filled the horizon, created by a stream of bodies, while the occasional flash of blue, white and yellow could be seen among the domineering scene. I was early, so I wasted some time by looking around the United megastore, a truly unpleasant experience. I once visited the Nou Camp while on holiday in Spain and it had the same sort of feel as Barcelona's club shop – dozens of bloodthirsty, celebrity-

Wigan's manager Paul Jewell celebrated their 2–0 win at West Ham. Contrary to rumours, the game was not being televised by Arab TV in a Hindley pub.

High spirits for the Wigan fans leaving for Arsenal for their Carling Cup semi-final second leg.

obsessed tourists buying anything and everything with a club logo on it from pencil sharpeners to blow-up lilos. Football truly had become a consumer industry.

After finally finding the exit I breathed a sigh of relief and decided to have a walk around the old stadium. Only thing was I couldn't find any sign of the old stadium. The place is a metropolis and, despite their unrivalled success over the past two decades, I'm sure some of the locals must look back with sadness on a time when the Stretford End really was an end, and the bloke stood next to you had heard of Burnage.

The stewards who searched the Latics fans as they entered the ground were thorough to the extreme and inside the atmosphere turned sour when a couple of supporters were thrown out, apparently for nothing according to those around them.

Battered and bruised from four Premiership defeats, Wigan provided little resistance to Wayne Rooney and United and the game was a formality as the hosts

Jason Roberts's goal at Highbury triggered euphoric scenes among the Wigan fans. 'It was one of the purest and most exhilarating moments I've had while watching Wigan,' said O'Brien.

deservedly ran out 4–0 winners. Striving to savour the occasion and blank out the result, the travelling fans taunted their rivals with chants about 'the Manchester Dolphins'.

Wigan eradicated any concerns of a drop down the League with two consecutive home wins before flying down to London to play West Ham. Due to work commitments I couldn't make the mid-Christmas match but one of my mates had heard that a pub in Hindley was showing the game on Arab TV. It wasn't.

We tried six other pubs across Wigan and it wasn't being shown anywhere, so we ended up straining to listen to the radio in an empty Pear Tree while Latics recorded a 2–0 win. Apparently, the celebrations in the Upton Park away end weren't quite matched back in the sleepy Wigan pub, but I looked ahead to another new ground the following Monday, 2 January, as it was back on the M6 to Birmingham.

Arriving at St Andrews with two hours to spare we trudged away from the ground, over a nondescript retail park and into a pub that we were assured had 'loads of Wigan fans in'. I think my mate had forgotten that Birmingham also play in blue. We squeezed into the tap room where a group of locals were playing dominoes, another group cards, while a well-used dartboard was also being taken advantage of. The scene probably hadn't changed for 30 years and there was something to cherish in that sense of community.

On weaving our way out of the pub we walked past dozens of Wiganers who were mixing happily with Birmingham fans and back over an empty car park to the ground. I always thought of St Andrews as a traditional old ground with banks of mad Brummies swaying and surging over huge open terraces. Maybe it was like that at some point, but what stands there now is another acceptable if uninspiring stadium. It could have been anywhere in the country and Paul Jewell was equally unimpressed as his tired-looking side slumped to a 2–0 defeat.

Wigan fans invaded Cardiff for the Carling Cup Final at the Millennium Stadium.

Wigan's 4–0 defeat at the hands of Manchester United made for painful viewing.

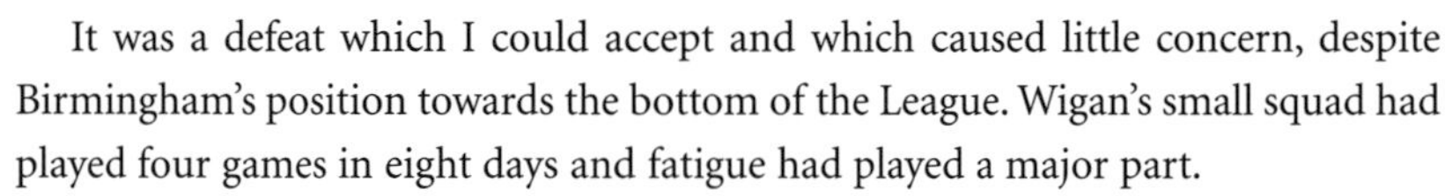

It was a defeat which I could accept and which caused little concern, despite Birmingham's position towards the bottom of the League. Wigan's small squad had played four games in eight days and fatigue had played a major part.

With the crucial trip to Highbury for our Carling Cup semi-final approaching I ducked out of Middlesbrough away – unsurprisingly, as I wasn't there we won – so my next Premiership game on the road was Bolton Wanderers on 4 February.

Arsenal away is covered elsewhere on these pages and anyway it would be difficult to succinctly describe exactly what happened when Roberts slotted home that last-gasp goal to send the team to Cardiff and 2,000 or so die-hard fans into rapture. It was one of the purest and most exhilarating moments I've had while watching Wigan. I'll have to leave it at that or this may turn worryingly pornographic.

Needless to say the FA Cup fourth-round defeat at Man City the following Saturday came nowhere near the ecstatic scenes at Highbury. The only consolation was that I'd finally seen Latics get past the third round. The last time had been 19 years ago, as a freckle-faced seven-year-old peering over a whitewashed wall to see us lose 2–0 to Leeds in the quarter-final. The wait definitely wasn't worth it.

Bolton, on the other hand, was a different prospect. One ground I'd always wanted to visit was Burnden Park and latterly the Reebok Stadium. For some reason my dad saw fit not to take me to Burnden but took my brother instead – a source of much delight on his part. We'd never been lucky enough to get a trip to Horwich in either Cup and had to earn our chance by joining them in the Premiership.

My dislike of Bolton began when as a terrified youngster I had to ask my dad why there were hundreds of Bolton fans in our end at Springfield Park. It was reinforced by a science teacher who insisted that Bolton's closest rivals were Manchester United. However, by the time we came to play them away we'd already beaten them twice at home and were cruising along in the Premiership, so the game didn't have the same significance and blood-boiling hatred that I thought it might.

I'd heard about a bus laid on for Wigan-based Bolton fans (is there such a thing?) which left from Wigan bus station and took a colourful route to the Reebok. Although empty as it departed, it slowly filled up as we headed through Hindley, Haigh and Aspull and weaved along the narrow roads of Little Scotland before the replica-clad Bolton masses piled on in Blackrod, perplexed by the occupied seats.

As we crossed over the motorway bridge in Horwich, the sight of Latics shirts streaming towards Winter Hill was long overdue. Despite forking out the top price, £36, our seats were ridiculously high up and we peered down as the fireworks exploded into the light blue sky.

A scrappy game looked to be falling from Wigan's grasp when Stelios scored for the home side, but Andreas Johansson – dubiously dubbed Teddy for his Sheringham-esque skill – came off the bench to earn us a draw. It was an excellent point which was made even sweeter by the grammatically dodgy chant of 'You'll never beat the Wigan!'

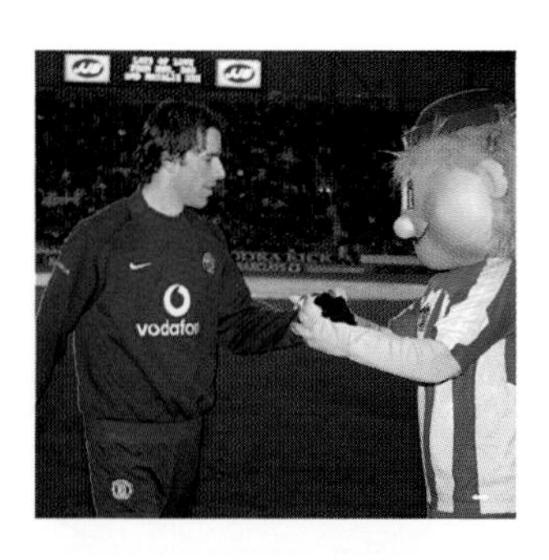

Latics mascot B meets Ruud van Nistelrooy as Wigan Athletic prepare to play Manchester United at the JJB Stadium, nine days after the Carling Cup Final.

At this stage of the season all our thoughts were dominated by Latics' impending trip to Cardiff to face Man United in the Carling Cup Final. Again that debauched weekend is covered in more detail elsewhere on these ebullient pages and the game itself is one that I'm not too keen on reliving. Not just because of the result, but because for 90 minutes it was an altogether unsavoury experience – for one thing, football should not be played under a roof. That said, the weekend on the whole was unforgettable, from the Saturday night staying on a *Withnail and I* style farm in Ross-on-Wye to being cheered on by every Cardiff local we passed on our way to the Millennium Stadium on Sunday morning.

'Good luck today boys,' they'd shout, leaning out the car window. 'Is Kavanagh playing for you today?'

'He is, yeah' we'd bashfully reply.

'I hope you stuff those idiots then boys, good luck!'

Before the game it felt like we'd already won as we sung and danced our way round iridescent Cardiff. Even after the 4–0 defeat the pubs and streets were full of smiling Wigan faces – not a red shirt in sight – and the welcome we got from everyone was impeccable.

Anyway, because of the strains the historic trip to South Wales had put on my overdraft, I decided to rein in the amount of away days. I managed to avoid Sunderland and Manchester City, but when the Blackburn game came round I felt myself strangely drawn to deepest Lancashire. It was a Monday night match and I was planning on nipping to the pub to watch it, but as I listened to a smug Mark Hughes on TV, who was under the impression that it'd be three easy points for his side, I felt that we'd get something at Ewood Park and therefore accepted my mate's offer of a lift.

Captain Arjan De Zeeuw and manager Paul Jewell salute the travelling fans at the City of Manchester Stadium.

We parked up at a nearby school and headed down a steep terraced cottage-lined road to the ground. A couple of hundred yards from the away entrance is an away fans only pub, which we headed for after picking up our tickets. Being met by smiling bouncers was a strange experience and made a refreshing change from being treated like an invading army. We left to pleas of 'come again' and 'have a good game,': hopefully this sort of generosity would continue inside the ground, I thought. Unfortunately nobody had explained the concept of 'rationality' to referee Phil Dowd, who made a number of baffling decisions and failed to spot a foul on John Filan for their equaliser. A point was a good result in hindsight, but three would have made the chants of 'We're all going on a European tour' more believable. We scuttled back up the hill, along the closed road, with the Blackburn fans, who were also bemoaning Dowd's performance. By the time we got back in the car Jewell's scathing comments about the gesticulating official were already on the internet and on my mate's phone. 'He's certain to get banned for that', I said to the others.

Amazingly the FA demonstrated that under-used commodity, common sense, and didn't fine or ban Jewell, so after the home draw against Birmingham he took his place on the St James' Park touchline for the Newcastle game. Three of us

The Wigan fans, high up in the rafters at St James' Park.

The view the travelling Wigan fans enjoyed in Tynecastle.

travelled up on the morning of the match and rolled over the River Tyne a couple of hours before kick-off. This was one trip most Latics fans had looked for when the fixtures were first released back in June and it was also to be my last away game of a season that looked set to change the club forever.

Some fans look back warmly, possibly through rose-tinted glasses, at our days at Springfield Park and long for the camaraderie that was created in those humble surroundings. There are a lot of new faces at the JJB Stadium and, for both good and bad, the club has changed beyond recognition. Personally I welcome anyone who is prepared to come and support their hometown club, no matter how belated that support may be. What I dislike is some of these fans proclaiming to be lifelong supporters and professing to be experts on everything Wigan Athletic. They need to express some humility and respect the club's long and under-valued heritage, which stretches back more than 70 years. The club was arguably cherished more by the 2,000 or so regulars who stood by the team no matter what division they were in, but that spirit hasn't evaporated into the Rupert Murdoch-polluted air. It still exists somewhere in that die-hard band of supporters who have travelled the length and breadth of the country to see their side in the Premiership. When Roberts scored that late goal at Arsenal in the semi-final it was there, when Bullard grabbed our first Premiership away win it was there and when 1,700 fans trekked up 14 flights of stairs to their seats at St James' Park it was there.

Growing up in Wigan for me was always about football, and I instinctively supported my hometown club. In the past 20 years I've witnessed dramatic changes but try never to forget what the club means to me and what it would have meant as a 14-year-old, who told his school mates that Ian Benjamin was going to be the greatest player Latics had ever had, to travel to the likes of St James' Park.

That's why, as we took our seats in the rafters of Newcastle's impressive stadium, I couldn't help but smile. For the first time ever I was on the front row and our view was simply breathtaking. When we trotted up the steps to get into the ground I couldn't see it, the ground that is. I could only see blinding blue sky and the murky

Sunderland horizon. Then the pitch finally came into view and, as I turned round, a massed bank of blue, white and yellow.

From my perch there wasn't a single obstruction, nothing but crisp fresh air between me and the corner flag. I could even cut out the black and white shirts if I didn't look down. For the first few minutes I leaned on the white steel barrier, resting my head on my hands, taking in the sublime sight. The only concern was that if we scored and jumped up to celebrate we might lose our balance and plunge onto the home fans below. That worry fled my mind when, at our end, Jimmy Bullard curled an exquisite free-kick past a static Shay Given. Unfortunately injuries led to our makeshift defence succumbing to Shearer and Co. and we lost 3–1, but Bullard's goal was worth the hike.

That evening we were staying at a mate's house in South Shields, so we enjoyed the delights of Newcastle by night. As I passed the Angel of the North the following morning I wondered what next season would bring on the road.

Jimmy Bullard celebrates a wonderful strike against Newcastle.

Phil O'Brien (right) will be able to tell his grandchildren he witnessed Alan Shearer's last goal – and game – at St James' Park.

14: February: The Big Four 'O

Dave Whelan says that despite his denials, Paul Jewell would love to coach England one day.

A COLLECTIVE sigh of relief rang around the town as the transfer window finally slammed shut. Never mind that Paul Jewell wanted to put a brick through it, most Wiganers would happily have brought out the hammer and nails and boarded the thing up.

As one cheesy old country star (Kenny Rogers) sang, 'You got to know when to hold 'em'. And we had. Paul Scharner, plus Reto Ziegler, Neil Mellor and David Thompson in for no outs, left the string bean squad somewhat fattened.

Not that this put a halt to speculation about who would be leaving, and when. 'In all the years I've been here I haven't had to turn down too many approaches, which is amazing,' reflected Paul Jewell. 'I didn't want Ellington to go, but I couldn't stop that. I've heard all the talk about Jimmy Bullard and Jason Roberts, but I haven't had an offer for any player that I was in danger of losing.'

Jewell had himself been linked to the vacancy at Newcastle, amply filled by Glenn Roeder. He reacted to it with typical vim: 'There are all sorts of rumours flying around linking different people, but I tend to take no notice of rumours because that's all they are.' The rumours centred around a supposed game of golf that had been played between Dave Whelan and Newcastle's charming chairman Freddy Shepherd. 'I spoke to my chairman two days ago, and he is in Barbados, but he never mentioned playing golf with anyone from Newcastle,' added the manager. 'I have said I would like to be the manager of a team that is challenging for the top honours. Yet here I was at Wigan playing for one of the big three trophies in English football. Of course, you want to achieve what you can in football and if you said I could achieve what Alex Ferguson has achieved, that would be fantastic.'

One hotseat Jewell was not going to end up in though was the England manager's – despite the farcical situation that had arisen when Sven was told his services would not be required after the World Cup. Chairman Dave Whelan put it most succinctly: 'I've never seen a Liverpudlian appointed to any major footballing position in my life. I know Paul says he wouldn't take it, but I will tell you if they came to his door and said "Paul Jewell will you be the next manager of England?" he would take it. He's done a fantastic job here and I don't think he will be thinking about leaving us to go to Newcastle, why would he? I can't see him leaning towards a move. But if Newcastle approach him about the job and Paul wants to go then that's his decision. I wouldn't stand in his way. But I know he's very happy here at Wigan and wants to stay.'

Despite bolstering the squad, Wigan's next two games against Liverpool and Bolton would become the tale of their nearly men. It was a strange phase of the season. Wigan's eyes had been turned toward the Carling Cup, injuries had begun to tot up and their next two opponents weren't at full strength.

Bolton had lost four main players to the African Nations' Cup, while Wigan were without Henri Camara, Connolly and the banned Jason Roberts. Latics' last win at Bolton had come on 7 April 1987, in a 2–1 win which saw Paul Jewell on the scoresheet.

A point at the Reebok 'fortress' Stadium made it three games unbeaten against their local rivals in the season and kept Wigan's hopes of a top-six finish alive thanks to forgotten man Andreas Johansson. Latics' number eight grabbed a surprise equaliser against the Trotters just 11 minutes after climbing off the substitutes' bench. He showed he had (Swedish meat) balls and a bit of class to react quickest in the box after Jussi Jaaskelainan had spilled a Reto Ziegler free-kick. 'I'm really happy to get my first goal in the Premiership,' Johansson said. 'To get a point was great because it's tough to come here. I just made a guess for the goal. Ziegler made a really good strike and the 'keeper couldn't hold the ball. I just followed up and got my foot on it. It was a hard game because Bolton were very physical. We were glad to have got the point in a really big derby game. A lot of teams have come here and lost.'

Graham Kavanagh makes a challenge on Bolton's Stelios Giannakopolous.

At that point, only Blackburn, Aston Villa and Liverpool had taken a point at Wanderers, while Everton were the only team to manage all three after the second

David Thompson celebrates with Jimmy Bullard after Andreas Johansson levelled the scores.

Mike Pollitt applauds the away support at Bolton.

Saturday 4 February 2006

Bolton Wanderers 1 Wigan Athletic 1

BOLTON: Jaaskelainen 6, O'Brien 7, Ben Haim 7, N'Gotty 7, Gardener 7, Nolan 7, Fadiga 6 (Hunt 23 7), Nakata 6, Jansen 7 (Vas Te 45 7), Davies 7 (Borgetti 52 6), Stelios 8.

WIGAN: Pollitt 7, Chimbonda 8, De Zeeuw 7, Henchoz 6, Baines 7 (Thompson 65 6), Teale 6, Kavanagh 8, Scharner 7, Bullard 8, Ziegler 7, Mellor 6 (Johansson 65 7). Wigan star man: Bullard.

Goals: Stelios (63), Johansson (77)
Half-time: 0–0
Referee: Steve Bennett
Attendance: 25,645

game of the season. Johansson joined the distinguished company of Marcus Bent, Juan Pablo Angel, Steven Gerrard and Luis Garcia in cracking the tough Bolton nut when he found the back of the net on their patch with 13 minutes to play.

Make no mistake, this was a great point for Latics under the circumstances and underlined how important their away form was to become. Paul Jewell's men boasted the third best points-per-game ratio away from home, trailing only Chelsea and Manchester United.

You will have read this next sentence before in this book... but Latics could so easily have taken all three points from this match. They looked to be heading for their fifth defeat in seven on the road after Stelios put the hosts ahead through a set-piece on 63 minutes. Wigan had the upper hand for the last period as the game hotted up. Johansson had a header saved before Bullard wasted a glorious opening when he fired wide after running from his own half. If he'd looked up Scharner would have surely netted his second goal in a week. That really would have been the perfect ending.

The Wigan side hadn't fluked their way among the country's front-runners. They showed resilience, character and battling qualities needed to salvage a deserved share of the points. 'Once Bolton get in front here they very rarely surrender the lead, so I'm more than pleased with the point,' Jewell said. Bolton manager 'big' Sam Allardyce had a slightly different take on it. 'I think we deserved to win the game. We took the game to Wigan and got our noses in front,' he fumed afterward.

The Bolton chief was clearly angered when Johansson won the free-kick, which led to the equaliser, under a Bruno N'Gotty challenge. Allardyce, never a man to hide his feelings on the touchline, said: 'We had a doubt that it was a free-kick. But we should have done better in defending it. It wasn't a great shot from the free-kick, but the wall didn't do its job properly and then Jussi couldn't quite push it to one side and they capitalised on it.'

Sorry Sam, but this season's bragging rights were royal blue and white.

Throughout the season, Jewell had managed to ignite that little spark in his players. At times, Jason Roberts, Jimmy Bullard and Pascal Chimbonda had their touch paper lit by the manager. And the next in that line was... Gary Teale?

The flying Scotsman had started to show glimpses of his ability, as his confidence slowly returned, with close control, blistering pace, an improved crossing ability and a greater awareness of just when his right-sided counterpart Chimbonda would be burning up the flank behind him. 'He's a winger and they are at best inconsistent,' said Jewell. 'But he's as quick as anything in the League and when he's full of confidence he's a big asset to us.'

Jewell revealed that Teale covered more distance on the pitch than any of his teammates, with Jimmy Bullard just behind him in second place. 'Against Arsenal Tealey ran 19k (11.8 miles) and that's an awful lot over the two hours of football,' Jewell said. 'It's shown on the Pro Zone stats he runs more than anyone. He does more work than anybody, he might not be a tackler, but he covers an unbelievable amount of ground.'

Teale, 27, is often to be seen on a Saturday afternoon taking an ear-bashing from his manager and fans alike. And while some players may have buckled under such criticism, Teale never shirks a challenge or goes missing. 'He's had more stick from

Team captains Steven Gerrard and Arjan De Zeeuw with referee Rob Styles as the coin is tossed for the kick-off.

What the opposition said...

'I will be moaning soon that we are drawing too many games. But in the last two games we've played Everton and Bolton who are both on good runs. When we don't play well we've got to try and get something. It's a hard place to come and when you don't have your strongest 11 it's even more difficult.' – Bolton manager Sam Allardyce.

What the Wigan fan said...

'It was a great result because it's hard to get anything from Bolton at the Reebok. Our midfield really dominated the game and we could quite easily have got three points, although no one is complaining with one point!' – Wigan fan Luke Samuel.

me than any player,' Jewell conceded. 'He drives me mad more than anybody, but at the moment he's well worth his place in the team. It's a credit to him because he's had a lot of set-backs since he's been here. He's had stick from supporters and from me, but he's responded properly and he's a great pro. He's got a lot of potential.'

Another of Latics' nearly men would take centre stage in the forthcoming home match against Liverpool – one of the most hotly anticipated games of the season. Latics would start the game without Henri Camara (in Africa), Jason Roberts (suspended), Neil Mellor (unavailable) and David Connolly (injured), meaning

	P	W	D	L	F	A	Pts
Chelsea	25	21	3	1	52	13	66
Man Utd	25	15	6	4	49	26	51
Liverpool	23	13	6	4	30	15	45
Tottenham	25	12	8	5	34	21	44
Arsenal	24	12	4	8	38	19	40
Wigan	25	12	3	10	30	31	39
Bolton	23	10	8	5	29	22	38
West Ham	25	11	5	9	36	34	38
Blackburn	24	11	4	9	31	30	37
Man City	25	10	4	11	33	28	34
Everton	25	10	3	12	18	32	33
Aston Villa	25	7	9	9	31	33	30
Charlton	23	9	3	11	28	34	30
Fulham	25	8	5	12	30	36	29
Newcastle	24	8	5	11	22	28	29
West Brom	25	7	5	13	23	32	26
Middlesb'h	24	6	7	11	30	44	25
Birm'ham	24	5	5	14	21	34	20
Portsm'th	25	4	6	15	17	42	18
Sunderl'd	24	2	3	19	17	45	9

Gary Teale gets his pass away as Xabi Alonso lunges in. Teale was praised by Jewell for his starring, energetic performances.

Captains reunited, as Arjan De Zeeuw battles with Steven Gerrard in the air.

Saturday 11 February 2006

Wigan Athletic 0 Liverpool 1

WIGAN: Pollitt 7, Jackson 7, De Zeeuw 7, Henchow 6, Ziegler 8, Teale 7, Kavanagh 6, Bullard 6, Thompson 6, Scharner 6, Johansson 6 (Baines 84). Wigan star man: Ziegler.

LIVERPOOL: Dudek 7, Finnan 7, Hyypia 8, Carragher 7, Riise 7, Gerrard 7, Hamman 7, Alonso 7, Kewell 6, Fowler 7 (Kromkamp 66), Morientes 6 (Cisse for Morientes 71).

Goal: Hyypia (30)
Half-time: 0–1
Referee: Rob Styles
Attendance: 25,023

Sami Hyypia celebrates his goal with teammates as Wigan look dejected.

'Andy' was the only thing that even looked like a forward at Wigan's disposal. The ex-Djurgardens man, an attacking midfielder, was happy to be playing his part. 'We didn't have that many strikers at that moment,' he reflected. 'It's not a problem for me if the manager wants me to play as a striker. My natural position is in midfield. But here I've been playing as an attacking midfielder and as a striker.'

Johansson joined Latics from his homeland club Djurgardens in January 2005 for £450,000. It had been a bumpy ride for the Swedish international, but he said he'd never thought about quitting the JJB Stadium in search of more regular football, remaining loyal to the club and showing a willingness to fight for his place when other players might have chosen to ask for a move. 'It never crossed my mind to leave,' said Johansson. 'I like it over here. When I arrived here I had a problem with my fitness for a year. It took me longer than I thought to get myself right.'

The build-up to entertaining Liverpool at home, though, was all about Henri Camara. Would the Senegalese make it back from the African Cup of Nations in time for the 12.45pm kick off on 11 February? It would be a sort of early Valentine for the fans. Senegal were ousted from the tournament against the host nation and eventual winners, Egypt, in the semi-finals. But they had a third place play-off game against Nigeria on 8 February. That gave Henri just 48 hours to make it back to Wigan. 'We just want him back ASAP,' insisted Jewell ahead of the match. 'If we can get him back so he can play some part or be in the squad against Liverpool, then we will endeavour to do that. We've had difficulties just trying to get hold of him, with someone from the club having spoken to his uncle. There's been talk of them returning to Senegal for a big reception, so I don't know what's happening. I know Henri wants to get back quickly, but it's quite political with the Senegalese, and we don't want to jeopardise his future with them.'

There had been a suggestion that Senegal's Barclays Premiership players would be pulled out of the game in order to return to their clubs. But the mysterious striker kept us all waiting. The talk of the terraces even in the minutes leading up to the squad being announced was, 'Is he back?' 'Where's Henri?'

But as the names were read out at the JJB, it became apparent that Latics had sent out a makeshift side. Paul Scharner had been drafted in as an emergency striker, scouser David Thompson started on the left and Pascal Chimbonda was missing, so stalwart Matt Jackson was drafted in at right-back – the position he started out in all those years ago at Everton. 'We're certainly not going to feel sorry for ourselves. We will have 11 players out there who will be committed, and we will see what we get out of the game,' said Jewell.

Wigan's perseverance, bravery and willingness never to surrender saw their opponents play the last 20 minutes of this clash with five across midfield and just Djibril Cisse as a lone striker. That's right: a severely depleted Latics side forced the European champions to sit in and scrap out a one-nil victory.

Scharner and Johansson ran their socks off all afternoon, but they were never going to pose as much threat to Sami Hyypia and Jamie Carragher as Latics' big guns would have done. Matt Jackson didn't look out of place in the absence of Chimbonda at right-back, showing a cool head, great positional sense and a determination to venture over the halfway line, even if he later dismissed his switch of roles as being 'a round peg in a very square hole.' Arjan De Zeeuw, making his 450th start in English football, and former Liverpool defender Stephane Henchoz, kept Anfield legend Robbie Fowler, Spanish international Fernando Morientes and latterly Djibril Cisse out of the game.

It was left to a freakish left-foot bobbler by Sami Hyypia to make the breakthrough. Mike Pollitt – beaten by a freak Peter Crouch strike at Anfield in December – admitted he shouldn't have been beaten by the Finn's winner on the half-hour. 'I thought he was going to absolutely smash it and it caught me by surprise,' the 'keeper said. 'I thought I'd saved it, but then I looked round and I couldn't believe it when it went into the net. As I went to flick it, it caught the inside of my arm. If he would have caught the ball cleanly I probably would have saved it. But the fact that it was bouncing and spinning caught me on the hop.'

No one was blaming the 33-year-old for Latics' slip to their fifth game without a win. Any 'keeper would have been proud of the stop he made to deny Morientes his only sight of goal on the stroke of half-time.

A new JJB Stadium capacity crowd of 25,023 witnessed a scratchy match, not helped by a rank JJB surface. The visitors shaded the first half, while Latics had the upper-hand after the break. Fowler saw an eight-yard header saved by Pollitt and the impressive Reto Ziegler, Wigan's best player, sent a 30-yarder just over the bar. He was given a start at left-back with Leighton Baines struggling with a groin injury. 'In the second half the lads rolled their sleeves up and gave a good account of themselves,' Pollitt said.

De Zeeuw had two decent opportunities with his head and, as Pollitt remarked, one of those hitting the target would have been 'a deserved point for us.' Johansson forced Jerzy Dudek to tip a header over and the 'keeper had to be alert to prevent Hyypia sliding the ball into his own net.

Pollitt made further saves from Gerrard and Cisse as the game fizzled out. 'People can say we've got our excuses ready because of lot of injuries and suspensions,' Pollitt added. 'But we went out there to get the three points.'

What the opposition said...

'We had to work hard against a good team who play with a high tempo. It was a difficult pitch to play on and it was an important result for us. Wigan work so hard for one another and have great team spirit.' – Liverpool boss Rafa Benitez.

What the Wigan fan said...

'Based on our second-half performance I thought we may have deserved a draw, but it was difficult without a recognised striker to get the equaliser. All credit must be given to the lads who played because several key players were missing for us. The atmosphere was great as expected, a JJB Stadium sell-out, such a huge game – it's what the Premiership is all about.' – West Stand season-ticket holder Martin Miller.

Paul Jewell shakes hands with Rafael Benitez after the game.

Matt Jackson, Jason Roberts, Leighton Baines and Alan Mahon during training ahead of their clash to Spurs.

	P	W	D	L	F	A	Pts
Chelsea	26	21	3	2	52	16	66
Man Utd	26	16	6	4	52	27	54
Liverpool	25	14	6	5	31	17	48
Tottenham	26	12	9	5	35	22	45
Arsenal	25	12	5	8	39	20	41
West Ham	26	12	5	9	39	34	41
Bolton	24	10	9	5	30	23	39
Wigan	26	12	3	11	30	32	39
Man City	26	11	4	11	36	30	37
Blackburn	25	11	4	10	31	31	37
Everton	26	11	3	12	19	32	36
Charlton	25	10	3	12	32	37	33
Fulham	26	9	5	12	36	37	32
Newcastle	25	9	5	11	24	29	32
Aston Villa	26	7	9	10	32	35	30
Middlesb'h	25	7	7	11	33	44	28
West Brom	26	7	5	14	24	38	26
Birm'ham	24	5	5	14	21	34	20
Portsm'th	26	4	6	16	18	45	18
Sunderl'd	25	2	4	19	18	46	10

It was a case of forgive and forget for Henri Camara. After missing a connecting flight from Paris to Manchester ahead of the Liverpool game, the jet-heeled frontman was back in action against Tottenham the following week, such was the scarcity of fit forwards at the club. 'Henri is an important player for us and there is no doubt we could have done with him fit on Saturday,' said Jewell. 'I told Henri I wasn't happy that he didn't make it back for the match, but I want him fully focused and committed for the massive games we have coming up. As far as I'm concerned the matter is now dealt with.'

Although exactly what happened remains a mystery outside the club, the 'difficulties' in having him returned hinged on the good grace of the Senegalese prime minister. That Henri returned at all was down to the magnificently named politician Macky Sall, who allowed the team to travel from Cairo to Paris on his private jet. But the flight was delayed overnight and only landed in France late on Friday evening. Camara was due at Manchester Airport at 6pm, but missed his connection. By then, considering the amount of football he had just played, the variations in climate and the shortness of time to rid himself of jet-lag, all in all, it was probably no bad thing that he missed the Liverpool game.

England coach Sven-Goran Eriksson watched Wigan at White Hart Lane.

As a final word about that dratted African Nations' Cup, Bill Green was sent there on a scouting mission to identify potential summer signings. Latics' football co-ordinator was dispatched to Egypt with a brief to find talent for next year. The Wigan boss has revealed his radar for new talent is stretching all around Europe as well as South America. 'It's all in the grand scheme of things towards trying to improve us,' said Jewell. 'I watched bits of it and saw some of Henri's games. There's the British market, Europe, South America – there are good players everywhere and it's up to us to find them.'

Planning for next season showed that Jewell was a multi-tasker of the highest order. Despite frequently telling both the media and his own players that he never looked beyond the next game, he had pulled off a piece of psychology worthy of Freud himself ahead of the Tottenham game. Knowing how important League survival was, Jewell had convinced his men that no name had been inked onto the teamsheet for the following week's Cup Final. He told the lads that places were still up for grabs and Latics fizzed their way across White Hart Lane.

A point would see Latics hit that magical 40-point safety mark – their suggested target at the start of the season. Jewell got this message out ahead of the London trip: 'I really don't know the team yet for the final. The team is nowhere near set in stone yet – there's a lot of places up for grabs. The Carling Cup will only come into the reckoning after the Tottenham game on Sunday. I can't start thinking about it. I'm telling the players not to start thinking about Cardiff. We haven't been basking in the glory. You do tend to see a pattern when a team reaches a final or after a final that their season can fizzle out. We're working really hard to make sure that doesn't happen,' he added, ominously.

Henri Camara, back in the side after missing the game against Liverpool because of a problem with his flight, battles with Edgar Davids.

And it was one in, one out in the squad. Jewell welcomed back Lee McCulloch after a double hernia operation, but Reto Ziegler was ineligible to face his ex-employers. 'We've been down to the bare minimum and we can't afford too many more injuries,' mused Jewell. 'Lee can play on the left-wing or up front for us and we've missed that versatility in the past couple of weeks. He was desperate to play and it just shows what an effect appearance money has!'

Sven-Goran Eriksson was in the stands as Wigan fought out a draw at Spurs, but when asked about likely successors, Wigan manager Paul Jewell insisted that ultimately the job should go to the best candidate regardless of nationality. Jewell told BBC Radio Five Live: 'It is quite interesting that Dave Richards [Premier League chairman] said British. I hope the best man for the job gets the job. It would be ideal if it could be an Englishman but give it to the best man. We'll see if we can win the World Cup with a Swede, that would be nice.'

Andreas Johansson puts the ball past Paul Robinson to score his first goal.

Saturday 25 February 2006

Tottenham Hotspur 2 Wigan Athletic 2

TOTTENHAM: Robinson 7, Stalteri 7, Dawson 7, King 7, Young-Pyo 7, Lennon 8, Carrick 8, Murphy 6 (Keane 73), Davids 6 (Huddlestone 85), Mido 8, Defoe 7.

WIGAN: Pollitt 8, Chimbonda 7, De Zeeuw 8, Henchoz 6 (Jackson 45 6), Baines 7, Bullard 7, Scharner 7, Kavanagh 8, Thompson 6, Johansson 8, Camara 7 (McCulloch 90). Wigan star man: Johansson.

Goals: Johansson (10, 67), Mido (23), Defoe (68)
Half-time: 1–1
Referee: Uriah Rennie
Attendance: 35,676

What the opposition said...

'We knew Wigan would be a tough side and they made it very difficult for us to get into any rhythm. We battled back well and you really have to take the positives out of the match. It was a bit disappointing to have thrown away the points but, although we could have won, it was a game from which we take a draw.' – Spurs manager Martin Jol.

What the Wigan fan said...

'We deserved to win the game. De Zeeuw was immense – what a signing he has been. He was at fault for their second goal, but he is only human. Apart from that he didn't put a foot wrong.' – Latics season-ticket holder Geoff Abernethy.

And Eriksson witnessed a tremendous Wigan performance, with a possible World Cup opponent scoring twice. Swede Andreas Johansson proved he was having a fabulous February, bagging a brace in a two-all draw. 'I'm just glad to have scored twice,' he said after the game in a manner typical of his countryman's level-headedness. 'It was really nice to score two goals, especially when you are playing as a striker.'

Andreas Johansson celebrates with Graham Kavanagh.

This was only Johansson's third League start for Wigan, but his brace against Spurs was the third time he'd found the back of the net in as many games. He was enjoying his best spell since he joined the club. And he said his equaliser at the Reebok Stadium two weeks earlier had given him a new lease of life. 'The goal at Bolton gave me more confidence,' he said. 'I think a weight has been lifted off my shoulders. I've not really been playing that much and I've been frustrated. But I know when you get a chance you've got to take it.'

Latics were left kicking themselves after twice taking the lead, only to be pegged back on both occasions. But, although a cliché of the highest order, it was a mark of 'just how far they've come', that they were disappointed with a point against a club in pursuit of a Champions' League place.

Johansson's first was a smart chest down and finish after Mike Pollitt's free-kick was flicked on by Paul Scharner. Wigan's resistance was undone midway through the half when they fell asleep at a throw-in. Paul Stalteri's cross deflected off Leighton Baines, Mido nipped in at the near post and flicked his shot into the far corner. The Spurs striker should have buried a free header shortly after from Aaron Lennon's cross as Wigan were let off the hook.

But Wigan had the better of the second period as Graham Kavanagh pulled the strings. Jimmy Bullard got himself more involved, while Camara and Johansson provided plenty of movement and ideas up front. Johansson struck again on 67 minutes as Kavanagh played him in. Johansson played a neat one-two with Camara and then passed the ball beyond Paul Robinson with his left foot. But the lead lasted less than a minute as Tottenham equalised from the kick-off.

Mido's flick was totally missed by De Zeeuw and Defoe was allowed to chip over the advancing Pollitt. It was the Dutch defender's slip at the JJB Stadium in

	P	W	D	L	F	A	Pts
Chelsea	26	21	3	2	52	16	66
Man Utd	26	16	6	4	52	27	54
Liverpool	26	15	6	5	32	17	51
Tottenham	27	12	10	5	37	24	46
Arsenal	26	12	5	9	39	21	41
West Ham	26	12	5	9	39	34	41
Blackburn	26	12	4	10	33	31	40
Wigan	27	12	4	11	32	34	40
Bolton	24	10	9	5	30	23	39
Man City	26	11	4	11	36	30	37
Everton	26	11	3	12	19	32	36
Charlton	25	10	3	12	32	37	33
Fulham	26	9	5	12	36	37	32
Newcastle	25	9	5	11	24	29	32
Aston Villa	26	7	9	10	32	35	30
Middlesb'h	25	7	7	11	33	44	28
West Brom	26	7	5	14	24	38	26
Birm'ham	25	5	5	15	21	37	20
Portsm'th	26	4	6	16	18	45	18
Sunderl'd	26	2	4	20	18	48	10

De Zeeuw, Scharner and McCulloch applaud the fans.

November which gifted Robbie Keane a goal. Scharner could have won it with four minutes remaining when he connected with Chimbonda's cross, but Paul Robinson kept him out superbly with a one-handed stop.

The result, and the way in which Wigan approached the game, left Dave Whelan calling for Paul Jewell to be named the Premier League Manager of the Year. And Whelan believed Jewell's outstanding achievements should be recognised by his fellow top-flight managers who were set to cast their votes. 'If Paul Jewell was made Manager of the Year I would not be surprised at all – he would get my vote,' he glowed. 'He's one of the best managers in this country. If he won it he would have my total and utter support. If anyone has earned it with hard work, Paul and his assistant Chris Hutchings have.'

FEBRUARY was best remembered as the month when Carling Cup frenzy swept through Wigan and for Latics chief executive Brenda Spencer, it proved the perfect way to mark her 20th year with the club...

Brenda Spencer sat in her office near to the JJB Stadium reception, her smile broadening as she spied the flowers presented to the club by the *Wigan Observer*. 'I'm just finishing our UEFA registration,' she revealed, before placing her pen on the desk. Despite frequent denials, thoughts of Europe then were, unofficially, on the mind of Wigan Athletic, who were about to play their first major Cup Final.

'It wouldn't do to win the Cup and not be able to play in Europe, would it?' she asked, adding that Europe could not be further from the club's thoughts before the season started. 'Everybody's goal when you start in the Premiership would be to finish fourth from bottom.'

All in all, it was a good Monday morning for Spencer, who was celebrating not only her team's progression to the Carling Cup Final and 20 years at the club – but also her birthday the previous weekend as well. 'It was a special one,' she said. 'But I'm not telling you which!'

At the time of the interview, Spencer should have been getting on a flight to Egypt for a well-earned holiday. 'I booked a Nile Cruise with a group of friends way back in October and, although I knew I'd miss Wigan's game against Tottenham at the time, well, the thought of being at the Carling Cup Final never entered my mind,' she says. 'Even travelling to Arsenal one-nil up, it still hadn't hit me there was a possibility I might not go on holiday. When Jason Roberts scored at Arsenal with seconds to go, I knew then there was no way I would miss the final. All thoughts of the holiday went out of the window.'

Although she had marked her birthday at the weekend, festivities would continue in Cardiff.

Brenda Spencer has not lost her personal touch. Here, Lee McCulloch and Graham Kavanagh look delighted as she delivers their wage slips.

'We've got a restaurant booked in Cardiff on Saturday night, there's about 20 of us,' she said.

Ahead of the semi-final, Latics were in the full glare of the national media spotlight. It was a far cry from the day Spencer walked through the gates of Springfield Park 20 years ago, into a Wigan Athletic owned by Bill Kenyon to become the his new group accountant.

'I was working for a local accountant's when Bill asked me if I'd join the staff at Latics,' she recalls. 'Yes, I was into football at the time, but no, I won't tell you which team I supported. All I'll say is that I've got blue blood through and through now. After a few years, Mr Kenyon sold the club to investors in London, and the deal was that I stayed with the club, to protect its interests. Dave Whelan bought us in February 1995 and made me chief executive. I remember the times at Springfield Park well.

Wigan Athletic chief executive Brenda Spencer at her desk in the JJB Stadium.

We've always had a friendly staff and a great team spirit and way of working among what you would call the backroom staff.

'The difference between then and now? Well, the stadium apart, we didn't know if at the end of each season, we would be able to pay the players' wages, or the staff wages for that matter. The holiday would start and you would think, "How the hell are we ever going to get through to the start of the next season?" People contributed to the club in whatever ways they could. I do miss Springfield Park, there was something about the place. But look at how far we've come.'

As for her management style, she's a pragmatic 'look after the pennies' sort. 'It makes me angry when people waste money,' she says simply. 'I get very angry when people spend money that is not necessary and also when people do stupid things at work without rhyme or reason. The most important piece of advice I've had is something my father told me. He said, "If you can't speak good of somebody then don't speak of them at all". It is something I have tried to adopt even though there are times when people get on your nerves but I often remember his advice when I hear worthless tittle-tattle.'

Through every off-season, the Latics walked a tightrope between existence and financial meltdown. 'That first game was always a big relief. Somehow we always made it through,' she adds. 'Dave Whelan brought us the financial stability we were lacking. Although the pressure to stay afloat has gone, those hundreds of pounds have now turned into millions.'

And looking after the millions takes a strong personality. All the more surprising, then, that Brenda is one of only four female chief executives in football. The others are Birmingham's Karren Brady, Luton's Cherry Newbery and Colchester's Marie Partner. But mixing with the likes of David Gill and Peter Kenyon doesn't faze this Lancashire lass. 'If you are good at your job, it doesn't matter whether you are a woman or not,' she says staunchly, adding that she has never come across sexism in the boardroom. 'If women are capable of doing the job, it shouldn't stand in the way just because they are female. The number of women chief executives will grow in the next 10 years. There are now far more female football club secretaries than males.'

Spencer admits she never expected her two-decade journey with Wigan would lead her and the club into the Premiership. 'Getting to the Championship was my goal for the club,' she said. 'I'm living the dream in the Premiership. I never thought we would be playing here. Whoever would have thought that Wigan could have travelled to Tottenham, played like that and got a result like that? We were almost happy in the end to come away with only a point but we deserved all three.'

But she refused to be drawn on naming her favourite players, despite the popularity of the likes of Arjan De Zeeuw, Jason Roberts and Leighton Baines with the town's female population (considering the previous question about sexism in football, Brenda played this one back with an extremely straight bat). 'They are a great bunch at the moment,' she revealed. 'Every year you say that this is the best we've ever had, and every year you get another group, and you think, "No, this is the best".'

And for the future? 'I think we are losing the stigma of "Little Wigan". We want to be an equal club in the Premier League. We want to cement our position there.'

For Spencer, Wigan is an extended family and there can be no better example of that than the fans: 'When I started we had about 800 season-ticket holders. One of the nice things is that you still recognise a lot of the supporters from those days. I have made so many friends, and I've been so lucky to have been involved in football for so long.'

15: The Millennium Adventure with True Romance

Wigan's Carling Cup campaign captured the heart of the nation.

THE clock on his car read 2.37am when Latics fan David Groom arrived back in Springfield on a cold January morning. 'I can't believe I went all that way to Highbury,' he said. 'Only to see them lose!' He laughed. He had laughed most of the way home.

Having driven all the way to London with his friend, Susie Melling, clinging to hope with one hand and a 1–0 first-leg win with the other, the 28-year-old was so elated driving back up the M6 he was practically flying. A season that had already delivered so, so much had just just taken an intriguing new twist. Jason Roberts's dramatic goal in the 120th minute of a pulsating game had pulled the score back to 2–1 and, suddenly, the phenomenon known as Wigan Athletic had begun a new chapter in their saga.

The following day, the euphoria was married to the surreal with the result of the other semi-final – Latics would be playing Manchester United. In the Carling Cup final. In the Millennium Stadium. In front of the world.

Rewind four months, and Wigan's glamorous Carling Cup journey began the previous September with a distinctly unglamorous home tie against humble League One side Bournemouth. The game drew just 3,346 fans, though such a lack of enthusiasm was not without precedent for the early rounds of the Carling (or League, Milk, Coca-Cola, Worthington) Cup competition, particularly given managers' tendency to field virtual reserve teams.

Jason Roberts spared Wigan's blushes against lowly Bournemouth in the opening round.

The game came just two days after Wigan's draw against Middlesbrough in the Premiership and Paul Jewell changed his entire starting line-up, challenging them to give him a selection headache. They didn't. Instead, it was left to substitute Jason Roberts to spare their blushes against plucky opposition so depleted by injury they could not name a full bench – and three of their substitutes were 16 years old.

'It could have been worse,' Jewell joked. 'It could have gone to extra-time. I'm glad it didn't because I don't think some of the Bournemouth players could have stayed up that late! I've got to give

Josip Skoko congratulates Andreas Johansson after his goal against Watford.

Tuesday 20 September 2005
Round two

Wigan 1
Bournemouth 0

WIGAN (4–4–2): Filan, McMillan, Jackson, Thome, Wright, Mahon, Taylor, Skoko, Teale (Connolly 58), Johansson (Roberts 58), Camara. Wigan star man: Roberts.

Goal: Roberts (86)
Half-time: 0–0
Referee: Steve Miller
Attendance: 3,346

credit to them, they played ever so well. But it was very unlike us because one of the things we have is a spot-on attitude, but some didn't do themselves justice. It must have been dismal to watch.'

The referee's petulance disrupted the flow of the game though the second half was far livelier than the first, and the introduction of Roberts and David Connolly stepped up the intensity and served as a catalyst for the rest of the team. Roberts, aware that he would be seen as the club's saviour, tried to deflect some of the praise onto his teammates. 'It can happen like that,' he argued. 'I've played in games like that when on paper you think you should be beating these sides, but you start badly and then it's hard to get in the groove.'

The following month, on the back of a 2–0 Premier League win at Aston Villa, Wigan again faced lower League opposition but again left it late to secure passage to the fourth round. They needed the cushion of extra-time to wrap up the win,

Stephane Henchoz puts pressure on Alan Shearer during Wigan's '1–0 hammering' of Newcastle.

with three goals in the final 23 minutes sparing them penalties against Adrian Boothroyd's side, who had reached the semi-finals of the competition the previous season. 'They should have been dead and buried by half-time,' fumed Jewell. When full-time arrived, he raced down to pitch side from his perch in the directors' box to fire up his players. 'I didn't appreciate having to go down there at full-time and get my shoes dirty on the pitch to sort them out,' he said. Just seven minutes into extra-time, which Wigan controlled, Mahon was up-ended by Chambers in the area and former Tranmere penalty-taker Taylor drove the spot-kick into the left corner. Mahon should have scored from eight yards, but blazed over, before he fed Johansson on the left and his shot beat Chamberlain via the inside of the far post. The Swede tapped in Mahon's pass to finish the game off.

Suddenly, people began to take the Carling Cup seriously. Could Wigan really do well in this competition? The team answered that question with a resounding yes when a virtual reserve side marched over a strong Newcastle team and into the quarter-finals.

Tuesday 25 October 2005
Round three

Wigan 3 Watford 0

WIGAN (4–4–2): Pollitt, Wright, Jackson, Thome, McMillan (Waterhouse 118), Taylor, Skoko, Bullard (Kavanagh 70), Mahon, Teale, Johansson. Wigan star man: Johansson.

Goals: Taylor (pen 88), Johansson (117, 120)
Half-time: 0–0
Referee: Andy Hall
Attendance: 4,531

David Connolly fires home his penalty against Newcastle.

Wigan won 1–0 but, in the words of Jewell, it was 'a 1–0 hammering'. David Connolly's last-gasp winner two minutes from time from the penalty spot was enough to see off the Geordies after a string of close scrapes from Andreas Johansson, Gary Teale and Alan Mahon. Latics' desire and commitment was brutally evident against a team boasting a string of big-name stars including former England captain Alan Shearer.

Encouraged by that victory, and a convincing 3–0 win over Charlton in the League, Wigan stormed into the last four of the competition five days before Christmas when a Jason Roberts brace provided Jewell with the perfect tonic for a bad cold that confined him to the directors' box.

Many strikers survive on their arrogance, but Roberts was modesty personified after his quarter-final heroics, choosing to salute the efforts of keeper Mike Pollitt rather than bask in the spotlight. Pollitt kept out Ricardo Vas Te from six yards when he flung himself to his left and Roberts beamed, 'It was an unbelievable save. It was as good as a goal for Bolton and then he did that… it was incredible.'

The breakthrough came in the 40th minute when Alan Mahon's inch-perfect pass found Andreas Johansson on the left, and his cross saw Roberts skip inside

Wednesday 30 November 2005
Round four

Wigan 1 Newcastle 0

WIGAN (4–4–2): Pollitt, Taylor, Jackson, Thome (Henchoz 30), McMillan (Baines 45), Teale, Skoko, Mahon, McCulloch, Connolly, Johansson (Roberts 69). Wigan star man: Skoko.

Goal: Connolly (pen 88)
Half-time: 0–0
Referee: Steve Bennett
Attendance: 11,574

Lee McCulloch is brought down by Bolton's Joey O'Brien.

Tuesday 20 December 2005
Round five

Wigan 2
Bolton 0

WIGAN (4–4–2): Pollitt, Taylor (Chimbonda 86), Jackson, De Zeeuw, Baines, Francis, Kavanagh, Mahon (Teale 70), Johansson (Camara 70), McCulloch, Roberts. Wigan star man: Roberts.

Goals: Roberts (40, 45)
Half-time: 2–0
Referee: Mike Dean
Attendance: 13,401

Radhi Jaidi and drill his shot passed Jussi Jaaskelainen. The Latics striker showed no mercy as he stroked home his second with ease minutes later. They were through to the semi-final.

Wigan were drawn against Arsenal – Manchester United had Blackburn – though Arsene Wenger's decision to field a virtual second-string team for the first leg at the JJB Stadium wiped a little of the gloss off the event. With the match live on Sky and Radio 5 Live, the crowd of 12,181 reflected the stretched overdrafts of many Wigan fans after a hectic festive period – this was the club's sixth home match since the weekend before Christmas.

Wigan, a by-word for fairytale by now, ensured the match survived long in fans' memories with an epic 1–0 win on 10 January. Paul Scharner had been in England just a few days following his £2.5 million signing and was handed a debut against the team he had supported most of his life. Boyhood allegiances counted for little, though. After coming off the bench for the injured Lee McCulloch on the half-hour mark, he rattled the Gunners with an all-action display that was crowned with a glorious 78th-minute header. 'I was ready to play, but I was really surprised when I got the chance to come on,' he said, in fluent English. 'Heading is one of my strong points and it was great to be in the right position to score.'

Jewell opted for Scharner to inject 'energy and enthusiasm' into his side after a muted opening half-hour. 'We did not show enough desire and at half-time I told them they might never get into another final,' said Jewell who, having secured the win, was unable to resist the urge to make a small joke. 'They had their wives and girlfriends watching – some have got both. I told them to go out in the second half and do it for them.'

The game was delayed for 13 minutes during a second-half power dip, which plunged the ground into darkness. The fall in power was automatically detected by United Utilities and the town was switched to an alternative supply almost immediately. But the dip was significant enough to cause the JJB's emergency systems – designed to ensure the stands and concourses are illuminated for fans – to kick in. And once this had occurred the club had to wait 10 minutes while the floodlights cooled before they could be switched back on.

'Our emergency procedures kicked in and worked like clockwork,' said club spokesman, Matt McCann. 'We knew instantly the game was never in doubt. The

match referee and both managers were told it would be a 10-minute delay and you can stay on the pitch or go off. They decided to go off.' As the players trotted off the pitch, Jimmy Bullard illuminated the moment with a typical prank by pulling down Freddie Ljungberg's shorts – the Swedish international was well known for posing in underwear for a Calvin Klein advertisement.

Paul Jewell and Arsene Wenger had a touchline bust-up during Wigan's 1–0 first-leg semi-final win.

Once the lights returned and the game resumed, Scharner struck the all-important goal. At one stage, Wenger and Jewell had a furious touchline bust-up when the Arsenal manager accused Roberts of sticking his boot in against 'keeper Manuel Almunia during a late challenge. Jewell responded by saying Arsenal had

The JJB Stadium semi-final was plunged into darkness by a power failure.

Paul Scharner applauds the fans after his debut heroics.

Tuesday 10 January 2006
Semi-final first leg

Wigan 1
Arsenal 0

WIGAN (4–4–2): Pollitt, Chimbonda, Henchoz, De Zeeuw, McMillan, Teale, Kavanagh, Bullard, McCulloch (Scharner 33), Roberts, Connolly (Johansson 23).
Wigan star man: Scharner.

Goal: Scharner (78)
Half-time: 0–0
Referee: Howard Webb
Attendance: 12,181

more red cards than any other club. 'To be honest I was trying to avoid the 'keeper,' insisted Roberts. 'We collided and I apologised to him. I'm told Arsene Wenger felt I left my foot in but the truth is I tried to evade him. We collided – and that's football. I was totally unaware of the controversy my challenge on Manuel caused until some of the boys told me afterwards.'

Wenger insisted after the first-leg match that, despite trailing 1–0, he would not be tempted to unleash his big guns at Highbury in the return leg two weeks later. 'We use this competition to play our younger players,' he said. He didn't. Instead, he rolled out World Cup-winners Thierry Henry and Gilberto, as well as established internationals Dennis Bergkamp, Sol Campbell and Lauren in a full-strength side and, suddenly, Wigan's chances were widely written off. 'Every Arsenal supporter expected them to walk over us,' admitted chairman Dave Whelan. Many believed Wigan's best hope was if Arsenal under-performed, but those were the same voices who had tipped Wigan for relegation months earlier.

Highbury had hosted many memorable matches in its 93-year existence, but few would have been as incredible and absorbing as the game that unfolded on 24 January 2006. The two teams slugged it out like heavyweight boxers and the Gunners thought they would land the first blow when Stephane Henchoz handled Henry's cross in his own area in the 22nd minute and Reyes had the chance to open the scoring from 12 yards. But Pollitt flung himself to his left to turn his penalty round the post. Latics should have been awarded a penalty of their own when Senderos fouled Roberts in the area.

Jason Roberts battles with Sol Campbell in the Carling Cup semi-final second leg at Highbury.

Frenchman Henry was denied superbly by Pollitt when he burst clear and then Roberts was pulled down again in the area, this time by Campbell, but referee Phil Dowd turned the appeals away. Pascal Chimbonda was brought down by Almunia after the break, but that also went unnoticed. 'We should have had three penalties,' claimed Jewell. 'But we were at Arsenal and we didn't get them.'

The second half was just as exciting, with Pollitt somehow keeping out Henry, who managed to break the deadlock in the 65th minute when he nodded home Hleb's cross, which tied the score 1–1 on aggregate and moved the game into extra-time. It was the first goal Jewell's men had conceded in the competition. Latics were the better side in the extra 30 minutes, but against the heavy onslaught from the visitors, substitute Van Persie's stunning free-kick in the second period made the aggregate scoreline 2–1 to Arsenal.

It looked like Wigan's dream was over. But with just 30 seconds remaining of an enthralling, gripping rollercoaster two hours, Graham Kavanagh pumped a hopeful long ball forward – and thousands of fans in the stadium and in the pubs, clubs and lounges of Wigan held their breath. The ball caused absolute havoc in the Arsenal defence.

Scharner, playing as an emergency centre-forward as the game moved towards its climax, clashed with Philippe Senderos. Campbell completely missed the ball

Dave Whelan with young fan Ben Kirkpatrick after Latics beat Arsenal to reach the Carling Cup Final.

and that allowed Roberts to nip in and send Wigan into the final with the all-important away goal.

But the jubilation was not instant. Many of the players, sections of the 1,600 travelling supporters and even chairman Dave Whelan did not realise the away goal rule (the scores were 2–2 on aggregate but Arsenal had not scored away) counted in the Carling Cup and were preparing for penalties. Jewell, though, was aware of its significance as he charged 30 yards down the touchline to celebrate. 'I thought it was a bit of a Mourinho moment,' he coyly admitted. 'I don't like to show my emotions too much, but I couldn't help it.'

As the news of the away goal rule seeped through – chief executive Brenda Spencer informed Whelan, while text messages from friends watching the television coverage confirmed to the travelling fans that another dream had been realised – the emotions flowed as freely as the beer and champagne long into the night. Jewell and his assistant Chris Hutchings led their players over at the final whistle to soak up the applause of their adoring fans. And they were followed by Mr Wigan himself, Dave Whelan, the man who had turned a dream into reality.

The travelling support were in full voice, mocking their Arsenal counterparts with a chant of 'Little Old Wigan – you're having a laugh!' before continuing the party in the streets around Finsbury Park tube station, with echoes of 'You are my

Mike Pollitt celebrates his team's progress into the Carling Cup Final.

sunshine' ringing through the London Underground. It was arguably the sweetest defeat ever.

Mike Pollitt emerged from the euphoric scenes as the real hero after his brilliant saves throughout the match. 'Mike Pollitt has become a legend tonight,' offered Sky Sports summariser Niall Quinn. Ironically, Pollitt had been sent off in his last League Cup appearance at Highbury while playing for Rotherham in October 2003, a sore point, as the Millers bowed out 9–8 to Arsene Wenger's side on penalties. But redemption presented itself in six top-class saves. 'This certainly makes up for the sending-off – this is the best night of my career,' the 33-year-old smiled, before admitting, 'I was getting ready for penalties, I didn't realise we'd won. I looked round and I saw everyone celebrating and that's when I knew. I knew the rules, but it just didn't click on because it all happened so quickly.'

Pollitt's efforts epitomised the difference between the two sides, according to Roberts. 'I think it's a statement that hard work and believing in each other works,' said Roberts, who had scored four goals in the competition. 'Arsenal were far superior technically to us on paper, but we were always confident.'

The Wigan squad continued celebrating as the team bus pulled away from Highbury under police escort, Graham Kavanagh grabbing the microphone for a loud rendition of Van Morrison's classic *Brown Eyed Girl.* Jewell rewarded his players by allowing them to drink on the coach home. 'Arsenal had given us a couple of crates of champagne, which helped,' said Dubliner Kavanagh. 'It was really good of them because they must have been disappointed. Anyway, for the first time ever the manager let us have a drink on the way home. Nothing silly, just a bit of fun and a good singsong. There were phone calls and text messages coming in from all over the world and it seemed a shame it all had to stop when we got home... although it was half past three in the morning.'

The following day – or later that day, to be precise – Whelan met the media at the JJB Stadium to reflect on their stunning achievement. 'There's an unbelievable buzz everywhere you go,' he said. 'This is the same as when we got promotion to the Premier League. This team has surprised everyone, including me. It's wonderful for a working-class town like Wigan to go down to a place like Arsenal and come away with us in the final. Everyone records the rewards of success in different ways. Mine will be watching Wigan Athletic step out in their first major final – it's fairytale stuff, but we've done this on merit.'

The result even made dispatches in the House of Commons. Prompted by Wigan MP Neil Turner during Prime Minister's Questions, Tony Blair – Arjan De Zeeuw's number one fan – said: 'At the risk of alienating every Arsenal supporter in the country, I would like to congratulate Wigan on their progress.'

In the four weeks before the final, Wigan went into Carling Cup overload. League games against Everton, Bolton, Liverpool and Tottenham were all well supported but they did not carry the same kudos as the Millennium Stadium date that was looming. When tickets went on sale, season-ticket holders were given two weeks to book their seats for the showcase event. That, though, did not stop them arriving at the JJB Stadium in their thousands with some sleeping overnight to guarantee their places. Many ignored advice to return later in the week – they were too excited to be cautious and did not, could not, run the risk of the tickets being sold out. 'It's a Cup Final no one expected us to get to,' admitted Jewell. 'United are one of the biggest clubs in the world – and it's going to be a great day out.'

Jason Roberts and Paul Jewell celebrate at Highbury.

Tuesday 24 January 2006
Semi-final second leg

Arsenal 2
Wigan 1 (Agg 2–2)

(Wigan won on away goal rule)

WIGAN (4–4–2): Pollitt, Chimbonda, Henchoz, Scharner, Baines, Teale, Bullard, Kavanagh, Mahon (Ziegler 63), Roberts, Mellor (Johansson 61). Wigan star man: Pollitt.

Goals: Henry (65), Van Persie (108), Roberts (120)
Half-time: 0–0
Referee: Phil Dowd
Attendance: 34,692

Arjan De Zeeuw pictured at the JJB Stadium after a press conference to preview the Carling Cup Final.

Sunday 26 February 2006
Final

Wigan 0 Manchester Utd 4

WIGAN: Pollitt (Filan 14), Chimbonda, Henchoz (McCulloch 62), De Zeeuw, Baines, Teale, Scharner, Kavanagh (Ziegler 72), Bullard, Roberts, Camara. Wigan star man: Bullard.

MANCHESTER UNITED: Van der Sar, Neville, Ferdinand, Brown (Vidic 83), Silvestre (Evra 83), Ronaldo (Richardson 73), Giggs, O'Shea, Park, Rooney, Saha.

Goals: Rooney (33, 61), Saha (55), Ronaldo (59)
Half-time: 0–1
Referee: Alan Wiley
Attendance: 66,866

Some of the Wigan squad had experienced these big events before – Stephane Henchoz was in Liverpool's treble-winning side, while Henri Camara had savoured a World Cup with Senegal. But for the bulk of the squad, this represented the pinnacle of their careers. Jewell had assembled his team largely from obscurity, and for a relative budget price: Jimmy Bullard, Graham Kavanagh and Mike Pollitt had spent nearly all of their careers in the lower leagues, Lee McCulloch and Gary Teale had been plucked from Scotland and Leighton Baines had developed through the Wigan junior ranks. 'This game will be the biggest of my career,' said Arjan De Zeeuw, without hesitation. 'Just the sheer occasion of it being against Manchester United as well and for me to be playing in it as captain of Wigan Athletic, where I have spent most of my career… it's fantastic. I'm 35 now and I haven't been to [a major final] in my career, so I intend to make the most of this one.'

Although Bullard had been signed by Wigan from Peterborough, he had started his career as an apprentice at West Ham alongside United's club record signing Rio Ferdinand. 'I can't wait to see him,' the dynamo enthused. 'I used to play against Rio when I was about 14 or 15 at county clubs, and he was always going to be a good player. Once he got to West Ham he just took off. I think he's an awesome player. I've always said I think he's one of the best we've got in England. I know how he trains and looks after himself and I know how talented he is, he's incredible. I saw him before the game at Old Trafford and we had a chat, it's one of those things that you see each other around and when you do you catch up, but we don't have each other's numbers any more.'

Commentators, rival players and managers all voiced their predictions (many, understandably, sided with United) although there were a few who had been convinced by Wigan's abilities to excel in their underdog status. 'They can beat anyone,' Liverpool manager Rafa Benitez said. 'They work so hard for each other and have the ability to create a lot of chances because they are always pushing forward.' Even Mr Blair, at the JJB Stadium for a function which staunch Labour supporter Sir Alex Ferguson attended, wished the team well.

Those who had played for Wigan on their path from the non-League to the Premier League never swayed from their allegiance to the club. Noel Ward, a member of the side elected to the Football League in 1978, stayed in Wigan after moving to the area from Aberdeen to play at Springfield Park. He settled in Beech Hill and had supported Wigan ever since retiring in September 1979 from a fractured right leg. 'Having been to places like Colchester on a cold Tuesday night there's no way I'd miss a Cup Final in Cardiff,' he said. 'My daughter Kerry queued for 10 hours on the day tickets went on sale.'

Wigan had not appeared in a major final since playing Millwall in the Autowindscreens Shield seven years earlier at Wembley in front of 55,349 fans. Paul Rogers had scored a sensational 92nd-minute winner for Wigan that day and before he retired, began to see the early, tentative steps being taken by Whelan in driving Wigan forward. 'Mr Whelan said he wanted the club in the Premiership within 10 years of taking over and got laughed at – I was one of them,' added Rogers.

Matthew Ashton and Charlotte Bibby Ashton, enjoyed their day in Cardiff.

The Latics squad travelled to the plush Celtic Manor hotel in the Usk Valley, in South Wales, three days before the final, with Jewell still unsure of his team. Andreas Johansson's sparkling form in the previous three weeks – he scored against Bolton and Tottenham – handed him an intricate problem. 'Some of the players are going to dislike me even more than they do now,' Jewell joked, before his tone

A pre-match publicity shot ahead of the Carling Cup Final.

turned serious. 'But it will be my toughest call as a manager. Whoever gets left out is going to be devastated. I was left out of the Freight Rover Trophy Final for Wigan against Brentford in 1985 and it was the worst thing that's happened to me in football.'

One player who had already resigned himself to a bit-part role was David Thompson, who had scored during a 27-minute spell for Blackburn against Charlton and was consequently unavailable due to the Cup registration rules. 'It's a sickener for sure,' said Thompson, who travelled down with the rest of the squad for the match. A former England squad player, Thompson had faced big occasions before and was a soothing presence in the Wigan camp. Kavanagh, a natural leader and a vastly experienced Irish international, was also keen to help calm nerves. 'I've been trying to tell the younger lads in the squad that something like this doesn't happen every single year in your career,' he offered. 'When you are 21 you can think it will happen. We just have to concentrate on our own game because if we worry about the talent United have we won't sleep from this day to the final.'

Paul Jewell congratulates Wayne Rooney.

Finally, 26 February arrived. Hours before kick-off, convoys of cars, minibuses and coaches took to the road with scarves draped from their windows and signs and badges proudly displayed. At the motorway service stations, old friends and work colleagues bumped into each other and shared jokes – as well as optimistic predictions – before invading the historic city, the narrow streets awash with rich blue and white colours and fans overflowing out of pubs and onto the pavements.

Inside the Millennium Stadium the Wigan fans were marginally out-numbered but never out-voiced, as they sang and celebrated and partied. Then, when the teams emerged, the ground erupted and even those Wiganers who had gone for the occasion were touched by goosebumps. Such emotions had been felt before: against Chelsea, Arsenal and even Reading the previous season when promotion was secured. But never on such a grand stage.

The presence of £19 million Ruud van Nistelrooy, the Premiership's top goalscorer, on United's substitutes' bench underlined the gulf between these two clubs. The game signified so much for so many. Here was a romantic, swashbuckling tale of how a team put together on a shoestring – in relative terms – could overcome Bolton, Newcastle and Arsenal, and it stood as a beacon of hope for other smaller clubs.

Not even a 4–0 defeat – the same scoreline as at Old Trafford in November – could dampen those spirits. 'This Cup Final was a massive bonus on top of a great season,' insisted fan Alison Kennedy, from Appley Bridge, outside the stadium. 'I feel like we have won despite the score.'

Arjan De Zeeuw leads the teams out at Cardiff.

Wigan tried, fought and battled, but having fallen 2–0 down – a goal either side of half-time – and in striving to rescue the game, they fearlessly went in pursuit of a goal. Their strategy contributed to their downfall, as it left them vulnerable to United's deadly counter-attack and Ferguson pointed out that, perversely, the final scoreline served as a tribute to Wigan's bravery. 'His team aren't afraid to have a go and the consequences are if you don't score you can concede goals,' the Scot added.

Arjan De Zeeuw and John Filan show their frustrations after Wayne Rooney's goal.

Rooney teased and tormented the Wigan defence so much that the faithful blue half of the Millennium Stadium could not help but marvel at his skills. 'He is one of the best I have seen and played against. We tried everything to try and stop him,' lamented Paul Scharner, who had faced the England superstar on the international stage.

Bullard was still fighting back the tears when he left the dressing room after the game, gulping down water as if trying to drown his sorrows. After the final whistle had blown, he appeared to take defeat the hardest, throwing himself down onto the pitch as if looking for a piece of turf that would subside and swallow him up. 'We're all gutted and it's really hard to take,' he shrugged. 'I don't think I'll be able to bring myself to watch a video of the game. But you've got to hold your hands up, United were a different class.'

Just three minutes into the match, Mike Pollitt went down clutching his hamstring. He disappeared down the tunnel with just 14 minutes played and missed most of the game as he had to go for a random drugs test. 'I felt really sorry for Polly and all his family up in the stands,' Bullard added. But even Wigan's Highbury hero would have struggled to fare any better than his replacement John Filan in preventing the four goals which followed. Rooney had already hit the bar with a header in the seventh minute before the opener arrived, Saha's flick sending Rooney through.

Leighton Baines was close to tears.

Bullard and Kavanagh tried to wrest control of the midfield from United and it almost paid off, as Bullard set Henri Camara free only to see his drive blocked by Edwin Van der Sar. It was to prove a costly miss, as 10 minutes later United had rattled in another three with a blistering show of execution. Filan superbly stopped Saha's effort but could not keep out the second attempt, then, when Henchoz's poor clearance fell to the feet of Saha, Ronaldo capitalised. With half an hour still left to play, Rooney tapped in Ryan Giggs's free-kick.

Latics' endeavour never waned as they fought until the final whistle, earning respect and bolstering their reputations, even if the scoreline remained the same. The result left the players devastated, their emotion highlighting their lofty expectations. 'I was trying not to shed a few tears,' admitted left-back Leighton Baines. 'I tried to stay out and watch the presentation, but when United were getting the trophy I had to come in. I was thinking that it could have been us and it was a difficult pill to swallow.'

In the official after-match press conference, Paul Jewell marched in a proud man and handled himself with diplomacy, humour and honesty. 'Obviously, the better side won,' he stated. 'I thought we'd catch them on a bad day because I hear they've slipped down to the second richest club in the world! But I'm proud of my players, proud of my staff and proud of our supporters.'

Jewell was too competitive not to be affected by the defeat. But the realist in him took over as he acknowledged the strides the club had made under his guidance. Just four-and-a-half years earlier, Wigan had been tumbled out of the LDV trophy by Wrexham in a 5–1 mauling, watched by less than 1,600 fans.

Delving into Wigan's past, it was easy to find gauges of their progress. 'We've just played Man United in a Cup Final and last season we got knocked out by Grimsby,' Jewell continued. 'It's been a wonderful adventure. In the grand scheme of things, Wigan Athletic won no matter what.'

By contrast, his United counterpart cut a disconsolate figure as he met his enemy – the Press. He was grilled about his selection policy and his own position before he turned on the tabloid journalists sat on the front row, 'You guys don't have a clue. Not a clue. Honest. And on that note…'

Jewell was right. In so many ways, Wigan were the winners. Fans savoured their day in the spotlight and revelled in the occasion. 'The scoreline is disappointing but we have had the greatest day of our lives,' said 40-year-old Worsley Mesnes resident Les Crawford, who travelled with 20 family members and friends to the match.

The final was a celebration of Wigan's journey. The story may not have finished as the Hollywood scriptwriters would have wanted. This fairytale, it seemed, didn't have a happy ending. But it was still a fairytale. Wigan were still heroes. Nothing could change that.

Wigan's FA Cup campaign fizzled out in the fourth round but it did produce a wonderful game when Wigan beat Leeds in a third-round replay. Jason Roberts celebrates his goal.

The FA Cup

MENTION WIGAN'S Cup run of the 2005–06 campaign, and few would think of the FA Cup. One of the most famous competitions in the world did not figure highly on an agenda that already had a debut season in the Premiership and a blistering Carling Cup run on it. But it did feature one of the most entertaining matches in Wigan's season. Having drawn 1–1 in their third-round tie with Leeds United in early January, Wigan travelled to Elland Road two weeks later and played their part in a thrilling replay that was pushed all the way to penalties.

It was a match Paul Jewell and his counterpart Kevin Blackwell did not want to take place. Both clubs were enjoying successful League campaigns and when they met on 7 January at the JJB Stadium, they cared as much that there was a result one way or the other than what the result actually was. They were clamouring for the outcome to be decided by full-time, but were left disappointed. 'A draw's the result that we both didn't want,' Jewell admitted. 'We didn't want a replay.'

Rob Hulse's late equaliser cancelled out David Connolly's opener in a rather forgettable match. Ryan Taylor had to be carried off the pitch with a broken foot after Wigan had already made their three allocated substitutions, meaning the hosts had to play the remainder of the game with 10 men in near-Arctic conditions. To add to Jewell's woes, the Football Association forced his side to face Leeds just two days after their Premiership clash with West Brom. Leeds had earlier refused Wigan's request to postpone the match by 24 hours.

'It's because it's "Little Old Wigan",' Jewell raged. 'We feel if we were Manchester United we wouldn't have to play again two days after a game. The players shake hands with the opposition before the game and all that nonsense for fair play, but I don't see it as fair play asking a team to play 48 hours after a tough Premiership game.'

The quick turnaround in matches stretched Wigan's resources (third-year apprentice Luke Joyce won a place on the bench) and challenged their resolve, but their gritty work ethic once again served them well in a tense, edge-of-the-seat match which was only decided by a dramatic penalty shoot-out. The two sides couldn't be separated at the end of the 120 gripping minutes of end-to-end action.

Jason Roberts thought he'd done enough to book Wigan's passage through with a brace that followed Andreas Johansson's opener. But Blackwell's resilient unit clawed their way back three times, the last of which was a stunning long-range strike from Gary Kelly with five minutes to go.

'That goal was worthy of winning any cup tie,' raved Blackwell, with strong justification. Journalists in the Elland Road press box were already filing copy back to their sports desks for the following days papers when Kelly forced them to scrap their reports and start again.

The game came down to who could hold their nerve. Jimmy Bullard, Gary Teale, Jason Roberts and Graham Kavanagh all converted their penalties to see the visitors through. David Healy and Rob Hulse sent their spot-kicks high into the Don Revie stand. 'It was a good game to be involved in,' Roberts said. 'We managed to keep our heads during the shoot-out and put the balls in.'

Latics' fourth-round tie took them to the City of Manchester Stadium to face Stuart Pearce's side. Wigan were seeking FA Cup revenge against Manchester City – 35 years after being knocked out of the competition by the Blues. The two clubs met at Maine Road on 2 January 1971 in the third round of the Cup. Latics player-manager Gordon Milne saw his Northern Premier League outfit push the Division One side all the way, before bowing out to a Colin Bell strike.

The clash at City's new home on 28 January was far from memorable. Andrew Cole, the man responsible for dumping Latics out of the League Cup in December 2002, ended their Cup run with six minutes left. It came as a relief – a replay would have just been too much for Paul Jewell's stretched squad. 'The treble has gone now,' he said. 'We feel a bit sick because we've lost and we don't like losing. But we've had an awful lot of games lately and a replay was the last thing we needed.'

Saturday 7 January 2006
Third round

Wigan 1
Leeds 1

WIGAN (4–4–2): Filan 7, Taylor 6, Jackson 7, Henchoz 6, McMillan 7, Johansson 6, Skoko 6, Francis 6, Mahon 6, Connolly 6, McCulloch 8. Subs: Teale 6 (for Mahon 57), Kavanagh (for Johansson 72), Roberts (for Skoko 72). Wigan star man: Lee McCulloch.

Goals: Connolly (47), Hulse (88)
Half-time: 0–0
Referee: Graham Poll
Attendance: 10,980

Tuesday 17 January 2006
Third round replay

Wigan 3
Leeds 3

WIGAN (4–4–2): Filan 7, Chimbonda 6, De Zeeuw 7, Jackson 7, Baines 8, Teale 8, Kavanagh 8, Francis 6, Skoko 6, Roberts 8 Johansson 8. Subs: Bullard (for Francis 78), Joyce (for Skoko 100). Wigan star man: Graham Kavanagh.

Goals: Johansson (23), Healy (40, pen 64), Roberts (50, 103), Kelly (115)
Half-time: 1–1
Referee: Graham Poll
Attendance: 15,243

Saturday 28 January 2006
Fourth round

Wigan 0
Manchester City 1

WIGAN (4–4–2): Filan 7, Chimbonda 6, Scharner 7, Jackson 6, Baines 7, Mahon 5, Francis 5, Skoko 5, Ziegler 5, Johansson 5, Mellor 5. Subs: Roberts 6 (for Mellor 59), Bullard 6 (for Mahon 65), Henchoz (for Skoko 70). Wigan star man: Paul Scharner.

Goal: Cole (84)
Half-time: 0–0
Referee: Howard Webb
Attendance: 30,811

16: **March: Doubles up**

Gary Teale, back from Scotland duty, clears the danger from Wayne Rooney at the JJB Stadium.

GARY Teale had made his first major Cup Final appearance and Scotland debut within days, but the results could not have been worse for the winger, regularly a blue blur haring down the touchline. Three days after Wigan were humbled 4–0 by Manchester United in the Carling Cup, Teale's international blooding was overshadowed by the disappointment of a 3–1 home defeat by Switzerland.

'It was good to get my first game but you don't want to be ending up getting beaten 3–1 so overall I'm disappointed,' he lamented. 'But obviously I can learn from the experiences. I just want to play these type of games more often and take it as a learning curve.'

And the blond bomber said his form domestically, coupled with additions to his game, had helped him make the step up. 'When you're playing in the Premiership you've got to wise up,' he added soberly. 'Before I was probably more a luxury-type player whereas now I'm more of a right midfielder. I think defensively, team positioning and everything else, that's where I've improved and that's credit to the manager. In the Premiership you're on your toes, you need to be really concentrated in every game, for 90 minutes you have to be on top of your game. And our teamwork, everyone's in it together, that's been drilled into us.'

But not all Latics' prospects were finding international honours forthcoming. Young Leighton Baines, courted by the wee lassies that clamour for autographs as the players make their way into the ground ahead of each game (you wouldn't have got that at Springfield Park), was being haughtily ignored by England manager Sven-Goran Eriksson. 'If Leighton Baines played for anyone but Wigan then he might have been in the squad by now,' moaned manager Paul Jewell. 'I think he has been tremendous. He has made massive strides this season, but maybe Wigan aren't sexy enough for some people at the FA.'

The left-back role was becoming problematic for England ahead of the World Cup. Both Ashley Cole and Wayne Bridge struggled for form and fitness for the majority of the season, and while West Ham's Alan Pardew was trumpeting the claims of his shaven haired bone-cruncher Paul Konchesky, Jewell believed the infinitely more pristine Bainesy was well worth a look.

Unlike previous years, where all talk of championships or play-off places were strictly taboo while the team attempted to garner as many points as possible, both the players and the club's management were positively striving for a European berth. Before a March ball had been kicked, Graham Kavanagh believed Latics needed at least 15 more points to finish sixth and qualify for the UEFA Cup.

Rio Ferdinand takes a tumble under pressure from Jason Roberts.

Wigan missed out on their first chance for a European berth in next season's competition after the Carling Cup disappointment. 'We have set ourselves a new target. We want to try and get 55 or 60 points now and see if we can get into Europe,' Kavanagh asserted. 'We got 40 points going into February which no one expected us to have. That was our target all along. I think we could definitely pat each other on the back, but the manager and all the players weren't taking their foot off the gas.'

The squad needed no more motivation to springboard their season toward a European place than a rematch with Manchester United. You could say after a 4–0 loss in a showcase event, that Wigan's players would want to bury their heads in the sand, never mind face their tormentors, Rooney and Ronaldo, again so soon. But what's that saying about falling off a horse?

Wigan were bursting to get the game underway. They had a point to prove. And so did their manager. At this moment in time, Paul Jewell had the unenviable record of shipping four goals each time a side under his stewardship had played the Red Devils.

The year's two 4–0 losses were two too many for the combative Liverpudlian, never mind the previous pair of 4–0 defeats when he was in charge of Bradford. 'Every time we've had a setback over the last three years here we've managed to kick on again and that's what I would expect,' he said. 'The Carling Cup was a big occasion for us, but nothing will ever take the place of the Premiership in my eyes.'

The visit of Manchester United to the JJB stadium on 6 March was only the second in their history. Sir Alex Ferguson's men opened the £28 million-structure on 4 August 1999 with an exhibition of football from their global superstars which was thought well beyond the realm of any Wigan player.

Jimmy Bullard celebrates with Paul Scharner after taking the lead against Manchester United – a goal that sent the JJB Stadium wild.

Oh, how times had changed. On home turf, Wigan knew they could have the edge – if they played to their potential. With a packed JJB stadium bristling with indignation at their supposed inferiority, and the crowd baying for Red blood, a wolfish Wigan side hunted the 2006 superstars down in packs. Hustling and harrying, playing the pressure game that the wide open spaces of Cardiff didn't allow for, Messrs Rooney and Co. didn't get a kick during the first half.

Wigan threw everything at United. Skipper Arjan De Zeeuw set the tone in the opening minutes by flinging himself at Christiano Ronaldo. It was one of those occasions where a team 'gets' at a star player, especially one who invites tackles with close control and dribbling skills. De Zeeuw was letting Ronaldo and the rest of his side know that Wigan meant business, that they would get close enough to see the whites of their opponents' eyes. He was booked, but no Wigan fan begrudged him that.

But it wasn't all blood and thunder. When Wigan had the ball, they played simple, stylish football at great pace and with a surety of touch. Their wide men, McCulloch, Teale, Chimbonda and Baines, pressed far up the pitch and it was all Wigan. How many a schoolboy fan dreamed of saying that while kicking a casey around his patch of concrete?

Teale, Roberts and Camara all had superb opportunities within the first 25 minutes. United started valiantly, but realised their opponents had the greater desire and had to simply hang on to Wigan's coat tails and hope they wouldn't be out of sight at the interval. But seven chances missed Van Der Sar's net by the interval. Had Wigan's chance slipped away?

Monday 6 March 2006

Wigan Athletic 1
Manchester Utd 2

WIGAN: Filan 7, Chimbonda 7, De Zeeuw 8, Scharner 8, Baines 8, Teale 7, Kavanagh 7, Bullard 7, McCulloch 8 (Ziegler 89), Roberts 7, Camara 7. Wigan star man: Scharner.

MANCHESTER UNITED: Van Der Sar 7, Neville 7, Ferdinand 7, Brown 7, Silvestre 6 (Evra 85), Ronaldo 8, Giggs 7, O'Shea 6, Park 6 (Van Nistelrooy 71), Saha 7, Rooney 8.

Goals: Scharner (60), Ronaldo (74), Chombonda (og, 90)
Half-time: 0–0
Referee: Steve Bennett
Attendance: 23,574

Paul Scharner and Ruud van Nistelrooy look for the advantage.

United had improved by the second half – they seemed instinctively to know the importance of the first goal. Rooney missed United's gilt-edged chance when, unmarked, he sent a diving header over the bar from a few yards. Instead Wigan claimed what should have been the crucial opener. Bullard's corner saw De Zeeuw's header cleared off the line by Ryan Giggs. McCulloch touched into the path of Roberts, but Giggs again kept it out. There was no denying Scharner, though, as he poked home at the third attempt. The stadium almost exploded.

Wigan stuck with the enterprising, edgy style that had so far brought so many rewards, but it was a game of roulette in footballing terms. When Kavanagh lost the ball upfield, Wigan were left with too little cover at the back. Van Nistelrooy, freshly on as a sub, mis-hit a cross shot which fell at the feet of Ronaldo, who planted the ball into an empty net. It was their first attempt on target. Undeterred, Wigan went in search of a second.

If the equaliser was a sickener, what unfolded in the second minute of injury-time was a gut-wrenching blow.

Ronaldo's cross saw Louis Saha's shot come back off the bar and the ball hit Chimbonda before rolling agonisingly over the line. It was as big a robbery as the £50 million Securitas heist in Kent coupled with the Great Train Robbery. United won 2–1, despite registering just one shot on target.

Chimbonda wanted the ground to swallow him up. 'I'm very disappointed. We were outstanding all the way through the game,' said a sombre Paul Jewell afterwards. 'We were in their faces from the off and I couldn't ask for any more from my players. They beat us fair and square and easily in the Carling Cup Final, but we definitely deserved something this time.'

He now had to raise the players again for the rest of the season.

'It was one of those unfortunate things for the defender. It came down on top of him and I don't there was much he could have done about it – it was unlucky,' reflected Sir Alex Ferguson after Chimbonda's last-minute misfortune.

'We all felt really sorry for Pascal. He knows he couldn't avoid it,' said his gutted teammate Lee McCulloch. 'He didn't say much afterwards. I asked him what happened and he said there was nothing he could have done about it. It came off him a yard out – it could have happened to anyone.'

But the close-knit nature of the team meant Chimbonda was exonerated in the post-match recriminations. All were sure United had the luck of a leprechaun with a four-leaf clover. Malcolm Glazer sprang to mind.

Again, all the talk was of the positives, of Wigan playing for a European place, a point reiterated by their manager, who juggled a couple of footballing clichés at the same time. 'We've got to keep going until the end of the season and give it our best shot,' he told the press corps.

What the opposition said...

'I don't think we've had a harder game away from home this season. I thought Wigan were absolutely brilliant. We really had to work hard and fight hard and at the end of the day we've had a bit of luck. Wigan were terrific and I don't think they deserved that result, but it was a very important win for us.' – Sir Alex Ferguson.

What the Wigan fan said...

'We had 11 heroes out there in blue and white jerseys. We deserved at least a point out of the game. The winner was a sickener. Who would have ever thought we'd be disappointed to have not at least got a draw against Manchester United?' – West Stand season-ticket holder Andy Wareing.

	P	W	D	L	F	A	Pts
Chelsea	28	23	3	2	56	17	72
Man Utd	27	17	6	4	54	28	57
Liverpool	28	16	7	5	33	17	55
Tottenham	28	13	10	5	40	26	49
Arsenal	28	13	5	10	43	22	44
Blackburn	28	13	4	11	36	34	43
Bolton	26	11	9	6	33	27	42
West Ham	27	12	6	9	41	36	42
Man City	28	12	4	12	38	32	40
Wigan	28	12	4	12	33	36	40
Newcastle	28	11	6	11	29	30	39
Everton	28	11	4	13	21	36	37
Charlton	28	10	6	12	32	37	36
Aston Villa	28	8	10	10	33	35	34
Middlesb'h	27	9	7	11	36	44	34
Fulham	28	9	5	14	37	43	32
West Brom	28	7	5	16	25	42	26
Birm'ham	27	6	5	16	22	38	23
Portsm'th	28	4	6	18	18	48	18
Sunderl'd	28	2	4	22	19	51	10

Sir Alex Ferguson hailed Wigan as the toughest side he had faced on his travels.

John Filan kept Wigan in the game against Sunderland with a string of stunning saves.

Up next was a sure-fire three-pointer against Sunderland's Black Cats, who, weighed down by the forces of history, were anchored to the foot of the League. Sunderland were still to win at home and had lost 10 on their own patch, managing just four draws so far. The north-east club had only scored nine at home, not scored more than one in a home game and had conceded 27.

Yet McCulloch warned his teammates to prepare for a backlash after Sunderland sacked the largely blameless, but equally hapless, Mick McCarthy in the week before the game. 'We needed to pick ourselves up for Sunderland. We knew this was going to be another tough game for us,' he reasoned. 'It definitely wasn't to be an away banker, especially with their manager going. Their players all had a point to prove.' A great example could be found just up the road from the Wearsiders. Their great rivals Newcastle were six games unbeaten after dumping Graeme Souness.

The Stadium of Light crowd was not expecting a good game. The previous season, Sunderland scraped a jammy 1–0 win at the JJB by playing a physical, pressure game, high on puff, but low on finesse. Yet the turgid affair was lit by a moment of singular brilliance. Henri Camara took a bouncing ball on the edge of the box and, swivelling, caught it on the volley. Crack!

As it whistled into the far corner of the net, just under the angle of post and crossbar, Sunderland's goalkeeper Kelvin Davies managed to move only one part of his body. His jaw dropped as he remained rooted to the spot. Only eight minutes of the match had gone, but so had Sunderland's stomach for the fight. Camara was certainly due a goal after going five games without finding the net, and had he ever scored a better one?

It was the worst Wigan played all season and won. But, after what had happened at the JJB Stadium the previous Monday, Jewell's troops were due a bit of luck. 'We

Saturday 11 March 2006

Sunderland 0 Wigan 1

SUNDERLAND: Davis 6, Nosworthy 6, Caldwell 7, Collins 7, McCartney 7, Delap 7 (Le Tallec 64 6), Whitehead 7, Leadbitter 7, Arca 6 (Lawrence 45 6), Kyle 6, Elliott 7 (Stead 86).

WIGAN: Filan 8, Chimbonda 6, Scharner 6, De Zeeuw 7, Baines 6, Teale 6 (Thompson 59 6), Bullard 6, Kavanagh 6 (Ziegler 63 6), McCulloch 7, Camara 8 (Johansson 82), Roberts 6. Wigan star man: Camara.

Goal: Camara (8)
Half-time: 0–1
Referee: Mike Riley
Attendance: 31,194

Arjan De Zeeuw congratulates Henri Camara at the Stadium of Light after the goal of the season.

didn't deserve to win,' Arjan De Zeeuw confessed. 'Sunderland made us fight tremendously hard. But we got the breaks that we didn't get against United.'

'It was an awful game,' sighed a relieved Paul Jewell. 'But we got three points. We didn't have any drive or energy and only for our 'keeper we would have lost the game. John made three or four really good saves.' One 'keeper gets injured, his replacement puts in a man of the match performance. What a terrible headache for a manager.

Wigan's win in the north-east saw them repeat the same scoreline against the Black Cats after Jason Roberts's 12-second penalty at the JJB Stadium back in August.

'We weren't that bad in the home game,' Jewell warned. 'Over the two games, though, Sunderland had been better than us.'

March was all about doubles. First Sunderland and now big north-west rivals Manchester City could surrender all six League points to Wigan. Doing the double over City especially would put a spring in the step and a twinkle in the eye of many a fan who remembered a certain Shaun Goater 'goal' in a play-off semi-final not too

What the opposition said...

'We created a lot of chances but didn't hit the back of the net. I remember thinking we could have done without that today, it was an unbelievable goal, but these things happen. I'm disappointed with the result but pleased with the performance.' – Sunderland caretaker manager Kevin Ball.

What the Wigan fan said...

'Wigan started off like they were still playing Manchester United and we scored with a fantastic Henri Camara strike. But for some reason we then started playing like a Sunday League side. I don't think we'll see Wigan score a better goal this season.' – Season-ticket holder Jay Taylor.

	P	W	D	L	F	A	Pts
Chelsea	29	24	3	2	58	18	75
Man Utd	28	18	6	4	56	28	60
Liverpool	29	16	7	6	34	19	55
Tottenham	29	13	10	6	41	28	49
Arsenal	29	14	5	10	45	23	47
Blackburn	29	14	4	11	38	34	46
Bolton	27	12	9	6	37	28	45
Wigan	29	13	4	12	34	36	43
West Ham	28	12	6	10	42	40	42
Man City	29	12	4	13	39	34	40
Everton	29	12	4	13	24	37	40
Newcastle	29	11	6	12	29	32	39
Charlton	29	11	6	12	34	38	39
Aston Villa	29	8	10	11	33	37	34
Middlesb'h	28	9	7	12	37	46	34
Fulham	29	9	5	15	38	46	32
West Brom	29	7	6	16	26	43	27
Birm'ham	28	6	6	16	23	39	24
Portsm'th	29	5	6	18	20	49	21
Sunderl'd	29	2	4	23	19	52	10

Paul Jewell admitted Sunderland had been the better side despite scraping a 1–0 win – completing their second double in as many weeks, following a victory over Manchester City.

Wigan's Lee McCulloch sends a header into the back of the net at the City of Manchester Stadium.

many (blue) moons ago. May 1999 to be precise. And everyone at the club was pulling, or pushing the same way.

On the pulling front, David Connolly decided not to do any more damage to himself – returning to action for the reserves after 12 games out with a tweaked hamstring – and Ryan Taylor's recovery from a metatarsal break was almost complete.

On the pushing front, Europe was still on the horizon, and Latics were singing from the same hymn sheet.

Wigan's only blip against City came when they were knocked out of the FA Cup in the fourth round in Manchester back in January. But there was plenty of cause for confidence in the Wigan camp. Lee McCulloch celebrated the arrival of his second child, Jack, the previous Tuesday, 14 months after his first son Callum, with a thumping header in Manchester, which kept Latics firmly on course for Europe.

Unfortunately, Wigan's first consecutive League wins of 2006 didn't propel them any further up the table after Bolton and Blackburn both won, meaning they remained eighth. But Latics' first-ever victory at City in five attempts and against a side who had won their previous seven on home soil, was the perfect tonic for McCulloch on the back of his first decent night's kip in a week. 'I've had some sleepless nights over the last week,' he said, rubbing his eyes. 'I managed to get a good night's sleep in the hotel, though. We knew it was such a big game and to get all three points is a great result. It was a scrappy game, but the most important thing for us was the points.'

The match was remembered for some calamity keeping from David James. When his attempted clearance from a hard-hit back pass spooned behind the goal, McCulloch swooped at the resulting corner.

City's best chance of the game came when John Filan's attempted throw-out bounced off Sylvain Distin's bonce a couple of yards in front of him and landed on the bar before landing safely.

Saturday 18 March 2006

Manchester City 0 Wigan 1

MANCHESTER CITY: James 5, Mills 6, Distin 7, Sommeil 6, Thatcher 6, Sinclair 7, Ireland 6, Reyna 6 (Croft 66), Sun 6, Wright-Phillips 6, Sibierski 5 (Samaras 27, Miller 61).

WIGAN: Filan 7, Chimbonda 7, Scharner 8, De Zeeuw 7, Baines 7, Teale 7, Kavanagh 6, Bullard 7, McCulloch 8, Roberts 7, Camara 7 (Johansson 85). Wigan star man: Scharner.

Goal: McCulloch (55)
Half-time: 0–0
Referee: Martin Atkinson
Attendance: 42,444

As if March hadn't been stormy enough to begin with, boy were fans to wake up to a bombshell on the morning of 15 March. 'Lindsay appointed to Latics' board of directors' ran the headlines. Maurice Lindsay, for so long a centre of power in rugby league, specifically Wigan Warriors, had been made a director of Wigan Athletic. No one really knew why.

Not to go over old ground too much, Dave Whelan said it would 'bring his two clubs together'. Latics' vice-chairman Phillip Williams and director Brian Ashcroft had correspondingly joined the Warriors' board. At the time Paul Jewell said: 'There is a saying that I've used a lot recently, which is, "If you can't please everyone, just please yourself."' He basically meant Mr Whelan had trusted in his own judgement by appointing Lindsay, but Jewell did say that he had 'the club's best interest at heart' and 'wouldn't do anything which would jeopardise that.'

And the man at the centre of the storm? 'I am not a one-eyed supporter,' said Lindsay defiantly. 'By that I mean I don't think it's absolutely essential to only love one sport. You are much richer in life if you love all sports. I have been watching football all my life, one of my best friends is Nat Lofthouse. I am sure that there are still a few people who harbour old-fashioned grudges, which I believe have no place in the modern world or modern Wigan. To be honest, what was once known as a rugby league town is now a sporting town and I think everybody should be behind that principle. I suppose you can't please all the people all of the time, but we used to have this problem between rugby league and rugby union. That enmity has now been buried and we have all grown up.'

Ecstatic Jimmy Bullard congratulates scorer Lee McCulloch with Jason Roberts at Manchester.

Latics' vice-chairman Phillip Williams diplomatically pointed out, 'both clubs already share so much. We have the same home, facilities, medical expertise, infrastructure and ultimately the same pride in our great town. It's time to share the talent, ideas and inspiration that both clubs possess.'

On a lighter note, Paul Jewell was remembering what it was like to be on a football field, taking a starring role in a game of ex-pros versus TV personalities in Halifax. The game raised money for Tommy Gildert, the fitness co-ordinator for the Shaymen for the past 10 years who had been diagnosed with terminal cancer. Jewell certainly made his mark as he claimed a left-footed drive any striker would have been proud of.

Back to the football, then, and Jimmy Bullard told his teammates that four more wins would bring European qualification. The former trainee Hammer piped up in

What the opposition said...

'We brought our club captain and two international full-backs back. There were one or two youngsters but in the main the performance was responsible for the result rather than the team selection. We did not compete well enough, or get the ball down and play when we did compete with them.' – Manchester City manager Stuart Pearce.

What the Wigan fan said...

'We thoroughly deserved to win the game. We had a lot of the ball and could have scored more goals in the end. City only had one chance and that said it all. Scharner had a good game – the defence has looked a lot better since he's been playing next to Arjan De Zeeuw.' – season-ticket holder Stuart Waterworth.

	P	W	D	L	F	A	Pts
Chelsea	30	24	3	3	58	19	75
Man Utd	29	19	6	4	58	29	63
Liverpool	31	18	7	6	42	21	61
Tottenham	30	14	10	6	43	28	52
Arsenal	30	15	5	10	48	23	50
Blackburn	30	15	4	11	41	36	49
Bolton	28	13	9	6	39	28	48
Wigan	30	14	4	12	35	36	46
Everton	30	13	4	13	28	38	43
West Ham	29	12	6	11	44	44	42
Man City	30	12	4	14	39	35	40
Newcastle	30	11	6	13	30	35	39
Charlton	30	11	6	13	34	41	39
Fulham	31	10	5	16	40	51	35
Aston Villa	30	8	10	12	34	41	34
Middlesb'h	29	9	7	13	39	49	34
West Brom	30	7	6	17	27	45	27
Birm'ham	29	6	6	17	23	41	24
Portsm'th	30	6	6	18	24	51	24
Sunderl'd	30	2	4	24	19	54	10

Dave Whelan (second from left), benefactor of Wigan Warriors and Wigan Athletic, announced a board shake-up with Latics directors Philip Williams (left) and Brian Ashcroft (second from right) also taking a role with the rugby club and Warriors chairman Maurice Lindsay (centre) given a role with Wigan Athletic. Also pictured is John Martin (right), director of the Warriors.

the week before facing his old club. 'We still owed them one from a couple of years ago when they stopped us getting into the play-offs,' he recalled. 'That was the lowest point of my time at Wigan when Brian Deane popped in that header in the last minute. We'd worked so hard all season and to miss out like that was gutting. We were determined they wouldn't stop us this time as we pushed for Europe.'

The crafty Cockney was also professing his interest in playing for the Germans at the summer World Cup. He qualified for the Jerries through his maternal grandmother but didn't know whether boss Jurgen Klinsmann was interested in him. 'I'm still waiting for my phone to ring, I'd jump at the chance if it came,' he bubbled. A week later he was to do a Sky Sports interview, in which he was stumped when asked who played for the current German side. 'You said you wouldn't ask me that!' squealed the Soccer AM regular, before going on to remember that Oliver Kahn and Jens Lehmann guarded the sticks.

Despite the jocularity, Bullard's week took a turn for the worse after the game. It had always been his dream to score the winner against West Ham – but not for them with three seconds to play. After outplaying West Ham for the best part of 90 minutes, Wigan had suffered another sickening home reversal.

A clearly gutted Bullard diverted Teddy Sheringham's last-ditch cross into his own net. The strike was credited to West Ham skipper Nigel Reo-Coker, but the Latics midfielder knew different. 'It came off me in the end – I had the last touch and kicked it in,' Bullard moped. 'It was very lucky how it happened. Teddy scuffed the cross and Bainsey jumped to try and block it and it went under him. It went to Reo-Coker and he didn't even kick it, it clipped my foot and went into the back of the net. I couldn't believe it. That's twice now that West Ham have done it to us in the last minute.'

Jason Roberts tussles with West Ham's Hayden Mullins at the JJB Stadium.

Latics' goal came from a Lee McCulloch 25-yard rocket, which left Shaka Hislop static. But West Ham were on level terms after a slip-up at the back. Paul Scharner's back header lacked the required pace and allowed Marlon Harewood to nip in and walk the ball around Mike Pollitt and into the empty net.

Again Wigan went chasing a game, and again, they paid the price for it in the cruellest of fashions.

After a blistering debut season in the Premiership, Jewell had seen his team spend the majority of the year in the top six. And with just seven games to go, eighth-placed Latics were still in the hunt for Europe. 'Our own European ambitions were still there for the players,' Jewell said. 'I never said Europe was a

Lee McCulloch shows his disappointment after a late defeat by West Ham.

Saturday 25 March 2006

Wigan 1
West Ham 2

WIGAN: Filan 6 (Pollitt 45 6), Chimbonda 7, Scharner 6, De Zeeuw 8, Baines 8, Teale 6 (Thompson 70), Kavanagh 6 (Ziegler 75), Bullard 6, McCulloch 7, Roberts 6, Camara 6. Wigan star man: Baines.

WEST HAM: Hislop 7, Scaloni 7, Collins 6, Gabbidon 6, Konchesky 6, Benayoun 7 (Newton 90), Reo-Coker 7, Mullins 6, Etherington 6 (Zamora 71), Ashton 6 (Sheringham 82), Harewood 6.

Goals: McCulloch (45), Harewood (52), Reo-Coker (90)
Half-time: 1–0
Referee: Dermott Gallagher
Attendance: 18,736

A disconsolate Jimmy Bullard holds his hand up for West Ham's winning goal, admitting it came off his foot.

These fans travelled all the way from Holland to watch Wigan and make a plea to get Arjan De Zeeuw in the Dutch squad.

What the opposition said...

'You could see the hangover in the first half, but in the second we were more like ourselves, and this was a great win for us. Now there's a chance of glory and we have to grasp that opportunity. The FA Cup is a chance to win a trophy. Sixth or seventh place in the Premiership doesn't really enthrall me as much as winning silverware.' – West Ham manager Alan Pardew.

What the Wigan fan said...

'It's the second time we've thrown three points away in successive home matches. We should have won this game. Don't get me wrong, West Ham are a quality side, but we gave them the first goal and at this level you can't afford to do that.' – West Stand season-ticket holder Bill Melling.

	P	W	D	L	F	A	Pts
Chelsea	31	25	3	3	60	19	78
Man Utd	30	20	6	4	61	29	66
Liverpool	32	19	7	6	45	22	64
Tottenham	31	15	10	6	45	29	55
Blackburn	31	16	4	11	42	36	52
Arsenal	30	15	5	10	48	23	50
Bolton	29	13	9	7	42	32	48
Wigan	31	14	4	13	36	38	46
West Ham	30	13	6	11	46	45	45
Everton	31	13	4	14	29	41	43
Charlton	31	12	6	13	37	42	42
Man City	31	12	4	15	39	37	40
Newcastle	31	11	6	14	31	38	39
Middlesb'h	30	10	7	13	43	52	37
Fulham	32	10	6	16	40	51	36
Aston Villa	31	8	11	12	34	41	35
West Brom	31	7	6	18	28	47	27
Birm'ham	30	6	6	18	23	44	24
Portsm'th	30	6	6	18	24	51	24
Sunderl'd	31	2	4	25	19	55	10

target or aim at the start of the season. But I always knew it could be a possibility if we played to our maximum.'

Latics were up against Blackburn next, with their opponents banging on the door of the Champions League. 'They beat us 3–0 earlier this season and I have to say it was one of the best performances against us this term,' recalled Jewell. 'The attacking players were some of the best around. Craig Bellamy, Morten Gamst Pedersen and David Bentley were all fine players. Like all of the best teams in the Premier League they mixed that with a great workrate.'

The growing murmurs of contracts and players' comings and goings – around seven were due contract talks at the end of the season – were swiftly silenced by the manager, who decided to draw his team's focus to the here and now. 'We still had an awful lot still to play for,' he said, neatly underlining the point. 'I briefly mentioned it to the chairman, but he said he wanted to get to the end of the season before sitting down and looking at it. That was his choice because he made the decisions on money and what the players are paid. I didn't want the contract situation to be an issue. We had enough of that last summer with Nathan Ellington.'

Forward Neil Mellor, on loan from Liverpool until the end of the campaign, had already spoken of his desire to return to Anfield in the summer, and in fact was to leave Wigan sooner rather than later.

The first to be winging his way out of the exit door was Alan Mahon with the club's best wishes ringing in his ears. The popular Irishman joined Burnley on loan and was given a three-year contract by the Clarets. He joined Wigan from Blackburn in February 2004, making 56 appearances in all competitions and scoring 10 goals. 'He was one of the best pros I've worked with and everyone at the club is genuinely saddened he is leaving,' said his old manager Paul Jewell, proving his fairness and loyalty to players who he thought had rewarded him well. 'He's too good a player to be sitting on the bench.'

WIGAN Athletic used 29 players during their debut season in the Premier League. Objectivity goes through the window as *Season of Dreams* runs the rule over each and every one of the Latics players from their dramatic, historic and unforgettable debut top-flight campaign.

John Filan
Mr Dependable – the 'keeper not only made the odd wonder-save (think Villa Park) but, crucially, he made very few bloopers. The amiable Australian was forced to play second fiddle for the majority of the season but when he got his chance he proved he was good enough to still play at the top level, following a stint in the Premiership with Blackburn.
Appearances: 20. Goals: 0. Rating: 8.

Pascal Chimbonda
A revelation – Chimbonda swiftly progressed from unknown Frenchman, to cult hero, to the PFA's right-back of the year. He played like the energetic schoolboy striker asked to play in defence, such was his deceptive pace and natural attacking tendencies. Solid at the back, Chimbonda also covered more ground than any other full-back in the League. He only missed one League game but his Wigan stay turned sour on the final day.
Appearances: 43. Goals: 2. Rating: 9.

Arjan De Zeeuw
Captain fantastic – the prodigal son (pictured right) returned to the club to lead them into their historic campaign and was an absolute inspiration. The experienced Dutch centre-back showed the kind of courage that soldiers win medals for. Consistently brilliant, De Zeeuw led by example with his fearless challenges to win the Supporters' Player of the Year award and confirm his status as a genuine Wigan Athletic legend.
Appearances: 35. Goals: 0. Rating: 10.

Paul Scharner
Instant impact – the Australian international arrived in breathtaking style in January by netting a late winner against Arsenal in the first leg of the Carling Cup semi-final. He was brought in as a centre-back, but demonstrated he's as equally at home in the middle of the park. Rescuing a point against Everton and also scoring against Manchester United, he calmed his occasional tendency to over play in defence.
Appearances: 19. Goals: 4. Rating: 8.

Leighton Baines
International bright young thing – an exceptional debut campaign for the full-back, who showed experience well beyond his years. Never fazed by any opponent, Baines stood up to everything thrown at him and was a dangerous customer in the opposition's half – traits that compensated for the absence of a goal. He starred for England U–21s and Paul Jewell called for him to be considered for a full cap. No Wigan fan disagreed.
Appearances: 43. Goals: 0. Rating: 9.

Gary Teale
Flying Scotsman – no player polarised opinion quite like Gary Teale, but no one ever questioned the Scot's blistering pace, which only a handful of players in the Premiership could come close to

matching. The winger covered more ground than any other player during the season and when he was on song, so were Wigan. Teale showed he was more than good enough to play in the Premiership.
Appearances: 33. Goals: 0. Rating: 8.

Jimmy Bullard
A one-off – there will never be another Jimmy Bullard. The energetic midfielder took to the Premiership seamlessly and while others would buckle under such intense pressure and media scrutiny, Bullard went about his business with a smile. His infectious personality and remarkable skills helped him revel in even the biggest of stages. His journey mirrored the rise of Wigan, and it was with reluctance that he left.
Appearances: 43. Goals: 4. Rating: 9.

Graham Kavanagh
Major Kav – Manchester United proved they could succeed without a battling, Irish midfielder in the heart of their side, but Kavanagh was a lynchpin of Wigan's success. His contrasting style with Bullard complemented the midfield, Kavanagh thriving in the anchor role in front of the back four. He never scored, but his leadership and competitive streak proved invaluable and earned him the nickname Major Kav.
Appearances: 42. Goals: 0. Rating: 8.

Lee McCulloch
Muscled up – McCulloch chipped in with five goals from midfield, a decent return considering his campaign was hampered by injury. A real aerial threat, the Scot added some muscle out on the left that worried plenty of right-backs. His stamina to work up and down the line was almost as impressive as his screaming goal against West Ham. Another player to follow the club up from the old Division Two.
Appearances: 35. Goals: 5. Rating: 8.

Jason Roberts
Proved a point – Roberts led the line full of guts, determination and with new-found maturity. Many strikers get trapped in the notorious grey area of being too good for the lower leagues, but not good enough for the Premiership. Roberts was initially and unfairly pigeon-holed in that category, but he proved his class by troubling the best defences in the League. His end-of-season dip didn't overshadow a remarkable campaign.
Appearances: 43. Goals: 14. Rating: 9.

Henri Camara
French polish – he arrived with a reputation as an *enfant terrible* but thrived under Paul Jewell's astute leadership. Would Latics have qualified for Europe if he hadn't missed 10 games in January due to African Nations Cup duty? His frightening pace blew defences away at times – his hat-trick against Charlton a memorable highlight. Camara also grabbed the goal of the season at Sunderland.
Appearances: 32. Goals: 11. Rating: 8.

Mike Pollitt
Highbury hero – plucked from the relative obscurity of Rotherham for a measly £200,000, Pollitt made a strong case for being Paul Jewell's shrewdest ever signing. He never ceased to impress, while his heroic display at Highbury in the Carling Cup semi-final will go down as one of the finest individual performances of the season. Niall Quinn said at the time, 'Mike Pollitt has become a legend tonight.' Amen to that.
Appearances: 30. Goals: 0. Rating: 9.

Matt Jackson
Sure and steady – limited to just eight Premiership starts, the experienced professional and club captain never let anyone down when he came into the side and didn't look out of place. His pace may not have been what it was during his Everton heyday, but his positional sense and knowledge of the game proved vital and he was an incredibly popular figure in the camp.
Appearances: 23. Goals: 0. Rating: 7.

Stephane Henchoz
A warhorse (a neutral one; he's Swiss) – arrived on a free transfer and proved good business as he added Premiership experience to the back line. The ex-Liverpool defender made up for his lack of pace with his ability to tackle, harass and block. After a disappointing Carling Cup Final performance he fell out of favour but did enough to earn a World Cup call-up.
Appearances: 32. Goals: 0. Rating: 7.

Andreas Johansson
Swede success – started the season with a missed chance against Chelsea and ended with a sending off at Arsenal. In between, he played some productive football. The versatile player proved a valuable member of the squad and finished with seven goals, despite only playing a bit-part during the season. Never one to moan, Johansson played up front, on the left and in midfield and scored twice at Spurs.
Appearances this season: 24. Goals: 7. Rating: 8.

Steve McMillan
Cursed – it was another season blighted by injury for the unlucky Scottish left-back, who only managed to start four games because of a troublesome knee problem. But every time he was in action he always showed he had a trusted left boot, admirable composure and the ability to handle whatever was thrown at him.
Appearances: 7. Goals: 0. Rating: 7.

Ryan Taylor
Perfect (if) fit – Taylor proved a cracking £750,000 buy from Tranmere, starring at both right-back and in midfield. Bags of potential, played for England U–21s but saw his season ravaged by injury. Broke his metatarsal (think Beckham, World Cup, 2002) against Leeds in January and then broke his leg during his comeback in the reserves.
Appearances: 16. Goals: 1. Rating: 7.

Reto Zieglerr
Loan ranger – Tottenham's highly-rated Swiss star joined on loan in January and quickly settled into the side when he got his chance at left-back or in midfield. A great technician with the ability to deliver from set-pieces. Gave the side good balance and was unlucky not to score on a couple of occasions.
Appearances: 13. Goals: 0. Rating: 7.

Josip Skoko
Struggled – limited to just 11 games for Wigan before he went to Stoke on loan until the end of the campaign. The Australian international played a significant part in the club's Carling Cup win over Newcastle in the fourth round, starring in a second-string side, but never really excelled in the chances he was given.
Appearances: 11. Goals: 0. Rating: 6.

Damien Francis
Faded – started the season well as a powerful, attacking midfielder and got the winner at Goodison Park in September. But his confidence melted and his campaign went downhill after the defeat at Liverpool in December. After refusing to go to Stoke on loan, he found himself on the sidelines in the New Year, restricted to a cameo role.
Appearances: 24. Goals: 1. Rating: 6.

David Connolly
No luck of the Irish – Latics didn't get an immediate return from the £2 million spent on the Irishman at the start of the season. He burst onto the scene with a stunning goal at West Brom, but then spent 10 weeks out in the New Year with a hamstring injury.
Appearances: 20. Goals: 3. Rating: 6.

Alan Mahon
Fond Farewell – one of the personalities at the club, whose sense of humour gave the squad much of its strong sense of togetherness, he left in March when he joined Burnley. He only appeared 13 times in their Premiership campaign, such was the competition ahead of him, but the Irishman scored a cracker at Villa Park in October.
Appearances: 13. Goals: 1. Rating: 7.

David Thompson
A fair Kop – signed in January until the end of the season from Blackburn, the ex-Liverpool and Blackburn star provided cover on the right side of midfield. He claimed an important goal at Middlesbrough in January and starred at Arsenal on the final day, scoring a stunning goal.
Appearances: 9. Goals: 2. Rating: 7.

Neil Mellor
Down after the Riverside – managed just five games as he struggled with a knee injury and his fitness. He was sent back to Liverpool in April, but did help claim all three points at the Riverside Stadium with a last-minute winner.
Appearances: 5. Goals: 1. Rating: 6.

David Wright
Limited chances – the defender appeared just four times as he suffered with injuries throughout the campaign. He also spent a month at Norwich at the end of 2005.
Appearances: 4. Goals: 0. Rating: 6.

Emerson Thome
End of the road – played two games against Bournemouth and Watford before his two-and-a-half-year stay at the JJB Stadium came to an end.
Appearances: 2. Goals: 0. Rating: 6.

Luke Joyce
To Elland back – the young midfielder came on in extra-time during the Cup clash at Leeds and moved to Carlisle on loan in March.
Appearances: 1. Goals: 0. Rating: –.

Joey Waterhouse
In reserve – the young defender came on for the last two minutes of extra-time against Watford. Highly regarded.
Appearances: 1. Goals: 0. Rating: –.

17: April and May: A glove affair turns sour

PAUL Jewell built his reputation on the backbone of a strong character. A manager steadfast in his beliefs. Noble values from his own upbringing as well as schooling at the famous Liverpool academy instilled virtues like honesty, integrity and fairness – and his own, unwritten rules served him so purposefully throughout his career that he would rarely deviate from them. The beginning of April was one of those rare occasions.

Unlike many managers, Paul Jewell doesn't criticise referees publicly. Doesn't moan about their decisions. Doesn't blame them for results not going his way. But at Ewood Park on 3 April, he witnessed a challenge on keeper John Filan that left him raging at referee Phil Dowd.

Arjan De Zeeuw thinks he has scored against Blackburn, but referee Phil Dowd ruled his goal out for offside.

Controversy again, as Blackburn's Shefki Kuqi equalises despite a challenge on John Filan.

Monday 3 April 2006

Blackburn Rovers 1
Wigan Athletic 1

BLACKBURN: Friedel 8, Neill 6, Nelsen 7, Khizanishvili 6, Gray 6, Bentley 6 (Tugay 58 6), Savage 7, Reid 7, Pedersen 7, Bellamy 7, Dickov (Kuqi 58 6).

WIGAN: Filan 8, Chimbonda 7, Scharner 6 (Jackson 45 7), De Zeeuw 8, Baines 7, Teale 8, Kavanagh 7, Bullard 7, McCulloch 7, Roberts 7, Johansson 7. Wigan star man: De Zeeuw.

Goals: Roberts (53), Kugi (84)
Half-time: 0–0
Referee: Phil Dowd
Attendance: 20,410

The official had already ruled out a legitimate goal from Arjan De Zeeuw and then allowed Shefki Kuqi's equaliser to stand six minutes from time. Lucas Neill's challenge on Filan, which led to the Finn's strike, belonged in cage wrestling, not football, and had Wigan won they would have moved up to seventh in the table.

Even the risk of an FA penalty, a heavy fine and a touchline ban could not silence Jewell's anger. 'We were robbed in the first half and robbed at the end, but I suppose that's about right for Phil Dowd isn't it?' he raged. 'I don't think John was fouled at the end – I think it was GBH. It was a nonsensical performance from the referee. Everyone has a bad game, but it's just incompetent. One Premiership manager told me he's the worst referee we've got in the League and he's not wrong. I'm at a loss.'

It was not the first time Jewell had been left incensed by Dowd's performance. 'We had the same referee at Arsenal (in the Carling Cup semi-final) and we should have had three penalties there and he gave them one,' he said.

Before the match, Latics were already up against it going into their first League clash at Ewood Park. Jewell's battlers had only won two of 11 in all competitions prior to kick-off and, with Henri Camara granted leave to return to Senegal following the death of his grandmother, they took the game to Rovers.

Jimmy Bullard's free-kick was headed on to Arjan De Zeeuw by Ryan Nelsen, the ball went goalwards and the Latics captain slammed home the lose ball. Zurab Khizanishvili was playing both Scharner and Roberts onside, leaving the decision shrouded in mystery.

'There was no way my goal was offside,' offered De Zeeuw afterwards. 'You can clearly see from the replays that the linesman has made a big mistake.'

Brad Friedel produced a sensational stop to deny Lee McCulloch from point-blank range but the American was helpless to stop Roberts netting his 14th of the campaign from the resulting corner. But the equaliser arrived in the 84th minute when Reid's cross saw Neill flatten Filan, and Kuqi slotted in the loose ball.

In the aftermath, as Jewell sweated on whether he would face an FA rap for bringing the game into disrepute, the Wigan manager elaborated on his remarks and, as many had come to expect from him, his comments were more common sense than controversial. Defending his outburst, he was angered that he had been asked for an explanation from the game's governing body. 'That's quite interesting because of the other 32 League games so far, they [the referees] have been great and I've said that,' he said. 'And I've never once had anyone from the FA ring me up to thank me for that. I consider myself an objective manager. A passionate one, but an objective one, and I'm disappointed that I've got to explain those comments.'

What the opposition said...

'I felt we were hard done by when Morten Gamst Pedersen had a goal chalked off in the first half when Paul Dickov was pulled up for a supposed foul on John Filan. It was a valid goal. We showed a great reaction after going behind and it's always difficult against Wigan because they stopped us playing our normal game. They came here and had a real go at us, but we still had some good chances.' – Blackburn Rovers manager Mark Hughes.

Paul Jewell argues with referee Phil Dowd and later said Stevie Wonder wouldn't have awarded Blackburn's goal.

What the Wigan fan said...

'The referee determined the outcome of the game with some really bad decisions. A point at Blackburn may not be a bad result, but we deserved all three. He was terrible and cost us the game. Someone like Phil Dowd would be better off refereeing in the non-League.' – season-ticket holder Mark Fulton.

	P	W	D	L	F	A	Pts
Chelsea	32	25	4	3	60	19	79
Man Utd	32	22	6	4	64	30	72
Liverpool	33	20	7	6	47	22	67
Tottenham	32	15	10	7	46	32	55
Arsenal	31	16	5	10	53	23	53
Blackburn	32	16	5	11	43	37	53
Bolton	30	13	9	8	43	34	48
Wigan	32	14	5	13	37	39	47
West Ham	32	13	7	12	46	46	46
Everton	32	13	5	14	31	43	44
Charlton	32	12	7	13	37	42	43
Newcastle	32	12	6	14	34	39	42
Man City	32	12	4	16	39	38	40
Middlesb'h	31	11	7	13	44	52	40
Fulham	33	10	6	17	41	54	36
Aston Villa	32	8	11	13	34	46	35
West Brom	32	7	6	19	28	49	27
Portsm'th	31	7	6	18	27	52	27
Birm'ham	31	6	7	18	23	44	25
Sunderl'd	32	2	5	25	21	57	11

Video replays clearly vindicated Jewell's comments, but that wasn't the point. He stood by the theory that referees make mistakes but, over the course of the season, the close calls balance themselves out.

Jewell had been in trouble with the FA before. He was handed a two-game touchline ban and given a £1,000 fine after lambasting Paul Robinson after he sent off Filan at Reading in November 2003. Again, that was another rare occasion when he contradicted his own, self-imposed rule of not questioning the referee. 'Some go for you and some don't and I accept that, especially the marginal ones,' he continued. 'If I have to watch a replay of something and then view it again I think, "Well, the referee is only human and he's only seen it once". There's only me and about two other managers who go to the referee to give them the team-sheet myself – at other clubs they send a coach or a kit man, but I show them the courtesy and respect and I know everyone makes mistakes – even me. Sometimes. But these weren't dubious – I don't think Stevie Wonder would have given that goal on Sunday.'

The incident led to the debate resurfacing about whether technology should be introduced into football. Jewell, as perhaps expected, took the traditional stance – 'I'm definitely not one for change' – though not for traditional reasons.

'You go back to when Newcastle played here (in October, Wigan beat Newcastle 1–0 in a game that saw visiting striker Alan Shearer have a goal ruled out when it was cleared by Leighton Baines despite strong claims the ball crossed the line). I've seen the video and I think Shearer gets the ball over the line. But how far do you go back? Because before that, Shearer definitely took out Arjan De Zeeuw and so I'm not one for technology, because it's the small instances that lead to the big instances.'

Andreas Johansson celebrates his goal against Birmingham but Wigan's home curse was to strike again.

Having been robbed of points on their travels, Wigan were hoping to collect some at home. They had won just one point out of a possible 15 at home since the start of 2006 and, with visitors Birmingham embroiled in a relegation dogfight, they had the perfect chance to end their difficult run.

The game marked Steve Bruce's first at the JJB Stadium since turning his back on Wigan five years earlier. Bruce, the ex-Manchester United skipper, was in charge at the JJB Stadium for just eight games in 2001 before bailing when they lost their Second Division semi-final play-off clash against Reading to join Crystal Palace just two days later. 'It was a tough decision to leave Wigan and move my family down south, but I felt it was a commitment I had to make at the time,' he said ahead of the match, with his side languishing second from bottom in the Premiership and two points adrift from safety.

Bruce was only at Palace five months before breaking his contract to join Birmingham in 2001 and though he infuriated Dave Whelan for walking out on the club, he said he spoke regularly to Jewell. Soon after joining Birmingham, Bruce recruited John Benson from Wigan and though the former manager and director

Saturday 8 April 2006

Wigan Athletic 1
Birmingham 1

WIGAN: Filan 8, Chimbonda 8, Scharner 6, De Zeeuw 6, Baines 6 (Ziegler 43 6), Teale 7, Kavanagh 6, Bullard 6, McCulloch 7, Roberts 7, Johansson 7 (Camara 79). Wigan star man: Pascal Chimbonda.

BIRMINGHAM: Taylor 8, Tebily 7, Cunningham 7, Taylor 7, Sadler 7, Pennant 7, Izzet 7 (Dunn 65), Jarosik 7, Johnson 6, Sutton 6 (Forssell 65), Heskey 7.

Goals: Johansson (49), Dunn (77)
Half-time: 0–0
Referee: Howard Webb
Attendance: 18,669

What the opposition said...

'Considering the position we're in we've rounded off a very good week for ourselves. Wigan have had a fantastic season. It's never easy coming here, but let's hope this is the point that keeps us in the Premier League. We've got a good point, which we deserved. But we're a little bit disappointed because we had enough chances to have nicked it.' – Birmingham manager Steve Bruce.

of football was unpopular with many Latics fans, Jewell told a different story. 'There are a lot of misconceptions among Wigan fans about John – he took a lot of flak for stuff that was nothing to do with him,' said Jewell. 'He was solid and he really helped me when he was here. He actually interviewed me when I got this job.'

Club media manager Matt McCann interrupted to joke that Benson must have been drunk at the time. 'John's a moped like you, Matt,' Jewell quipped. 'Two pints and you're both full!'

Two days before the game Paul Scharner invited his teammates to his new home in Warrington for a house-warming party. Ironically, Scharner could have so nearly been lining up against Latics for Birmingham that weekend if Paul Jewell hadn't hijacked the deal.

Scharner was a walking, talking contradiction. A dedicated athlete yet a showman; an intelligent, caring family man who dyes his hair and has a life coach. He had his own website, while his passions were bridge jumping, skydiving… and Mozart. Graham Kavanagh says 'clubs need diverse characters to make a team' and that Scharner's eccentric qualities do not mask the fact that he is 'a top lad and a top player'.

That was unquestionable. Unfortunately, the game against Birmingham was not one of his best.

The Austrian defender allowed Emile Heskey to skip past him with 13 minutes left to set up substitute David Dunn for an equaliser that was fully deserved. Scharner, who had been substituted at Blackburn five days earlier, got the nod over Matt Jackson but his late error allowed the Blues a share of the spoils. 'We backed off Heskey too much,' Jewell conceded.

The Premiership table still made fabulous reading, with Latics remaining eighth, but this was the third consecutive home game in which they had tossed away a winning position.

Andreas Johansson, making only his fifth Premiership start, put the home side ahead four minutes after the re-start with his seventh of the campaign. But after that strike, it was Birmingham who flew into the ascendancy, and the longer the game went on, the more it became apparent the visitors were going to hit back.

In the end Latics were glad to hear the final whistle.

Lee McCulloch and Graham Kavanagh on the Christopher Park training ground as they prepare for the end of season run-in.

Jewell at least received some positive news, albeit two days after the match, when the FA confirmed he would not be punished for his verbal assault on referee Phil Dowd, a victory for common sense. But concern over his team's attacking prowess was beginning to creep in.

Having seen his team go 14 games since winning by more than one goal, he had the thankless task of balancing his workload between ending the campaign on a high and beginning to plan for the following season. With the transfer window reopening at the end of the campaign, the option of delaying all future plans until after the final game would have been career suicide.

'We've scored 38 goals all season and it's not good enough,' he said. 'We've got one eye on next season and improving the squad, and the team as a whole don't score enough goals. We've had a fabulous season, but being analytical you look at each area and we've got the lowest goals for in the top half of the table.'

Jason Roberts was the leading scorer with 14 at the time, Henri Camara had nine and Andreas Johansson had chipped in with seven, but Jewell added, 'It's not just the strikers, it's all over the pitch. A draw at home to Birmingham at the start of the season would have been seen as a decent result,' he added. 'But it's not.'

One of the many joys of being promoted was visiting new stadiums and the trip to the 53,000-capacity fortress in the heart of Newcastle was certainly one of the most eagerly anticipated. Wigan had played there before – half a century earlier. Latics, then playing in Lancashire Combination Division One under the watchful eye of Ted Goodier, staged one of their finest ever come-backs on 9 January 1954 against a star-studded Magpies outfit boasting six internationals to draw 2–2 and set up a replay at Springfield Park.

There were 52,222 lucky enough to witness the epic inside the ground, including 4,000 travelling fans who made their way in three special trains as well as convoys of coaches and cars.

'Ted said we had nothing to fear because it was only 11 against 11,' recalled Bert Lomas, the goalkeeper that day. Newcastle legend Jackie Millburn broke Wigan's hearts when he brought the scores level with 14 minutes to go and Lomas added,

What the Wigan fan said...

'Birmingham finished the stronger and deserved to score. We went in front, but then sat back and invited them onto us. Our midfield was getting over-run when we should have been pushing forward trying to get another goal. I think the concentration at the back let us down in the end.' – West Stand season-ticket holder Bill Downall.

	P	W	D	L	F	A	Pts
Chelsea	33	26	4	3	64	20	82
Man Utd	33	23	6	4	66	30	75
Liverpool	34	21	7	6	48	22	70
Tottenham	33	16	10	7	48	33	58
Blackburn	33	16	6	11	45	39	54
Arsenal	32	16	5	11	53	25	53
Bolton	32	13	9	10	43	36	48
Wigan	33	14	6	13	38	40	48
West Ham	33	13	7	13	47	50	46
Newcastle	33	13	6	14	36	40	45
Everton	33	13	6	14	31	43	45
Charlton	33	12	8	13	37	42	44
Man City	33	12	4	17	40	40	40
Middlesb'h	32	11	7	14	45	54	40
Aston Villa	33	8	12	13	34	46	36
Fulham	33	10	6	17	41	54	36
Birm'ham	33	7	8	18	25	45	29
West Brom	33	7	7	19	28	49	28
Portsm'th	32	7	7	18	29	54	28
Sunderl'd	32	2	5	25	21	57	11

John Filan, having recovered from his 'GBH' challenge at Blackburn, faces Newcastle. The Aussie was used to big crowds – he competed in the 1992 Olympics (in football, obviously).

'We held out for the remainder of the match and danced off the pitch when we held them. We had six full-timers, I think we were the first non-League team to engage professionals. I think we were paid £12 a week. I was on £7 as a part-timer.' Newcastle won the replay 3–2 at Springfield Park four days later in another edge of the seat thriller. Many things had changed in the intervening decades but there was one thing that hadn't – the hostility of the St James' crowd. Wigan 'keeper John Filan was used to big occasions (he is an Olympian – he played for Australia in the 1992 Barcelona Games) and played his last match for Blackburn in the Premiership at the famous Tyneside ground. 'Any game up at Newcastle is going to be tough because of the crowd they have behind them,' said Filan.

The teams walked out to a wall of noise and, with the home fans even more raucous because of Alan Shearer's pending retirement, the visiting players faced their biggest crowd since the Carling Cup Final. Yet despite a stunning goal from Jimmy Bullard, Wigan had to take a back seat to Newcastle's favourite son. Shearer tormented the reshuffled defence and scored two goals to seal a 3–1 home win.

Bullard's goal was sublime, and he did not deserve to belong to the losing side. But unable to get the win, he got the next best thing – Shearer's iconic No.9 home shirt. 'It's always going to be tough when you're up against someone like Alan Shearer – he's one of the best around,' said Leighton Baines. 'He did really well and proved what a handful he is.'

Once again Wigan took the lead for the fourth consecutive match after Bullard and Graham Kavanagh finally settled who would take the fifth-minute free-kick, 25 yards from goal. But injuries to Wigan's two centre-backs disrupted their hopes of clinging onto the slender lead. Matt Jackson injured his knee in a collision with John Filan and Shola Ameobi. From the resulting corner Arjan De Zeeuw broke his collarbone when he was clattered by Stephen Carr and disappeared down the tunnel, before Jackson soon followed, unable to continue.

Scharner joined the action to forge an emergency centre-back pairing with Pascal Chimbonda and though they tried to settle into their unfamiliar surroundings, Shearer instantly sensed his opportunity. The hosts were level when Michael Chopra tripped over his own boot laces at the back post, but the assistant referee Mike Cairns decided Ziegler had pushed him and referee Uriah Rennie pointed to the spot for Shearer to convert. 'I don't think it was a penalty,' Baines said. 'Reto just stood there. He went down very easily.'

Baines produced a great block on the line to deny Chopra a tap-in but minutes later Titus Bramble nodded in a free header from Nolberto Solano's corner, then as the game crossed the hour mark Shearer beat the offside trap to slot home. The cruel injuries, and Shearer's experience, decided the outcome. 'A make-shift centre-back pairing of Chimbonda and Scharner, who will have never come up against someone like Alan Shearer before, was a shock to the system,' concluded Jewell.

As Jewell spoke, Arjan De Zeeuw was being driven to Euxton Hospital, his collarbone hurting and his season prematurely cut short. And all of this just a day before his 36th birthday. 'I'm absolutely gutted and I'm feeling very down about it,' he admitted. 'It wasn't the best way to celebrate my birthday – I was having to cut my cake with one hand!'

De Zeeuw, regarded by many as the consummate professional, was disappointed with the challenge. 'I'm not very happy with Stephen Carr about it,' he said. 'I knew

Saturday 15 April 2006

Newcastle 3 Wigan 1

NEWCASTLE: Given 7, Carr 7, Moore 7, Bramble 8, Elliot 7, Solano 8, Bowyer (Faye 9 6), Dyer 6 (Clarke 74), N'Zogbia 8, Ameobi 6 (Chopra 18 7), Shearer 8.

WIGAN: Filan 6, Chimbonda 7, De Zeeuw 6 (Scharner 17 6), Jackson 6 (Baines 20 7), Ziegler 7, Thompson 7, Kavanagh 7, Bullard 7, McCulloch 5 (Camara 44 5), Roberts 5, Johansson 5. Wigan star man: Jimmy Bullard.

Goals: Bullard (5), Shearer (28, 66), Bramble (36)
Half-time 2–1
Referee: Uriah Rennie
Attendance: 52,503

What the opposition said...

'I'm pleased for many reasons, but for two especially. It was the first time that we've come from behind to win a game in more than two years and Wigan haven't been beaten away from home in the League for six games. Wigan have been terrific this year and deserve great credit. We were comfortable, though, for long periods.' – Caretaker Newcastle manager Glenn Roeder.

What the Wigan fan said...

'I think a draw would have been a fair result. There was a couple of big decisions which went against us and the injuries to De Zeeuw and Jackson cost us. We stayed over for the weekend and the Newcastle fans were great with us. It's the best stadium I've been to this season.' – Wigan supporters' club chairwoman Caroline Molyneux.

Jimmy Bullard celebrates his stunning goal at Newcastle.

Arjan De Zeeuw, with his arm in a sling, chats to Paul Scharner – a man whose hobbies include sky-diving, bridge jumping... and Mozart.

	P	W	D	L	F	A	Pts
Chelsea	34	27	4	3	66	20	85
Man Utd	34	23	7	4	66	30	76
Liverpool	35	22	7	6	49	22	73
Tottenham	34	17	10	7	49	33	61
Arsenal	34	17	6	11	57	27	57
Blackburn	34	16	6	12	45	40	54
West Ham	34	14	7	13	48	50	49
Bolton	33	13	9	11	43	38	48
Newcastle	34	14	6	14	39	41	48
Wigan	34	14	6	14	39	43	48
Everton	34	13	6	15	31	44	45
Charlton	34	12	8	14	38	44	44
Man City	34	12	4	18	40	41	40
Middlesb'h	33	11	7	15	45	55	40
Aston Villa	34	9	12	13	37	47	39
Fulham	34	11	6	17	43	55	39
Portsm'th	34	8	8	18	31	55	32
Birm'ham	34	7	8	19	26	48	29
West Brom	34	7	7	20	29	52	28
Sunderl'd	33	2	6	25	21	57	12

as soon as he hit me it was serious – I was in agony.' His injury compounded the misfortunes for Wigan, who had slipped to 10th on the ladder and had some mentioning the proverbial bubble bursting. Not for the first time, Jewell questioned the sanity of his critics. 'They have no idea about football,' he added. 'You have to remain realistic in your targets. Our hopes at the start of the season were to finish 17th and anything above that would have been a bonus.'

Three days later Wigan returned to the JJB Stadium and ended their home voodoo in style by securing their third double of the campaign, beating Aston Villa (their other home-and-away wins had been over Sunderland and Manchester City).

The Three Amigos were in the crowd – Isidro Diaz, Jesus Seba and Roberto Martinez earned cult status after signing for Wigan in 1995 – and they were treated to a frantic, pulsating spectacle. Henri Camara returned to the Wigan team and scored twice in the second half. He later dedicated his haul to his grandmother. But it was Bullard who once again stole the show with a wonderful volley that rocketed into the corner to open the scoring in the 25th minute.

The Three Amigos, Chimbonda's gloves... as if Bullard was feeling left out, he tried to set his own trend with a distinctive Alice-band. 'My hair's getting too long and it's getting in my eyes so I have to wear it,' he said, by way of defence. Would a haircut not be an option? 'No, I can't,' he said, before admitting with admirable honesty, 'I've got sticky out ears so I have to have long hair to cover them up.'

Arjan De Zeeuw is helped from the field at Newcastle.

Wigan had not won at the JJB Stadium since their Boxing Day thriller against Manchester City, and the open attacking game produced an engrossing spectacle – but made anxious viewing for Paul Jewell, who later emphatically ruled out any chance of Wigan taking part in the summer's Inter Toto Cup. 'I don't care, I'm on my holiday,' he laughed. 'Joking aside, we're not geared up for that and it may have an adverse effect. The most important thing is next season, and if we start in July it just makes the season even longer.'

A combination of injuries and Jewell's desire not to let the campaign fizzle out prompted him to make six changes to the side beaten at Newcastle. And the rotation injected some vigour into the Wigan side and they took a deserved 1–0 lead against Villa through Bullard.

Henri Camara scored two goals against Aston Villa and dedicated his double to his late grandmother.

Tuesday 18 April 2006

Wigan Athletic 3 Aston Villa 2

WIGAN: Filan 7, Chimbonda 7, Henchoz 7, Scharner 7, Baines 7, Teale 8, Francis 8 (Kavanagh 78), Bullard 8, Ziegler 8 (McCulloch 81), Camara 8, Roberts 8. Wigan star man: Bullard.

ASTON VILLA: Sorensen 8, Hughes 7 (De La Cruz 66), Cahill 6, Ridgewell 7, Samuel 6, Milner 6, Gardner 6 (Agbonlahor 45 6), Barry 8, McCann 7, Angel 7, Baros 7.

Goals: Bullard (25), Angel (53), Camara (56, 60), Ridgewell (67)
Half-time: 1–0
Referee: Peter Walton
Attendance: 17,330

What the opposition said...

'When we got back to 1–1 we lost two quick goals that should have been prevented, but our effort and commitment was not in doubt. It sums up our season. With the chances we created we should be scoring more than two goals. We needed more quality this season. The quality has been short in vital areas – at both ends of the pitch.' – Aston Villa assistant manager Roy Aitken.

What the Wigan fan said...

'That was a great game – it was edge-of-the-seat stuff from start to finish and I'm glad we finished on top. It was a terrific goal from Jimmy Bullard and a great way to end our barren spell at home.' – Wigan fan Luke Samuel.

Angel clawed a goal back, but just as fans began to curse another lead thrown away, Camara struck with his quickfire double. 'I think he celebrated so much after the second goal he had no more energy,' grinned Jewell. Villa grabbed a second in the 68th minute through Liam Ridgewell but Wigan hung on after an exciting finish.

The win pushed Wigan beyond the 50 point mark – to 51 – with three games to go. And with Jewell drawing up the proverbial shopping list of summer targets he realised that the flourishing season would make his job easier. He would not need to give a hard sell of ambition and hope – a copy of the League table was ample proof of Wigan's new status among football's elite.

Paul Jewell shakes hands with David O'Leary, the manager who at the start of the season said, 'Good luck, I hope you don't go down.'

Ever the realist, he was aware of the pitfalls that might lie in waiting. 'I'm going to be careful not to finish 10th and then say we've got to do better,' he added. 'Look at Everton – they finished fourth and at the start of the season people were asking questions about David Moyes's future. There's no surprise element with us.'

Jewell had been joined in the JJB Stadium stable by one of his neighbours from the Yorkshire village of Ilkley. New Wigan Warriors coach Brian Noble and Jewell had shared the occasional pint – Noble joked he was the one who usually paid – and the Latics boss gave his counterpart a glowing endorsement. 'I know Brian well, and he spoke to me about the job when he was offered it,' he said.

	P	W	D	L	F	A	Pts
Chelsea	35	28	4	3	69	20	88
Man Utd	35	24	7	4	68	31	79
Liverpool	35	22	7	6	49	22	73
Tottenham	35	17	10	8	60	35	61
Arsenal	34	17	6	11	57	27	57
Blackburn	34	16	6	12	45	40	54
Newcastle	35	15	6	14	43	42	51
Wigan	35	15	6	14	42	45	51
Bolton	34	13	10	11	43	38	49
West Ham	35	14	7	14	48	52	49
Charlton	35	13	8	14	40	45	47
Everton	35	13	6	16	31	47	45
Middlesb'h	34	12	7	15	47	55	43
Man City	34	12	4	18	40	41	40
Aston Villa	35	9	12	14	39	50	39
Fulham	34	11	6	17	43	55	39
Portsm'th	35	8	8	19	32	57	32
Birm'ham	34	7	8	19	26	48	29
West Brom	35	7	8	20	29	52	29
Sunderl'd	34	2	6	26	22	61	12

The first hint that Pascal Chimbonda could be leaving the club emerged in a short *Daily Mirror* story. As if cursed by bad timing (more of that later), the speculation over Chimbonda's future came days before he was named in the Professional Footballers' Association Team of the Year – a prestigious honour as the fictitious line-up is voted for by the players themselves, eradicating any of the typical awards-bash sentiment.

Chimbonda came ahead of a string of more established names, including Manchester United captain Gary Neville and Liverpool's Steve Finnan, and added to the charms of Wigan Athletic. 'I have had a superb time, and the fans have been fantastic,' he said at the plush London ceremony.

Wigan were fast becoming a big club, at least bigger than most could ever have dreamt, and Chimbonda's honour served as a timely reminder of that. But fans' faint hopes of qualifying for the UEFA Cup were dashed in London the day after the PFA Awards, as they fell 1–0 to Chris Coleman's Fulham.

Only four teams – West Ham, Manchester United, Arsenal and Portsmouth –

Wigan's Jimmy Bullard clashes with Fulham's Hieidar Helguson at Craven Cottage just days before announcing he would be moving to the London club.

Monday 24 April 2006

Fulham 1
Wigan Athletic 0

FULHAM: Niemi 8, Rosenior 7, Pearce 7, Knight 7, Bridge 6, Malbranque 8, Elliott 7 (Christanval 84), Diop 6, Boa Morte 8, Helguson 7 (Radzinski 71), McBride 6.

WIGAN: Pollitt 7, Chimbonda 8, Henchoz 7, Jackson 7, Baines 9, Teale 8 (Connolly 86), Kavanagh 7, Bullard 8, McCulloch 7, Roberts 7, Camara 7. Wigan star man: Baines.

Goal: Malbranque (45)
Half-time: 1–0
Referee: Rob Styles
Attendance: 17,149

What the opposition said...

'You have got to feel sorry for Wigan because they created a lot of chances. They deserved something out of the game and we were lucky to take all three points. But we have played just like they did in other games and not come away with anything. In the end I couldn't really give a monkey's because we need the points.' – Fulham manager Chris Coleman.

What the Wigan fan said...

'The defence seemed rather slow. Wigan were lucky not to concede another goal, as a pass through Wigan's defence was flagged offside by the linesman but, when shown on the replay, wasn't. Camara didn't have his "shooting boots" on in this match – he missed a few sitters! Pollitt had a good game, Chimbonda too, but it just wasn't our night.' – Wigan fan Matthew Brennan.

had won at Craven Cottage that season and Steed Malbranque's thunderbolt on the stroke of half-time ensured Latics would not be joining that elite group, even though they had dominated the early exchanges.

It really turned into a scrappy affair, but Wigan could have salvaged a point in stoppage time. Chimbonda's pass was on a plate for late substitute David Connolly, but he fluffed his lines with the goal at his mercy from all of 10 yards and Camara put the rebound into the side-netting. It summed up Wigan's night. 'That's three points we've thrown away,' lamented Gary Teale. 'We had so many chances... we just didn't have that final bit of composure or quality.'

With Ryan Taylor joining De Zeeuw on the sidelines after breaking his leg playing for the reserves, and John Filan out with hernia problem, Jewell accepted missing out on Europe was a blessing in disguise. 'For a club of our size and with it being our first year at this level, we're maybe not ready for Europe just yet,' he said.

With the game against Fulham over, the news was made public that Jimmy Bullard had agreed to join the Craven Cottage outfit the following season after they activated a clause in his contract that allowed him to leave if a club bid £2.5 million for him.

A hugely popular member of the squad and a firm fans' favourite, Bullard's departure from Wigan was greeted by sadness. In many ways, Bullard's own

Jason Roberts, Leighton Baines and Ryan Taylor are applauded off the pitch in the final home game of the season.

	P	W	D	L	F	A	Pts
Chelsea	35	28	4	3	69	20	88
Man Utd	35	24	7	4	68	31	79
Liverpool	35	22	7	6	49	22	73
Tottenham	35	17	10	8	60	35	61
Arsenal	34	17	6	11	57	27	57
Blackburn	34	16	6	12	45	40	54
Newcastle	35	15	6	14	43	42	51
Wigan	35	15	6	14	42	45	51
Bolton	34	13	10	11	43	38	49
West Ham	35	14	7	14	48	52	49
Charlton	35	13	8	14	40	45	47
Everton	35	13	6	16	31	47	45
Middlesb'h	34	12	7	15	47	55	43
Man City	34	12	4	18	40	41	40
Aston Villa	35	9	12	14	39	50	39
Fulham	34	11	6	17	43	55	39
Portsm'th	35	8	8	19	32	57	32
Birm'ham	34	7	8	19	26	48	29
West Brom	35	7	8	20	29	52	29
Sunderl'd	34	2	6	26	22	61	12

Henri Camara gets the party started against Portsmouth, but it was the visitors left celebrating the most after a dramatic great escape from relegation.

journey had represented Wigan's. Here was an unheralded player bought for a bargain, who went on to meet and beat many household names. And he did it with a smile on his face.

It was, Bullard admitted, a massive decision but one he felt obliged to take to move closer to his family. 'I've been away from them for three years and it's always been my dream to play in front of my dad on a regular basis,' admitted Bullard, who had arrived from Peterborough for £275,000 in January 2003. 'He will only be half an hour down the road from me now and can watch me every other week. He's not getting any younger and it swung my decision in the end. But making the decision to leave was heart-breaking. I spoke to Paul Jewell four times before I made the decision because it was so tough… but I wanted to go back to London and be with my family.'

In an interesting aside, a journalist and a photographer from the men's magazine *Nuts* had travelled to Wigan from London to present Bullard with a special award for his exploits... only to find he was in London at the time having talks with Fulham. It was not a wasted trip – they also had to present a trophy to a female Wigan supporter who had been voted 'Britain's Fittest Fan'.

Latics planned a party for their final home game of the season. The prospects of a great escape from the drop saw Portsmouth pack out their end and they helped create a carnival atmosphere with a 2–1 win which guaranteed their top-flight status.

On reflection, it should have been Wigan – eight places ahead of Pompey – celebrating the most, but the drama of Pompey's survival meant Wigan's champagne remained on ice. The party poppers never came out of their boxes. 'We're all gutted,' said Leighton Baines. 'We wanted to go out on a high for ourselves and for the fans.'

Wigan had enough chances in the first half to condemn the visitors to their biggest defeat of the season. Henri Camara opened the scoring in the 33rd minute and Lee McCulloch conceded, 'The game should have been dead and buried at half-time'.

Portsmouth equalised through Benjamin Mwaruwari and then Gary Teale was sent off with 20 minutes to go when he handled Benjani's goal-bound header, which led to Matthew Taylor's winning goal from the penalty spot.

Saturday 29 April 2006

Wigan Athletic 1 Portsmouth 2

WIGAN: Pollitt 7, Chimbonda 6, Henchoz 5, Jackson 6, Baines 7, Teale 6, Kavanagh 8 (Johansson 84), Thompson 6 (Scharner 72), McCulloch 6, Roberts 6, Camara 8 (Connolly 80). Wigan star man: Camara.

PORTSMOUTH: Kiely 7, Priske 7, Primus 7, Stefanovic 7, Taylor 8, O'Neill 8, Davis 7, Mendes 7, D'Alessandro 8, Benjani 8, Todorov 6. Subs: Pamarot 6 (for Davis 45), Hughes 5 (for Mendes 69), Routledge (for Todorov 90).

Goals: Camara (34), Benjani (63), Taylor (71)
Half-time: 1–0
Referee: Mike Riley
Attendance: 21,126

What the opposition said...

'It was a really tough game for us and we knew it would be because Wigan are a good side, but I thought we deserved it. To take 20 points from our last nine games is unbelievable – it has been a terrific run. When you look at the position we were in, what we have done is just fantastic and all credit to the players.' – Portsmouth manager Harry Redknapp.

For a team so able to upset the odds and make headlines of their own, Wigan were not used to taking a back seat. They certainly weren't used to being written off – their lofty 10th position in the table and their haul of prized scalps were no flukes. On their final game of the season, the day belonged to Arsenal – they deserved to celebrate the end of their Highbury home – but the fact that there was a game to play was all too conveniently overlooked.

'I was reading the reports and watching the television before the game and I didn't know Wigan had a game today,' said Paul Jewell, in a thinly-disguised criticism of the media coverage. 'I just thought it was Tottenham against West Ham and that we'd given Arsenal a bye. There was no mention of us coming here trying to get a result.'

The atmosphere was electric, and Arsenal did an exceptional job of celebrating their landmark by giving all the fans specially commissioned T-shirts to colour the terraces with red, white and – of course – blue.

Having fallen behind to a Robert Pires goal Wigan stormed back to take a magnificent 2–1 lead through a Paul Scharner equaliser and a breathtaking 35-yard David Thompson goal. 'It was planned,' beamed Thompson. 'I knew Lehmann favoured moving to his left and I just found the gap.'

Wigan were not overawed by the magnitude of the occasion or by

What the Wigan fan said...

'We didn't play in the second half. So many times this year we have taken the lead and then sat back and invited the pressure instead of killing teams off. We've lost some daft games this season. We've had a great season, though, but I think a bit of fatigue is to blame.' – West Stand season-ticket holder Stan Grimshaw.

Wigan fans soak up the occasion at Arsenal.

	P	W	D	L	F	A	Pts
Chelsea (c)	36	29	4	3	72	20	91
Man Utd	36	24	7	5	68	34	79
Liverpool	37	24	7	6	54	24	79
Tottenham	37	18	11	8	52	36	65
Arsenal	35	17	7	11	58	28	58
Blackburn	36	17	6	13	48	42	57
Newcastle	37	16	7	14	46	42	55
Bolton	36	14	10	12	47	40	52
Wigan	37	15	6	16	43	48	51
West Ham	36	14	7	15	49	54	49
Everton	37	14	7	16	32	47	49
Charlton	37	13	8	16	41	51	47
Fulham	36	13	6	17	46	56	45
Man City	36	13	4	19	42	43	43
Middlesboro'	35	12	7	16	47	56	43
Aston Villa	37	9	12	16	40	54	39
Portsmouth	37	10	8	19	36	59	38
Birm'ham(r)	37	8	10	19	28	49	34
W. Brom (r)	36	7	8	21	29	55	29
Sun'land (r)	35	2	6	27	23	63	12

Sunday 7 May 2006

Arsenal 4
Wigan Athletic 2

ARSENAL: Lehmann 6, Eboue 8, Campbell 7, Toure 7, Cole 7, Hleb 8 (Van Persie 78), Gilberto 7, Fabregas 8, Pires 8 (Ljungberg 74), Reyes 8 (Bergkamp 78), Henry 9.

WIGAN: Pollitt 7, Chimbonda 7, Scharner 7, Jackson 6, Baines 7, Thompson 8 (Johansson 73), Ziegler 6 (Francis 66), Kavanagh 7, McCulloch 7, Roberts 6, Camara 6 (Connolly 82). Wigan star man: Thompson.

Goals: Pires (8), Scharner (10), Thompson (33), Henry (35, 56, 76)
Half-time: 2–2
Referee: Uriah Rennie
Attendance: 38,349

their heavyweight opponents. But then came along a Frenchman named Thierry Henry. Highbury had been a hunting ground as well as a playground for the virtuoso striker, and he ensured the final day of the famous ground's 93-year history belonged to him by claiming a hat-trick. Thompson's only blemish on an otherwise fine display was to gift Henry his second with a sloppy back-pass.

The hosts flew into the ascendancy as Wigan started chasing shadows and Henry was given the perfect chance to claim his treble when substitute Andreas Johansson pulled fellow Swede Freddie Ljungberg down. He was shown the red card just 88 seconds after coming on and without touching the ball, to claim a Premiership record for the fastest sending off. 'It was nonsense,' insisted Jewell.

Henry dispatched the ball from 12 yards, knelt and kissed the hallowed turf. After the final whistle, Wigan's players and manager saluted his historic day. 'Only an elephant gun might have stopped him,' mused Matt Jackson. 'It was a great part of history for him, it's just a shame it had to be against us. But he's a gentleman and an outstanding professional. He deserves all the credit because he's a humble man as well.'

After shaking his hand, Jewell also applauded the prolific Gunner, saying 'the script was written for him to go out and do that.'

Jewell and his players soaked up the cheers of the Wigan fans inside Highbury, before turning and – almost reluctantly – heading back to the dressing room to bring the curtain down on an epic season.

But there was another shock awaiting Jewell before he left Highbury. As the players sat reflecting on their achievements, and others nursed their tired bodies in the showers, Pascal Chimbonda approached Jewell and handed him a note. It could, and should, have been a thank-you card for launching his career.

It wasn't. It was an official transfer request. 'He unzipped his bag, took the note out and handed it to the manager – he hadn't even taken his boots off,' revealed PR Matt McCann. 'The other players couldn't fail to notice what was going on and some of the senior pros were very angry.' Jewell was, in his own words, 'livid' and

David Thompson celebrates his wonder-goal against Arsenal.

Wigan fans helped ensure Highbury's last-ever match was a memorable occasion.

accused the Frenchman of showing a 'spectacular level of disrespect'. He then informed chairman Dave Whelan, who volunteered the development when approached by reporters in the reception area of Highbury. 'The timing of the request was absolutely diabolical,' Whelan ranted, before threatening to let Chimbonda rot in the reserves unless a club paid £6 million for him. Two days later, the player's agent Willie Mackay told the *Wigan Observer* that Chimbonda had 'always seen Wigan as a stepping stone to move on and play for someone bigger.' He dismissed the outcry over Chimbonda's bad timing, saying, 'I think what the chairman and manager have said is right – he should have got dressed first.'

The messy affair threatened to take the shine off the season, but it never really did. Chelsea boss Jose Mourinho was named the season's Manager of the Year, only to graciously say that Jewell would have been an equally worthy recipient.

The gushing praise brought some perspective to Wigan's season. No player was ever bigger than the club, at any stage during their history or their season, and that was not going to change. Having masterminded one of football's most daring adventures, having seen his side to an unassailable, unbelievable mid-table finish and having proved so many sceptics who had forecast an overdose of doom and gloom wrong, Jewell could reflect on the season with well earned pride.

'We have done fantastic this season – absolutely unbelievable,' he smiled. 'The players have been a pleasure to work with. They can look back this season with pride and satisfaction.'

Pleasure, pride, satisfaction. Those words seem too modest to describe Wigan's season. Jewell was right first time, when he described the past year as 'absolutely unbelievable'.

Absolutely unbelievable - a fitting epitaph to a season of dreams.

What the opposition said...

'I felt that Wigan gave us a hard time, but we had to deal with nerves as well. We went into the last week knowing that we had to win two away games, and one home game against Wigan. For the history of the club and for this building here, to finish on a high I am very proud. We would all have felt guilty to have walked out of here on a low after what has happened here for years.' – Arsenal manager Arsene Wenger.

Paul Jewell celebrates taking a 2–1 lead at Arsenal.

What the Wigan fan said...

'It was a great game. Thompson scored a cracking free-kick but the day belonged to Arsenal and Henry. It was great to be involved in such an historic occasion. We played really well and it was a terrific way of signing off the season.' – South stand season-ticket holder Simeon Yenulevich.

	P	W	D	L	F	A	Pts
Chelsea (c)	38	29	4	5	72	22	91
Man Utd	38	25	8	5	72	34	83
Liverpool	38	25	7	6	57	25	82
Arsenal	38	20	7	11	68	31	67
Tottenham	38	18	11	9	53	38	65
Blackburn	38	19	6	13	51	42	63
Newcastle	38	17	7	14	47	42	58
Bolton	38	15	11	12	49	41	56
West Ham	38	16	7	15	52	55	55
Wigan	38	15	6	17	45	52	51
Everton	38	14	8	16	34	49	50
Fulham	38	14	6	18	48	58	48
Charlton	38	13	8	17	41	55	47
Middlesb'h	38	12	9	17	48	58	45
Man City	38	13	4	21	43	48	43
Aston Villa	38	10	12	16	42	55	42
Portsm'th	38	10	8	20	37	62	38
Birm'ham(r)	38	8	10	20	28	50	34
W. Brom(r)	38	7	9	22	31	58	30
Sunderl'd(r)	38	3	6	29	26	69	15

What they said afterwards:

Steve Bierley, *The Guardian:* 'There can surely be no doubt that Jewell must be the manager of the year. What a fabulously improbable beginning Wigan have made to life at the top.'

Sky's Martin Tyler: 'They are the story of the season. They are Wigan Athletic.'

Dave Whelan: 'Jewell for England? Too right.'

Leeds manager Kevin Blackwell: 'They have turned the bookies over all season. They have been so refreshing... a team that many thought would be fourth from bottom at best have looked more likely to finish fourth from top.'

Gary Lineker: 'Paul Jewell has built a side capable of troubling the best.'

Jeremy Alexander, *The Guardian*: 'This season they have thrived in their new surroundings, making a mockery of those who predicted their stay would be short-lived. They have continued to shed reputations.'

Portsmouth's Harry Redknapp: 'Paul Jewell is my manager of the year and he should win the award. What he has done at Wigan is nothing short of sensational'.

Guy Hodgson, *Independent on Sunday:* 'They are a fairy story in a League where fantasy rarely intrudes.'

Wigan Athletic Premiership results 2005–06

Date	*H/A*	*Opponents*		*Score*	*Half-time*	*Goals*	*Attendance*
14 Aug 05	(H)	Chelsea	L	0–1	(0–0)		23,575
20 Aug 05	(A)	Charlton Athletic	L	0–1	(0–1)		23,453
27 Aug 05	(H)	Sunderland	W	1–0	(1–0)	Roberts 2p	17,223
10 Sep 05	(A)	West Brom	W	2–1	(1–1)	Connolly 40; Bullard 90	25,617
18 Sep 05	(H)	Middlesbrough	D	1–1	(0–1)	Camara 68	16,641
24 Sep 05	(A)	Everton	W	1–0	(0–0)	Francis 47	37,189
2 Oct 05	(H)	Bolton Wanderers	W	2–1	(0–0)	Camara 47; McCulloch 62	20,553
15 Oct 05	(H)	Newcastle United	W	1–0	(1–0)	Roberts 39	22,374
22 Oct 05	(A)	Aston Villa	W	2–0	(1–0)	Hughes (og) 31; Mahon 82	32,294
29 Oct 05	(H)	Fulham	W	1–0	(0–0)	Chimbonda 90	17,266
5 Nov 05	(A)	Portsmouth	W	2–0	(0–0)	Chimbonda 47; Roberts 78	19,102
19 Nov 05	(H)	Arsenal	L	2–3	(2–3)	Camara 27; Bullard 44	25,004
26 Nov 05	(H)	Tottenham Hotspur	L	1–2	(0–1)	McCulloch 87	22,611
3 Dec 05	(A)	Liverpool	L	0–3	(0–2)		44,098
10 Dec 05	(A)	Chelsea	L	0–1	(0–0)		42,060
14 Dec 05	(A)	Manchester United	L	0–4	(0–2)		67,793
17 Dec 05	(H)	Charlton Athletic	W	3–0	(1–0)	Camara 8, 50, 62	17,074
26 Dec 05	(H)	Manchester City	W	4–3	(3–1)	Roberts 10, 44; McCulloch 22; Camara 70	25,017
28 Dec 05	(A)	West Ham United	W	2–0	(2–0)	Roberts 42; Camara 44	34,131
31 Dec 05	(H)	Blackburn Rovers	L	0–3	(0–1)		20,639
2 Jan 06	(A)	Birmingham City	L	0–2	(0–2)		29,189
15 Jan 06	(H)	West Brom	L	0–1	(0–0)		17,421
21 Jan 06	(A)	Middlesbrough	W	3–2	(2–0)	Roberts 2; Thompson 29; Mellor 91	27,208
31 Jan 06	(H)	Everton	D	1–1	(1–1)	Scharner 45	21,731
4 Feb 06	(A)	Bolton Wanderers	D	1–1	(0–0)	Johansson 77	25,854
11 Feb 06	(H)	Liverpool	L	0–1	(0–1)		25,023
19 Feb 06	(A)	Tottenham Hotspur	D	2–2	(1–1)	Johansson 10, 67	35,676
6 Mar 06	(H)	Manchester United	L	1–2	(0–0)	Scharner 60	23,574
11 Mar 06	(A)	Sunderland	W	1–0	(1–0)	Camara 8	31,194
18 Mar 06	(A)	Manchester City	W	1–0	(0–0)	McCulloch 55	42,444
25 Mar 06	(H)	West Ham United	L	1–2	(0–0)	McCulloch 46	18,736
3 Apr 06	(A)	Blackburn Rovers	D	1–1	(0–0)	Roberts 53	20,410
8 Apr 06	(H)	Birmingham City	D	1–1	(0–0)	Johansson 49	18,669
15 Apr 06	(A)	Newcastle United	L	1–3	(1–2)	Bullard 5	52,302
18 Apr 06	(H)	Aston Villa	W	3–2	(1–0)	Bullard 25; Camara 56, 60	17,330
24 Apr 06	(A)	Fulham	L	0–1	(0–0)		17,149
29 Apr 06	(H)	Portsmouth	L	1–2	(1–0)	Camara 34	21,126
7 May 06	(A)	Arsenal	L	4–2	(2–2)	Scharner 10, Thompson	33,349

Subscribers

Ian Abbott
Ian John Abernethy
John Abernethy
Stephen Abram
Dave Ackers
Kit Acrey
In Memory of Stephen Thomas Adams
Stephen Adams
Tim Addison
Jordan Ainscough
Graham Stuart Ainsworth
Jordan Akkaya
John Alker
Ken Alker
Andrew
Darren James Andrews
Garry David Andrews
Jamie Appleton
Frank Armstrong
Christopher James Armstrong
Geoff Arthur
Ken Ashcroft
Benjamin Ashcroft
George Aspey
Mr. Nolan F. Aspey
Mr Freddie Aspey
Bernard Aspinall
Terry Aspinall
Mr J.P. Aspinall
Adam Astbury
Kenny B
Stuart D. Baddeley
"Jade, Erica" Baggaley
Ian Ball
Brian E. Banks
Geoff Banks
David Barker
Ken Barlow
Darren Barlow
Bri Barnes
Howard Barrow
Malcolm Barton
Andrew Barton
Robert Barton
Peter Bates
Adrian Baxendale
David and Adrian Baxendale
Stephen Baxter
John Baxter
Willy Baxter
Alan James Baybutt
Paul Benbow
Tezz Benbow
Jamie Bennett
Mick Bentley
Brian Bentley
David Douglas Berry
Emily Lucy Berry
Andrew Billington
Roy Billington
Andrew Birchall
Bob
Moz Bodey
John Bond
Matthew J. Boon
Bob Bootle
Rachel Borley
Julie Boughey
Colin Boughey
Steven Boughey

David Boughey
Mr Trevor Boulton
Paul Boulton
Simon Christopher Box
Kierstan Boylan
Christine Boyle
Jim Bradley
Bradley
Richard Bramwell
Ralph Brimelow
Victoria Briscoe
Kevin Brogan
Frank Brogan
Dean Brookwell
Stephen and Emma Brown
Peter Brown
Alan J. Brown
Paul Brown
Tom Brunton
James Brunton
Mark Bullock
Chris J Burdett
Anthony Burke
David Burrows
Keith Burton
Catherine & Alison Byrne
Martyn Caddick
Peter Calderbank
Ian Lennie Caldwell
Jack & Joe Callaghan
Dale Callaghan
Anita Callaghan
Raymond Capper
Paul and Janet Carey
Lauren Carroll
Paul Cartwright
Suzanne Catchpole
Alan Catterall
Terry Chadwick
Barry Chadwick
Mr Carl J. Chamberlain
Thomas Chapman
Tommy James Clark
Simon Clegg
Anthony Mark Clements
Jack Close
Jimmy Clough
Phil Coleman
Andrew Collier
Warren Collier
Matthew Collins
Frank Collins
Andy Conroy
Neil Cook
Brian Cooper
Joseph Cooper
Mr Stephen A. Cooper
Roy Ernest Cottom
Mr Andy Court
Frederick Cox
Edwin Coyne
Paul Crippin
Darren Critchley
Louis Critchlow
Brian Croft
Stuart Daniel Crompton
Amanda Crompton
Granville Crompton
David A. Crossley
Philip J. Crossley
Adelle Cunliffe
Martin A. Cunliffe
John Cunningham
Kenny Dalgleish
Graham Daniels
John S. Darbyshire
Drew Darbyshire
Peter J Darbyshire

Raymond Darwin
Chris Davies
Gordon Davies
Stephen Davies
Keith Davies
Owen Davies
Brian Davies
Lee (Travis) Davies
Shaune Dawber
David Dawson
Joe Dawson
Paul Day
N.J. and J. Deakin
Noel Dean
Andrew Derbyshire
Kirsty Dickinson
Barry Dixon
Neil Mark Donaldson
Mark Peter Donaldson
Anna-Marie Donnellan
George Dootson
Mike Downey
Rachel Draper
Phil Draper
Mike Draper
Andrew Duckworth
Michael Dugdill
Derek Thomas Eaton
Rod and Louise Eccles
Eddie
Christine Edwards
Mark Edwards
Jake Edwards
Gareth John Edwards
Gary Edwards
Stephen Edwardson
Martin Ellis
Horace Ensor
Margaret Evans
John Evans
Chloe Evans
David Fairbrother
Anne Fairhurst
William Fairhurst
Stephen John Fairhurst
Calum Fairhurst
The Shepherd Family
Keith W. Fanning
Bobbi Fazackerley
D. Fillingham
John Anthony Fillingham
David Fillingham (Filly)
Eric Finch
David J. Finney
Jeff and Richard Fishwick
Neil Fishwick
Stephen Fishwick
J. Flannery
Manny Flores
Eric Forshaw
Jack Forshaw
Julie Forster
Rob Foster
Graham Foster
Alan Foster
Kevin Foster
Brian Foster
John Fowler
Ben Frain
Michael France
Jason Frost
Mark Fulton
Alan Gambles
Andrew Joseph Gannon
John Gaskell
Nathan Gaskell
Gordon Gaskell
Andrea Gavaghan

Paul Gee
Richard Gibson
Ian Gill
Thomas Ivan Gleave
David Gostelow
Frank Gough
Oliver Goulding
Graham
Stewart Grant
Barry Gray
Percy Grayston
Tyran Green
Richard Green
Sam Green
Kevin Green
Max Green
Andrew Greenall
Philip Greenall
Jake Greenhalgh
John Greenwood
Mick Griffiths
Ryan Griffiths
Cliff Griffiths
Jamie Griffiths
Stan Grimshaw
Jennifer Grist
Stephen Grundy
April Grundy
Martin Gwinnett
Ryan Hale
Rebecca Hall
Gary Hall
Jonathon Hall
Stephen J. Halliwell
Chris Halliwell
Craig Halliwell
Neville Hampson
R and R Hamson
Eric Harley
Johnny Harpo
Peter Harris
Jacqueline Harris
Philip Hart
Nicholas Hart
Marcus Hart
Graham Hatch
Richard Hatherell
Angela Hatherell
Brian John Hayes
Mark Hayes
S.J. Hayton
James Heaton
Liam B. Heaton
Robert Heaton
David Hern
John Heseltine
Kevin Hesketh
Joseph Hetherington
Mr David Heyes
Ian Heywood
Valerie Higgens
Andrew Higham
Neil Highton
Darren Highton
Stephen Highton
Roy Highton
Philip Hill
James Hilton
Gareth John Hilton
Bradley Hilton
Ashley Alan Hitchen
Simon Hodkinson
Simon Hodkinson
Christine and Stephen Hogarth
Martin Holden
Dale Holford
Andy Holian
Tyler Holland

Andy Holmes
David & Adam Holmes
Elliot Hook
Carl Horrobin
Ste Horrocks
Gerry Houghton
John Houghton
Simon Howard
Bill Howarth
Bryan Howarth
Stephen Howe
In Memory of Christopher Hoy
Norman Hughes
Owen Hughes
David W. Hughes
Craig Darren Hughes
Brian Hughes
Martin Hull
David Humphreys
Simon Humphreys
Ron Hunt
Malcolm Hurst
Daniel Ibbetson
Rob Ingram
Claire Jackson
Dave Jackson
Malcolm James
Cliff James
Ben Johnson
Chris Johnson
Mick Jolley
Jim Jolley
Dean Jolley
Mal Jones
G. Jones
Mark Jones
David C. Jones
David Owen Jones
Sharon Jones

Keith Jones
Andrew Jones
Dawn Jones
Simon D. Jones
David Jones
Anthony Martin Kay
Lee Kay
Martin Keating
Andrew Keefe
David Keller
Geoff Kendrick
Mr. Peter Kevill
Peter Kevill
Eric King
Bob Kingswood
Caroline Kirk
Stephen Kirk
Trevor Knight
Terry Knowles
Barney Kong
David Kyte
Joanne Lally
John Lamb
Hamish Lancaster
Julie Large
Paul Latham
Carl Latham
Stuart Law
Harvey Tomas Lawrenson
Jade Leak
Dudley Leather
Diane Leech
Louise Leigh
Alan Lenagan
Frank Lewis
Martin Lewis
Steve 'Cockney' Leyland
James Leyland
Aung Law Ha Ling

Ken Liptrot
Martin Liptrot
Mr. Ken Littler
Stephen H. Lloyd
Mark Long
Colin Long
Derek Lorton
David Robert Lowe
Kevin Mackenzie
Stuart Maconie
Tommy Madden
Stuart Makin
Aaron Makinson
Andy Maloney
Kyle Markland
Stephen Marsden
David Marsden
Tony Marsden
Gary Marsden
Chris Marsh
Celia Marshall
Stephen Marshall
Keith Martindale
Ray Martindale
Allan Foster- Mascot in 1967
Gill Mates
Chris Mawdesley
Stuart Mayo
Stephen Mayoh
Michael McGrail
Steve McKeon
Paul McLoughlin
Thomas McManus
Rebecca McVean
Paul Meachem
Terry Meehan
In Memory of Stephen Melling
John Melling
Katie Melling
Derek Melling USA
Tony Middlehurst
Sean Middlehurst
Darren Middleton
Karen Miller
Phillip Millward
Howard Mitchell
Charlotte Molloy
Jim Molloy
Paul David James Molyneux
Angela Molyneux
Bert Molyneux
Paul Moorcroft
Ronnie Moore
David Moore
Julian Morgan
Paul Moseley
Georgia Victoria Moss
Derek Moss
Nick Moulson
Alan Muir
Andrew and Christopher Mullins
Darcy Mullins
Jacqueline Mulvaney
Peter Murphy
Anthony Murray
Tony Musker
Sarah Napper
Keith Nelson
Helen Nicholl
Liam O'Connor
Bethany O'Connor
Martyn Ode
Ian C. Ogden
Shaun O'Hara
Scott Andrew O'Neill
Andrew O'Neill
Stephen O'Neill
Nick O'Neill

Stuart O'Neill
Naing Naing Oo
Dave Orrell
Geoff Owen
David Parkinson
David Parkinson
Andrew Parkinson
Dave Parkinson
Paul Parkinson
Mr Gwyn Parkinson
Geoff Parkinson
John Partington
Dean Partington
Malcolm Paton
David Peacock
Natalie Pearson
John Pendlebury
John Pengy
Craig Pennington
Lee Brian Pennington
Les Pennington
Thomas Penny
Peter W. Percy
Craig Perry
Phil
James Andrew Pickering
Mr Ian Pinkerton and Mrs Yvonne Pinkerton
Thomas Platt
David Pomfrett
Mr. H. Pomfrett
Alistair Pope
Wesley Potter
Neil Potter
Lawrence Power
Mark Prescott
David Prescott
Sam Prescott
David John Prescott
Colin Prescott
Royston J. Pugh
David Purdham
Ben Purdham
Shaun Quinlan
Bernard Ramsdale
David Ratcliffe
Garry and Joe Ratcliffe
Lewis Ratcliffe
Eli Ratcliffe
Michael Rawson
Albert Ready
Joe Redford
Peter A. Reece
John Reece
Liam Rees
Paul Reid
Michael Richardson
Miles Jason Richardson
Mark 'Blue Army' Rigby
Dave Rigby
Debbie Rigby
David Rigby
Ian Rigby
Paul Riley
Ian Ritchie
Emma Louise Roberts
David Roberts
Mark Roberts
Steven Robinson
Paul Roper
Paul Rosental
Jeff Rourke
Harvey Peter Stuart Rowe
David Rowlinson
Daniel Ruane
Jack A. Rubothan
T H Rudduck
John Rushton